Exposure Therapy for Child and

Adolescent Anxiety and OCD

ABCT Clinical Practice Series

Series Editor

Susan W. White, Ph.D., ABPP, Professor and Doddridge Saxon Chair in Clinical Psychology, University of Alabama

Associate Editors

Lara J. Farrell, Ph.D., Associate Professor, School of Applied Psychology, Griffith University & Menzies Health Institute of Queensland, Australia

Matthew A. Jarrett, Ph.D., Associate Professor, Department of Psychology, University of Alabama

Jordana Muroff, Ph.D., LICSW, Associate Professor, Clinical Practice, Boston University School of Social Work

Marisol Perez, Ph.D., Associate Professor & Associate Chair, Department of Psychology, Arizona State University

Titles in the Series

Applications of the Unified Protocol for Transdiagnostic Treatment of Emotional Disorders
Edited by David H. Barlow and Todd Farchione

Helping Families of Youth with School Attendance Problems
Christopher A. Kearney

Addressing Parental Accommodation When Treating Anxiety in Children
Eli R. Lebowitz

Forthcoming Titles in the Series

Exposure Therapy for Eating Disorders
Carolyn Black Becker, Nicholas R. Farrell, and Glenn Waller

Exposure Therapy for Child and Adolescent Anxiety and OCD

STEPHEN P. H. WHITESIDE,

THOMAS H. OLLENDICK,

AND BRIDGET K. BIGGS

OXFORD
UNIVERSITY PRESS

Oxford University Press is a department of the University of Oxford. It furthers
the University's objective of excellence in research, scholarship, and education
by publishing worldwide. Oxford is a registered trade mark of Oxford University
Press in the UK and certain other countries.

Published in the United States of America by Oxford University Press
198 Madison Avenue, New York, NY 10016, United States of America.

Library of Congress Cataloging-in-Publication Data
Names: Whiteside, Stephen P. H., author. | Ollendick, Thomas H., author. |
Biggs, Bridget K., author.
Title: Exposure therapy for child and adolescent anxiety and OCD /
Stephen P.H. Whiteside, Thomas H. Ollendick, and Bridget K. Biggs.
Description: New York, NY : Oxford University Press, [2020] |
Series: ABCT clinical practice series | Includes bibliographical references and index.
Identifiers: LCCN 2019040354 (print) | LCCN 2019040355 (ebook) |
ISBN 9780190862992 (paperback) | ISBN 9780190863012 (epub) |
ISBN 9780190863005 (updf) | ISBN 9780190863029 (online)
Subjects: LCSH: Anxiety disorders—Treatment. |
Obsessive-compulsive disorder—Treatment. | Explosure therapy. |
Child psychiatry. | Adolescent psychiatry.
Classification: LCC RC531 .W45 2020 (print) |
LCC RC531 (ebook) | DDC 616.85/22—dc23
LC record available at https://lccn.loc.gov/2019040354
LC ebook record available at https://lccn.loc.gov/2019040355

9 8 7 6 5 4 3 2 1

Printed by Marquis, Canada

CONTENTS

Mental health clinicians desperately want to help their clients and recognize the importance of implementing evidence-based treatments toward achieving this goal. In the past several years, the field of mental health care has seen tremendous advances in our understanding of pathology and its underlying mechanisms, as well as proliferation and refinement of scientifically informed treatment approaches. Coinciding with these advances is a heightened focus on accountability in clinical practice. Clinicians are expected to apply evidence-based approaches and to do so effectively, efficiently, and in a patient-centered, individualized way. This is no small order. For a multitude of reasons, including but not limited to client diversity, complex psychopathology (e.g., comorbidity), and barriers to care that are not under the clinician's control (e.g., adverse life circumstances that limit the client's ability to participate), delivery of evidence-based approaches can be challenging.

This series, which represents a collaborative effort between the Association for Behavioral and Cognitive Therapies (ABCT) and the Oxford University Press, is intended to serve as an easy-to-use, highly practical collection of resources for clinicians and trainees. The ABCT Clinical Practice Series is designed to help clinicians effectively master and implement evidence-based treatment approaches. In practical terms, the series represents the "brass tacks" of implementation, including basic how-to guidance and advice on troubleshooting common issues in clinical practice and application. As such, the series is best viewed as a complement to other series on evidence-based protocols, such as the Treatments That Work series and the Programs That Work series. These represent seminal bridges between research and practice and have been instrumental in the dissemination of empirically supported intervention protocols and programs. The ABCT Clinical Practice Series, rather than focusing on specific diagnoses and their treatment, targets the practical application of therapeutic and assessment approaches. In other words, the emphasis is on the *how-to* aspects of mental health delivery.

It is my hope that clinicians and trainees find these books useful in refining their clinical skills, as enhanced comfort as well as competence in delivery of evidence-based approaches should ultimately lead to improved client outcomes. Given the emphasis on application in this series, there is relatively less emphasis on review of the underlying research base. Readers who wish to delve more deeply into the theoretical or empirical basis supporting specific approaches are encouraged to go to the original source publications cited in each chapter. When relevant, suggestions for further reading are provided.

Even well-intending and highly trained clinicians may sometimes shy away from using exposure therapy to treat anxious children. This is a problem because exposure is a critical aspect of effective treatment within cognitive–behavioral treatment of anxiety disorders. *Why do clinicians do this?* They do so for a host of reasons, including discomfort with causing distress to the child, fear of doing it wrong, and unfamiliarity with the theoretical premise behind exposure.

This book details exposure "how to" and synthesizes the approach's research support and theoretical basis. It is a strong accompaniment to CBT treatment manuals that employ exposure. It is likely to become a must-read resource for clinicians in training. Seasoned clinicians are also likely to find this a good "refresher" on the conduct of exposure for a range of presenting problems in anxious children.

Drs. Stephen Whiteside, Bridget Biggs, and Thomas Ollendick comprise a world-renowned team of clinical scientists with expertise on this topic. In this volume, they share wisdom gleaned from their years of research and clinical experience working with children with anxiety disorders. The concepts are conveyed in a straightforward writing style and exemplified with case material. For these reasons, I suspect this will be a well-read resource in training clinics internationally.

Susan W. White, PhD, ABPP
Series Editor

ABOUT THE AUTHORS

Stephen P. H. Whiteside, PhD, ABPP, is a board certified Licensed Clinical Psychologist, Professor of Psychology in the Mayo Clinic College of Medicine and Science, and Director of the Pediatric Anxiety Disorders Program at Mayo Clinic in Rochester, Minnesota. His research focuses on improving access to evidence-based care for pediatric anxiety disorders and obsessive–compulsive disorder through the development of effective and efficient treatments facilitated by technology. He received a BA in Psychology from Northwestern University and a PhD in Clinical Psychology from the University of Kentucky. He completed a predoctoral internship in Pediatric Psychology at the Geisinger Medical Center and a post-doctoral fellowship in Child and Family Medical Psychology at Mayo Clinic. He has received research funding from the National Institutes of Health, the Agency for Healthcare Research and Quality, the International OCD Foundation, and the Mayo Clinic Center for Innovation. He has published more than 70 scientific articles, co-authored *Exposure Therapy for Anxiety: Principles and Practice* (second edition), and is the co-developer of *Mayo Clinic Anxiety Coach*, an iOS application.

Thomas H. Ollendick, PhD, is University Distinguished Professor in Clinical Psychology and Director of the Child Study Center at Virginia Polytechnic Institute and State University, Blacksburg, Virginia. He is the author or co-author of more than 350 research publications, more than 100 book chapters, and more than 35 books. He is the past editor of the *Journal of Clinical Child and Adolescent Psychology and Behavior Therapy*, as well as founding and current co-editor of *Clinical Child and Family Psychology Review*. He is also past president of the Association for the Advancement of Behavior Therapy (1995), the Society of Clinical Psychology (1999), the Society of Clinical Child and Adolescent Psychology (2007), and the Society for the Science of Clinical Psychology (2010). He received an Honorary Doctorate from Stockholm University in 2011 and holds Honorary Adjunct Professor positions at Roehampton University in London; Griffith University in Brisbane, Australia; and Sydney Institute of Technology in Sydney, Australia. He was awarded the Distinguished Research Contributions to the Field of Clinical Child Psychology in 2007 (American Psychiatric Association

[APA]), the Career/Lifetime Achievement Award from the Association for Behavioral and Cognitive Therapies in 2013, the Lifetime Achievement Award for Scientific Contributions from the Society of Clinical Psychology (APA) in 2017, and most recently recognized as a Pioneer of Behavior and Cognitive Therapy (ABCT) in 2019.

Bridget K. Biggs, PhD, ABPP, is a board certified Child and Adolescent Psychologist and Assistant Professor of Psychology in the Mayo Clinic College of Medicine and Science at Mayo Clinic in Rochester, Minnesota. She conducts research on childhood anxiety assessment and treatment; social factors related to children's and adolescents' mental and physical health; and improving access to behavioral interventions for children, adolescents, and their families. She earned a BA in Psychology and German at the University of Notre Dame, an MS in Clinical Psychology at the Pennsylvania State University, and a PhD in Clinical Child Psychology at the University of Kansas. She completed a pre-doctoral internship in clinical child psychology at the UCLA Semel Institute for Neuroscience and Behavior and post-doctoral fellowship in clinical child psychology at Stanford University. Her research has been supported by institutional and external funding sources, including the National Institutes of Health. She has published more than 30 articles and co-edited the book *Preventing and Treating Bullying and Victimization*.

Exposure Therapy for Child and Adolescent Anxiety and OCD

Overview and Background

Introduction and History

WHAT IS EXPOSURE?

The therapeutic value of confronting, rather than avoiding, difficult emotions and issues is integral to many approaches to psychotherapy (Foa & Kozak, 1986). Exposure therapy accomplishes this goal in the simplest, most straightforward manner. Although the principles of exposure are relevant to many emotional symptoms (Carey, 2011), this book focuses on its application to anxiety and obsessive–compulsive symptoms in children and adolescents. In this context, exposure embodies the colloquialism "face your fears." The goal of exposure therapy is to provide youth with an emotional learning experience to correct previous maladaptive beliefs, expectations, emotional responses, or behavioral patterns. For example, if a child is overly shy and fears others will respond negatively to her, she needs to practice talking to peers until she learns that conversations generally go well enough. If a child is anxious about having intrusive blasphemous thoughts, he needs to repeat those thoughts until anxiety is reduced and he learns thoughts are just thoughts and they cannot hurt him. Similarly, if a teen's life is disrupted by fear of panic attacks, she needs to purposely bring on physiological symptoms of anxiety through hyperventilation and other means until she learns that although feelings of panic are uncomfortable, they are not dangerous.

The opening chapters of this book (Section 1) provide an introduction to exposure, its applications and history, as well as a review of the theoretical models of how exposure therapy leads to symptom improvement. Section 2 covers the empirical support for exposure therapy. Section 3 details the application of exposure and constitutes the heart of the book. With the aim of this book being to guide the implementation of exposure, the techniques introduced in Section 3 are illustrated through case examples in Section 4. The book closes with a discussion of how to respond to common obstacles and where to find additional resources in Section 5.

WHY USE EXPOSURE?

One of the most common questions from patients, parents, and therapists is, "Why should I do exposure therapy?" This is a very reasonable question given

Exposure Therapy for Child and Adolescent Anxiety and OCD. Stephen P. H. Whiteside, Thomas H. Ollendick, and Bridget K. Biggs, Oxford University Press (2020). © Oxford University Press. DOI: 10.1093/med/9780190862992.001.0001

that exposure is often uncomfortable for everyone involved (youth, parents, and even therapists; Whiteside, Deacon, Benito, & Stewart, 2016). Youth or their parents may also wonder how exposure differs from the day-to-day struggles and challenges faced by someone with an anxiety disorder. The first answer, primarily for families, is that therapeutic exposure differs from unplanned daily life exposure in multiple important ways. Perhaps most important, exposure conducted in the context of therapy is designed to reduce or prevent escape and avoidance from the situation or thought, allowing the child to experience corrective learning. The child must remain in the situation long enough to evaluate the outcome without the cognitive distortions inherent during an anxious state. For example, a teen with social anxiety disorder may state that she confronts her anxiety every day when she attends school. However, if she avoids speaking to the peers who cause the most anxiety or tries to escape unavoidable conversations before she says the wrong thing, she will never have the chance to disprove her anxiety-causing beliefs. Therapeutic exposures are also conducted in a controlled, predictable, safe, and supportive manner that facilitates learning that anxiety in itself is not something to be feared and is manageable—conditions that are typically not present when feared situations are encountered in daily life.

The second major reason to engage in exposure therapy, primarily for clinicians, is that it enjoys the most empirical support of any treatment for childhood anxiety disorders and obsessive–compulsive disorder (OCD). In Section 2, we thoroughly review the literature supporting the use of exposure therapy. No other intervention, therapy, or medication has been evaluated as thoroughly as exposure-based treatments (Higa-McMillan, Kotte, Jackson, & Daleiden, 2017). This fact has three separate but related implications. First, there is sufficient evidence to encourage therapists to learn and implement exposure therapy as opposed to other traditional interventions, such as play therapy, relaxation, or general supportive therapy. Second, clinicians should be cautious about adopting the latest new trends in psychotherapy. Although innovations in therapy will undoubtedly lead to alternatives to exposure that may be as or more effective, initially promising approaches often fail to pan out. Until a new approach has been extensively supported by research, it should be viewed as a second-line approach to be used if exposure proves to be unsuccessful with a patient (Ollendick, Öst, & Farrell, 2018). Finally, in an age of increasing medicalization of mental health problems and emphasis on pharmaceutical interventions (Deacon, 2013), it may come as a surprise that exposure therapy rests upon a more substantial research base than medication for treating childhood anxiety disorders (Wang et al., 2017).

WHEN TO USE EXPOSURE?

Exposure therapy is most often associated with the treatment of excessive anxiety, fear, and worry. These symptoms occur within the disorders historically and/or currently categorized in the American Psychiatric Association's (APA) *Diagnostic and Statistical Manual of Mental Disorders* (DSM-IV [APA, 2000] and DSM-5 [APA, 2013]) as anxiety disorders: social anxiety disorder, selective mutism, separation anxiety disorder, generalized anxiety disorder, panic disorder, agoraphobia, specific phobias, OCD, and post-traumatic stress disorder (PTSD). Despite difficulties addressing the developmental context in which anxiety disorders occur (Whiteside & Ollendick, 2009), the DSM-5 diagnoses provide a convenient framework for summarizing a cluster of symptoms that are associated with specific treatment recommendations. Accordingly, throughout this book, we link our discussion of exposure to corresponding DSM diagnoses for anxiety and OCD (with more limited reference to PTSD). However, for a variety of reasons described next, this book is organized around the symptom target (i.e., external stimuli, thoughts, and bodily sensations) of the exposure rather than the diagnosis per se. Table 1.1 illustrates the connection between common exposure targets and DSM-5 anxiety-related diagnoses.

Categorization by symptom target promotes efficiency by emphasizing how a single technique can be applied across disorders (i.e., transdiagnostically). Rather than learning separate treatment protocols for approximately 10 different disorders, the underlying principles of exposure can be applied to all of them. In addition, the disorders treated with exposure are highly comorbid (Beesdo, Knappe, & Pine, 2009). Youth diagnosed with any one of the previously mentioned disorders typically also meet the criteria for some of the other anxiety disorders as well as additional non-anxiety disorders. Moreover, which anxiety diagnosis is primary and which diagnosis is secondary seems not to be important in the treatment of the disorders (Ollendick, Jarrett, White, White, & Grills, 2016). If therapy protocols were diagnosis specific, real-world practice would more often than not require therapists to integrate two or more protocols in the care of a single patient. A focus on symptom target, rather than diagnosis, is also compatible with the continuous nature of anxiety symptoms. For instance, fears and worries may warrant treatment even if they do not meet the criteria for one of the previously mentioned disorders or if they occur within the context of another disorder.

External Stimuli

The most commonly recognized application of exposure is in vivo exposure, in which patients confront external stimuli that provoke anxiety, specifically objects, situations, and activities. Example objects include animals for specific phobia and contaminated doorknobs for OCD. Example situations include riding elevators for specific phobia or going to crowded shopping malls for agoraphobia. Activities could include talking to peers for social anxiety disorder, stepping on cracks in the "incorrect" way for OCD, making small errors on homework for generalized anxiety disorder, or eating certain foods for a specific phobia of choking. These types of exposure are typically designed to approach the fear, ride out the anxiety without escape, and challenge the beliefs that something bad will likely happen (e.g., dogs will bite, germs on public surfaces lead to illness, people will react with annoyance, or imperfections on homework will lead to failure). Furthermore,

Table 1.1 EXPOSURE TARGETS AND DSM-5 DIAGNOSES

Target	Examples	DSM-5 Diagnoses
EXTERNAL		
Objects	Animals, sources of contamination, reminders of trauma	Specific phobia, OCD, PTSD
Situations	Elevators, attending school, site of traumatic experience	Specific phobia, agoraphobia, PTSD
Activities	Eating, talking to peers, stepping in the "wrong" place while walking	Specific phobia, social phobia, OCD
THOUGHTS		
Future worries	"I will fail the class"	GAD
Memories	Trauma narratives	PTSD
Intrusive thoughts	Blasphemous thoughts	OCD
BODILY SENSATIONS		
Panic	Hyperventilation, shortness of breath	Panic disorder
Being unwell	Upset stomach	Illness anxiety disorder, specific phobia

GAD, generalized anxiety disorder; OCD, obsessive–compulsive disorder; PTSD, post-traumatic stress disorder.

these exposures may also be designed to teach patients that they can handle the distress associated with reminders of a trauma, feeling panicky in public, feeling embarrassed during awkward pauses in conversations, or the sense that a pattern of walking is "just not right."

Thoughts

Thought exposure, also called imaginal exposure, involves confronting disturbing thoughts, memories, worries, or urges. Thought exposures should be used when the stimuli that produce anxiety are the thoughts themselves. This type of exposure is most often used with OCD, in which intrusive thoughts lead to ritualizing or other efforts to neutralize the thoughts, and with PTSD, in which traumatic memories are avoided because of the overwhelming emotions associated with them. For example, patients with fears of offending God may be prescribed to repeat the thought "I don't care about God" while refraining from ritualistic prayers (common escape behaviors that incidentally reinforce anxiety). Thought exposures for OCD frequently have the goal of demonstrating to patients that thoughts do not cause negative events, such as damnation or engaging in immoral behavior, even in the absence of rituals designed to undo the thought. Patients with PTSD may be assisted to recount the traumatic event without dissociating or suppressing emotions. When used with PTSD, narrative exposures commonly serve to demonstrate that although the traumatic memories will likely always be unpleasant, they do not have to be overwhelming and haunting and the patient does not need to avoid these thoughts to be safe. Based on success with OCD and PTSD, thought exposures can also be applied to future-oriented worries with the goal of demonstrating that thinking about a feared event does not cause it to come true and that the associated anxiety can indeed be tolerated and typically decreases with repeated exposure.

Bodily Sensations

Exposures to bodily sensations, or interoceptive exposures, are designed to elicit the physiological experience that triggers intense anxiety. These techniques were developed initially to address panic disorder and include exercises such as hyperventilation, breathing through a small straw, spinning in a chair, and running up and down stairs. The goal is to disconnect the typical bodily sensation (e.g., shortness of breath, dizziness, and heart racing) from the experience of anxiety, thereby teaching the patient that the physical sensations associated with anxiety and even intense panic may be uncomfortable but not dangerous. In addition to panic disorder, interoceptive exposures can be applied to other presentations in which the patient is afraid of the acute effect of the anxiety reaction. For example, hyperventilation could be applied to test anxiety if the child becomes anxious at the beginning of the test and then fears he will not be able to continue. Exposure to bodily sensations can also be used to address illness anxiety disorder, in which patients fear that physical symptoms such as dizziness or racing heart indicate the presence of an illness that might have long-term negative consequences.

Combining Exposure Techniques

Many anxiety presentations require the use of multiple exposure modalities. For example, a child with social phobia will need to do in vivo exposures that involve talking to peers but might also complete thought exposures to subsequent worries about the peers judging her. Moreover, multiple modalities can, and should, be combined together into a single exposure. Thought exposures can often be used to augment in vivo or interoceptive exposures. For instance, a boy with contamination-related OCD might repeat his feared thought, "I am going to get sick," while touching a hand railing in a public place. Moreover, to re-create the experience of panic attacks as closely as possible, a patient may hyperventilate while walking through a crowded hallway and repeating "I am going to pass out," thus combining all three exposure modalities.

Appropriate Emotion Targets

So far, we have focused primarily on using exposures to address anxiety, fear, and worry. However, exposure has also been successfully applied to other unpleasant emotions that can be impairing, such as disgust. Much of this research stems from work with OCD, a heterogeneous disorder that responds very well to exposure therapy. For example, exposure has been found to be successful for treating OCD symptoms stemming from disgust and the "just right" sensation (Abramowitz, Franklin, Schwartz, & Furr, 2003; Smits, Telch, & Randall, 2002). Whereas some children with contamination OCD fear that germs will lead to illness, others do not believe anything bad will happen, other than germs are disgusting and they will feel dirty until they wash themselves clean. Similarly, some children with OCD experience a sense that things are "not just right" if they tap a desk with one hand but not the other, chew their food an odd number of times, or write an imperfectly formed "e." For some children, the sense that something is "not just right" is linked to a fear that something bad will happen (e.g., a car accident), but many children simply fear that this uncomfortable feeling of incompleteness will never subside unless the item is "fixed" with a compulsion. Although disgust may not decrease as quickly as fear when doing exposures (McKay, 2006), both disgust and "not just right" sensations can be successfully treated with exposure. This finding also has implications beyond OCD as many specific phobias of animals have an element of disgust (Matchett & Davey, 1991).

As mentioned previously, exposure shares common components with many psychotherapeutic traditions—more generally the idea of confronting rather than avoiding unpleasant emotions. However, exposure differs from other approaches in the degree to which the negative emotions are purposely elicited and exaggerated. For example, a clinician treating an adolescent with social phobia would not merely have her talk about times she felt embarrassed and weigh the accuracy of those beliefs but, rather, would help her design exposures to purposely embarrass herself, experience the ebb and flow of anxiety, and learn that it was not as bad as she thought. As such, exposure tests the belief "something bad will happen" that is at the heart of fear and anxiety. Accordingly, this book is focused on the use of exposure to address anxiety (fear and worry), as well as some related experiences (disgust and "not just right"). Other emotions, including sadness and anger, require different therapeutic approaches. Certainly, some of the underlying treatment principles are similar, especially tolerating an emotion until it subsides. However, there is not a research literature demonstrating that purposely provoking heightened anger or sadness is an appropriate or effective treatment. For example, the behavioral treatment of depression primarily involves behavioral activation, which is designed to evoke enjoyment to decrease depression rather than to evoke sadness to demonstrate that it is tolerable. As such, first-line primary treatment of depression, disruptive behavior, eating disorders, autism spectrum disorders, psychosis, substance abuse, and other non-anxiety disorders is not addressed in this book.

Anxiety Disorders Versus Environmental Stress

Perhaps most important when determining whether to use exposure therapy with a patient is distinguishing between an anxiety disorder and environmental stress. Anxiety disorders are characterized by distorted overestimations of threat. For example, a socially anxious teen believes she is more likely than others to commit a social mishap and that it will be devastating if she does so, a child with separation anxiety believes he cannot handle being away from his mother for even a moment, a boy with a specific phobia of thunderstorms believes a tornado will occur whenever it gets cloudy outside and it will destroy his home and harm his family, a girl with generalized anxiety disorder worries about her grades even though she is on the A honor roll, and an adolescent with PTSD has nightmares about a car accident that occurred more than 1 year ago. In each case, the youth experiences intense anxiety and the need to avoid a situation that is generally safe and successfully navigated by other youth every day.

In contrast, environmental stress involves an anxiety reaction that is appropriate to the situation and similar to the response that would be expected by other youth in the same circumstance. Examples of environmental stress include a girl afraid to go to school because she is being bullied, an overly clingy child whose parents provide inadequate supervision due to substance abuse, a girl who worries about her failing grades related to poor reading skills, and an adolescent who fears his father's verbal and physical aggression. As can be seen from these examples, the difference between anxiety disorders and environmental stress is the degree of actual versus perceived threat.

Accurately evaluating whether a child's anxiety reflects an anxiety disorder versus environmental stress determines the course of treatment. As indicated previously, treatment of the former involves designing exposures to elicit anxiety and test the child's misperception. In contrast, treatment of environmental stress involves decreasing the child's anxiety through a variety of interventions, at times including avoiding the situation. Ideally, intervention for environmental stress results in fixing the problem, such as disciplining peers responsible for bullying, treating a reading disability, or providing family services. If the stressor cannot be removed, interventions may involve teaching coping skills, such as relaxation and problem-solving, and increasing the child's ability to manage stress, such as challenges related to experiencing a medical condition or family stressor. Although exposure is not the appropriate treatment for environmental stress, patient presentations in real life may not be so clear-cut. For example, at some point a child's reaction to a significant medical event could transition from expected stress indicating coping support to intrusive illness-related worries that are appropriate for exposure.

WHO USES EXPOSURE?

Exposure therapy has a long history of use with child anxiety. Mary Cover Jones, who worked with John B. Watson, recorded one of the first systematic examinations of various methods for eliminating fears in young children (Jones, 1924). Jones found that pure exposure, referred to as negative adaptation without additional re-educative measures, led to a reduction in fear and that pairing exposure with a positive activity—eating—engendered a positive response to the feared object. Although social imitation was also found to be successful, attempts to reduce the fear through discussion, ignoring, distraction, or social rebuke were unsuccessful. Because this study was a case series without the methodological rigor we have come to expect, its value is more of historical interest than probative (Ollendick, Sherman, Muris, & King, 2012). Nonetheless, the themes Jones examined remain relevant to modern treatment of childhood anxiety disorders. The interventions she found to be effective are precursors of using reinforcement and modeling to engage children in exposure therapy. In contrast, viewing clinical levels of anxiety as a phase that children simply outgrow is unlikely to be sufficient. The study also provides an inauspicious beginning for interventions that focus on discussing fears or distracting children from their fears rather than helping them face their fears (Ollendick & Muris, 2015).

Early on, exposure took the form of watching a model approach a feared object (i.e., vicarious learning; see Bandura, Grusec, & Menlove, 1967) and pairing anxiety with an incompatible physical state, typically relaxation (systematic desensitization; Wolpe, 1958). Research in the late 1960s and early 1970s witnessed the first randomized controlled trials (RCTs) of exposure therapy in children. Based on previous studies demonstrating the effectiveness of vicarious learning in the treatment of childhood phobias, Ritter (1968) compared group-based vicarious learning with and without contact desensitization (i.e., exposure) to a no treatment control. The children receiving exposure improved significantly more than did those without. This early study is of particular importance because it not only demonstrated that exposure was better than no treatment but also improved upon a treatment that had been previously found to be effective (Bandura et al., 1967). A second early RCT examined the effect of exposure apart from other aspects of systematic desensitization (Obler & Terwilliger, 1970). In order to treat specific phobias in children with neurological impairment, Obler and Terwilliger examined whether exposure could be successful without relaxation or awareness of the treatment procedures. The success of direct confrontation with feared stimuli encouraged through reinforcement in children regardless of intellectual ability suggested that exposure could be an effective stand-alone treatment. The effectiveness of exposure on its own as a superior treatment to vicarious learning was upheld two decades later in a seminal study conducted by Menzies and Clarke (1993).

The 1990s witnessed a surge in research into the treatment of child anxiety disorders, including three major advances. First, the application of exposure-based treatment was extended from specific phobias to include generally fearful and anxious children (Kendall, 1994), typically including children with separation anxiety disorder, generalized anxiety disorder (overanxious disorder in earlier studies), and social phobia (previously avoidant disorder). The second advance was that exposure therapy was combined with other anxiety management strategies such as relaxation, emotion identification, and cognitive restructuring into a treatment package called cognitive–behavioral therapy (CBT). This protocol most often took the form of introducing and building coping skills in the first half of treatment followed by completion of exposure exercises in the second half of treatment (Kendall, 2000). This structure was hypothesized to give children the skills they needed to tolerate and learn from exposures. The third advancement was adoption of modern experimental methods, including structured assessments, standardized questionnaires, and random assignment. The research in the 1990s established the efficacy of exposure-based CBT for child anxiety disorders, and much of the subsequent and current research into child anxiety treatment is rooted in this work.

Between 2000 and 2018, more than 100 RCTs of exposure-based treatments for childhood anxiety disorders were performed. Following the introduction of the individual-based CBT protocol, the intervention has been successfully adapted to group settings, family-based administration, brief formats, and electronic delivery. In addition to the diagnoses previously mentioned, exposure-based treatments have been applied to childhood OCD, panic disorder, and PTSD. The importance, tolerability, and effectiveness of exposure as a stand-alone intervention are increasingly being supported for anxiety and OCD (Ale, McCarthy, Rothschild, & Whiteside, 2015; Whiteside et al., 2015, in press). Overall, exposure-based therapies have a long history of use with childhood anxiety disorders and are the most thoroughly examined treatment option available.

SUMMARY

Exposure therapy shares with many other therapeutic interventions the goal of decreasing emotional and behavioral dysfunction through confrontation rather than avoidance of distressing emotional stimuli. Exposure stands apart from other interventions in its clarity of purpose and directness. Exposure therapy is designed to help patients tolerate anxiety without avoidance, thereby allowing natural anxiety reduction and providing patients with learning experiences that correct exaggerated beliefs about the likelihood and severity of negative events. In Chapter 2, we discuss various theories regarding the mechanisms through which the therapeutic benefits of exposure might occur. Exposure-based therapy has a long and extensive history of use and rigorous testing. In Chapters 3 and 4, we more closely examine the empirical support for exposure in general and with children in particular. When careful assessment suggests that a child's symptoms include anxiety (or the related disgust and "not just right" phenomena) related to overestimations of harm, rather than environmental stress, clinicians should consider use of exposure therapy.

REFERENCES

Abramowitz, J. S., Franklin, M. E., Schwartz, S. A., & Furr, J. M. (2003). Symptom presentation and outcome of cognitive–behavioral therapy for obsessive–compulsive disorder. *Journal of Consulting and Clinical Psychology, 71*(6), 1049–1057. doi:10.1037/0022-006X.71.6.1049

Ale, C. M., McCarthy, D. M., Rothschild, L., & Whiteside, S. (2015). Components of cognitive behavioral therapy related to outcome in childhood anxiety disorders. *Clinical Child and Family Psychology Review, 18*, 240–251. doi:10.1007/s10567-015-0184-8

American Psychiatric Association. (2000). *Quick reference to the diagnostic criteria from DSM-IV-TR.* Washington, DC: Author.

American Psychiatric Association. (2013). *Diagnostic and statistical manual of mental disorders* (5th ed.). Arlington, VA: American Psychiatric Publishing.

Bandura, A., Grusec, J. E., & Menlove, F. L. (1967). Vicarious extinction of avoidance behavior. *Journal of Personality and Social Psychology, 5*(1), 16–23.

Beesdo, K., Knappe, S., & Pine, D. S. (2009). Anxiety and anxiety disorders in children and adolescents: Developmental issues and implications for DSM-V. *Psychiatric Clinics of North America, 32*, 483–524. doi:10.1016/j.psc.2009.06.002

Carey, T. A. (2011). Exposure and reorganization: The what and how of effective psychotherapy. *Clinical Psychology Review, 31*, 236–248.

Deacon, B. J. (2013). The biomedical model of mental disorder: A critical analysis of its validity, utility, and effects on psychotherapy research. *Clinical Psychology Review, 33*, 846–861. doi:dx.doi.org/10.1016/j.cpr.2012.09.007

Foa, E. B., & Kozak, M. J. (1986). Emotional processing of fear: Exposure to corrective information. *Psychological Bulletin, 99*, 20–35.

Higa-McMillan, C., Kotte, A., Jackson, D., & Daleiden, E. L. (2017). Overlapping and non-overlapping practices in usual and evidence-based care for youth anxiety. *Journal of Behavioral Health Services and Research, 44*(4), 684–694. doi:10.1007/s11414-016-9502-2

Jones, M. C. (1924). The elimination of children's fears. *Journal of Experimental Psychology, 7*, 383–390.

Kendall, P. C. (1994). Treating anxiety disorders in children: Results of a randomized clinical trial. *Journal of Consulting and Clinical Psychology, 62*(1), 100–110.

Kendall, P. C. (2000). *Cognitive–behavioral therapy for anxious children: Therapist manual* (2nd ed.). Ardmore, PA: Workbook.

Matchett, G., & Davey, G. C. L. (1991). A test of a disease-avoidance model of animal phobia. *Behaviour Research and Therapy, 29*, 91–94.

McKay, D. (2006). Treating disgust reactions in contamination-based obsessive–compulsive disorder. *Journal of Behavior Therapy and Experimental Psychiatry, 37*(1), 53–59. doi:10.1016/j.jbtep.2005.09.005

Menzies, R. G., & Clarke, J. C. (1993). A comparison of in vivo and vicarious exposure in the treatment of childhood water phobia. *Behaviour Research and Therapy, 31*(1), 9–15. doi:0005-7967(93)90037-U

Obler, M., & Terwilliger, R. F. (1970). Pilot study on the effectiveness of systematic desensitization with neurologically impaired children with phobic disorders. *Journal of Consulting and Clinical Psychology, 34*(3), 314–318.

Ollendick, T. H., Jarrett, M. A., White, B. A., White, S. W., & Grills, A. E. (2016). Primary versus secondary diagnosis of generalized anxiety disorder in youth: Is the distinction an important one? *Child Psychiatry and Human Development, 47*(4), 548–553. doi:10.1007/s10578-015-0588-1

Ollendick, T. H., & Muris, P. (2015). The scientific legacy of Little Hans and Little Albert: Future directions for research on specific phobias in youth. *Journal of Clinical Child and Adolescent Psychology, 44*(4), 689–706. doi:10.1080/15374416.2015.1020543

Ollendick, T. H., Öst, L. G., & Farrell, L. J. (2018). Innovations in the psychosocial treatment of youth with anxiety disorders: Implications for a stepped care approach. *Evidence Based Mental Health, 21*(3), 112–115. doi:10.1136/eb-2018-102892

Ollendick, T. H., Sherman, T. M., Muris, P. E. H. M., & King, N. J. (2012). Conditioned emotional reactions: Beyond Watson and Rayner's Little Albert. In A. M. Slater & P. C. Quinn (Eds.), *Developmental psychology: Revisiting the classic studies* (pp. 24–35). London, UK: Sage.

Ritter, B. (1968). The group desensitization of children's snake phobias using vicarious and contact desensitization procedures. *Behaviour Research and Therapy, 6*(1), 1–6.

Smits, J. A., Telch, M. J., & Randall, P. K. (2002). An examination of the decline in fear and disgust during exposure-based treatment. *Behaviour Research and Therapy, 40*(11), 1243–1253.

Wang, Z., Whiteside, S. P. H., Sim, L., Farah, W., Morrow, A. S., Alsawas, M., . . . Murad, M. H. (2017). Comparative effectiveness and safety of cognitive behavioral therapy and pharmacotherapy for childhood anxiety disorders: A systematic review and meta-analysis. *JAMA Pediatrics, 171*(11), 1049–1056. doi:10.1001/jamapediatrics.2017.3036

Whiteside, S. P., & Ollendick, T. H. (2009). Developmental perspectives on anxiety classification. In D. McKay, J. S. Abramowitz, & S. Taylor (Eds.), *Current perspectives on the anxiety disorders: Implications for DSM-V and beyond* (pp. 303–325). New York, NY: Springer.

Whiteside, S. P. H., Ale, C. M., Young, B., Dammann, J., Tiede, M. S., & Biggs, B. K. (2015). The feasibility of improving CBT for childhood anxiety disorders through a dismantling study. *Behaviour Research and Therapy, 73*, 83–89. doi:10.1016/j.brat.2015.07.011

Whiteside, S. P. H., Deacon, B. J., Benito, K., & Stewart, E. (2016). Factors associated with practitioners' use of exposure therapy for childhood anxiety disorders. *Journal of Anxiety Disorders, 40*, 29–36. doi:http://dx.doi.org/10.1016/j.janxdis.2016.04.001

Whiteside, S. P. H., Sim, L. A., Morrow, A. S., Farah, W. H., Hilliker, D. R., Murad, M. H., & Wang, Z. (in press). A meta-analysis to guide the enhancement of CBT for childhood anxiety: Exposure over Anxiety Management. *Clinical Child and Family Psychology Review.*

Wolpe, J. (1958). *Psychotherapy by reciprocal inhibition.* Stanford, CA: Stanford University Press.

Theoretical Base and Mechanism of Action

Despite the strong empirical support for the efficacy of exposure therapy, disagreement remains regarding the theoretical underpinnings of how and why exposure works. To some, these theoretical distinctions will seem like splitting hairs; to others, they seem like foundational chasms. In this chapter, we endeavor to introduce the primary mechanistic theories of how exposure leads to symptom change and then provide a working model based on these theories. In the following chapters, we present guiding principles and specific steps for implementing exposure to youth with different disorders. These principles are grounded in the mechanistic theories reviewed here and integrated in the clinical model presented at the end of the chapter. The order of this presentation is based on our belief that understanding how exposure works allows therapists to apply this technique in situations that do not fit neatly within their previous experiences. Given the heterogeneity of anxiety problems, it is important to have a theoretical framework of the mechanisms of action to guide implementation and problem-solving. Establishing such an understanding is the goal of this chapter.

EXISTING THEORIES REGARDING EXPOSURE'S MECHANISM OF ACTION

Anxiety Inhibition

Early forays into exposure therapy often focused on replacing anxious feelings with a more appealing, and even reinforcing, experience. The theory suggested that if an individual repeatedly encountered a feared stimulus while experiencing an emotional state incompatible with anxiety, over time the more pleasant reaction would replace the initial fear reaction. For example, Mary Cover Jones (1924), in a method referred to as direct conditioning, paired a feared object with eating to help young children overcome anxiety. The most influential inhibition approach was *reciprocal inhibition*, in which relaxation strategies were used as an

Exposure Therapy for Child and Adolescent Anxiety and OCD. Stephen P. H. Whiteside, Thomas H. Ollendick, and Bridget K. Biggs, Oxford University Press (2020). © Oxford University Press.
DOI: 10.1093/med/9780190862992.001.0001

incompatible response to inhibit a fear response (Wolpe, 1958). *Systematic desensitization* refers to the gradual application of reciprocal inhibition to items arranged on a "stepladder" that produce increasing amounts of fear responses, commonly employing progressive muscle relaxation and imagery as strategies to inhibit anxiety. For example, Miller, Barrett, Hampe, and Noble (1972) first trained children in relaxation and then created a fear hierarchy. Once these items were in place, the children were instructed to relax and then imagine a feared scene. If the children became anxious, the therapist instructed them to switch to relaxation. Once the children could imagine the feared scenes without anxiety, treatment proceeded to in vivo tests. The goal of therapy was summarized as helping the children (and parents) "develop alternative responses which would inhibit fear" and allow the child to "experience the fear-inducing situation without anxiety" (p. 271).

Early research supported the effectiveness of systematic desensitization (Ollendick & Cerny, 1981). However, interest in the theory of reciprocal inhibition as the mechanism of action underlying treatment success and the associated application of systematic desensitization began to decline by the early 1980s (McGlynn, Smitherman, & Gothard, 2004). This decline was likely hastened by suspicion that the treatment was likely effective because of exposure to feared stimuli rather than inhibition of anxiety per se. Specifically, systematic desensitization shared with other effective treatments, such as flooding, the common element of exposure. Moreover, studies documenting that anxiety symptoms could be reduced through exposure without relaxation, such as that by Obler and Terwilliger (1970), questioned the theory that systematic desensitization led to change through inhibiting fear with a new and more desirable incompatible response. Concurrently, there was also a growing interest in the role of cognition in the presentation and treatment of anxiety disorders (McGlynn et al., 2004). Eventually, these two movements contributed to the development of new theories regarding how exposure works.

Habituation

As opposed to the theory that exposure works through the active process of working to calm one's body to inhibit fear, habituation posits a passive model to explain the process of exposure. Habituation is a basic behavioral learning principle that refers to a diminished response, in this case a fear reaction, resulting from repeated or prolonged stimulation, in this case exposure (Rankin et al., 2009). Although habituation alone is not generally presented as a complete theoretical explanation for the mechanism by which exposure leads to improvement, it has played an important role in the historical and current discussions of how exposure works. For decades, successful treatment with exposure was thought to require habituation consisting of (1) the activation of fear, (2) the absence or minimization of fear-reducing or "safety" behaviors, and (3) the reduction of anxiety within and between sessions (Benito & Walther, 2015). In other words, the patient needs to experience fear and have it subside without avoiding or escaping the fear. It is important to note that the habituation model posits that fear-inhibiting behaviors, such as relaxation exercises, rituals, reassurance seeking, and safety behaviors, are not only unnecessary but also counterproductive. As such, the habituation model shares confrontation of feared stimuli with the reciprocal inhibition model, but contrasts sharply on the prescribed behavior during that confrontation.

A number of empirical studies support the importance of habituation for successful exposure therapy. Most recently, a review of exposure sessions during treatment for pediatric obsessive-compulsive disorder (OCD) found that more habituation was related to improved outcome (Benito et al., 2018). In addition, the researchers found that higher levels of anxiety during exposures that did not habituate were related to poorer outcomes. This direct examination of child treatment is supported by other studies demonstrating that not only does anxiety generally decrease during exposure but also such decreases are directly related to better improvement (Benito & Walther, 2015). In addition, a number of studies with adults have documented the deleterious effect of safety behaviors to the success of exposure (Benito & Walther, 2015).

However, the empirical support for the importance of habituation, and thus its role in understanding the mechanism of action for exposure, is a topic of vigorous debate. It has not been clearly established that initial fear activation, a necessary precursor to the habituation of anxiety, is related to outcome (Craske et al., 2008). Moreover, in contrast to the studies described previously, the literature as a whole has not found that habituation during exposures, or between exposures, is necessary for treatment improvement (Craske et al., 2008). However, before disregarding the importance of habituation, one must acknowledge the potential barriers to examining the role of anxiety reduction during exposure (Benito & Walther, 2015). Most exposure sessions involve shifting the intensity of the exposure to match the patient's needs. This often means increasing the degree of challenge as the patient's anxiety decreases. Compare a patient whose end level anxiety is 70% lower than his peak anxiety after sitting in a room with a dog to a patient whose end level anxiety is 40% lower than peak anxiety but who began in a room with the dog and then gradually approached until she was standing next to the dog. In this example, the change in anxiety does not reflect the relative degree of habituation experienced by each patient. Actions performed during exposure by the patient or the therapist to reduce anxiety, such as ritualizing or decreasing the degree of challenge, also complicate the study of habituation (Benito & Walther, 2015). In these cases, decreases in anxiety do not reflect habituation but, rather, avoidance. For these reasons, and in light of recent research that addresses these barriers, the contribution of habituation to successful exposures continues to be a concept worthy of consideration (Benito et al., 2018).

Emotional Processing Theory

The centrality of habituation to exposure therapy has been most closely associated with the emotional processing theory first articulated by Rachman (1980) and later expanded upon by Foa and Kozak (1986). This theory proposes that "fear is represented in memory structures that serve as blueprints for fear behavior, and therapy is a process by which these structures are modified" (Foa & Kozak, 1986, p. 21). Reduction in anxiety occurs when the fear memory and related physiological arousal is activated and "corrective information" is introduced. During exposure, corrective information can take the form of the feared events either not occurring or being less aversive than anticipated, as well as anxiety or distress being more tolerable than expected.

To be informative, exposures must match the individual's fear structure as closely as possible. This match was operationalized as the activation of fear, often measured through physiological variables such as heart rate. Habituation was proposed as reflecting emotional processing and changes in fear structures. Moreover, habituation also directly provides corrective information that the stimuli do not necessarily need to be associated with a fear response and that the experience of fear dissipates without avoidance. Habituation within sessions was viewed as allowing a decrease in the expectation of harm and as a prerequisite for between-session habituation that reflects a decreased need for preparatory anxiety, which then subsequently results in symptom improvement. Foa and Kozak (1986) distinguish between a simple decrease in anxiety and habituation by emphasizing the importance of maintaining attention on the feared stimuli because avoidance during exposures will prevent learning even if anxiety decreases.

The adequacy and accuracy of emotional processing theory have been challenged based on the inability of research to consistently support the tenants of the theory. As mentioned previously, physiological measures of fear activation have not been consistently found to relate to outcome (Craske et al., 2008). However, such a direct relationship may not be necessary because (1) simply activating fear at any level may be sufficient, (2) a moderate amount of activation may be more effective than high or low activation, or (3) activation may be helpful if and only if the patient is allowed to habituate (Benito et al., 2018; Benito & Walther, 2015; Foa & Kozak, 1986). Of more concern, the inability of research to demonstrate that habituation during an exposure is necessary for treatment improvement substantially questions the tenants upon which emotional processing theory rests. However, as mentioned previously, the definitiveness of this research is open to debate, and Foa and colleagues have modified their theory in response to recent work (Foa, Huppert, & Cahill, 2006). Despite these uncertainties, the premise of emotional processing theory—that patients benefit from engaging with a feared stimulus long enough to experience corrective emotional information—remains valuable.

Cognitive Change

In contrast to the habituation-based models of exposure that emphasize change in emotional and physiological aspects of anxiety, cognitive models focus on changes to beliefs (Salkovskis, Hackmann, Wells, Gelder, & Clark, 2006). These models

were based on, and are supported by, theories and research recognizing that anxious individuals tend to have inaccurate beliefs, such as overestimating the likelihood of danger, that contribute to anxiety (Kendall, 1985; Ollendick, Öst, Ryan,
Capriola, & Reuterskiold, 2017; Ollendick, Ryan, Capriola-Hall, Reuterskiold, &
Öst, 2017; Rozenman, Vreeland, & Piacentini, 2017). Consequently, therapeutic
approaches (i.e., cognitive therapy) were developed that focus on changing maladaptive beliefs through techniques such as cognitive restructuring. In this approach, anxiety-provoking thoughts are identified, labeled as a specific type of
error (e.g., intolerance of uncertainty and danger expectancy), and challenged
through logical evaluation. Frequently, cognitive therapy involves "behavioral
experiments" during which patients engage in an activity to challenge their anxiety-
causing beliefs—a process commonly viewed as akin to exposure (Berman, Fang,
Hansen, & Wilhelm, 2015). With youth, cognitive change techniques are often
combined with exposure in cognitive–behavioral therapy (CBT). In this model,
training in cognitive techniques is viewed as necessary to prepare children to
learn from behavioral exposures (Kendall, 1985). In either application, from a
cognitive change perspective, exposure disconfirms the anxiety-provoking catastrophic misconceptions by demonstrating that the feared events do not occur.

In support of this theory, fear-related cognitions change with successful treatment (Ollendick, Öst, et al., 2017; Ollendick, Ryan, et al., 2017). In addition,
behavioral experiments may improve upon habituation-centered exposure, although the literature suffers from significant limitations (McMillan & Lee, 2010).
More broadly, enthusiasm for cognitive theories of change is tempered by the general inability to find that cognitive interventions improve upon exposure or that
cognitive change is necessary for, or a cause of, symptom improvement (Kendall
et al., 2016; Longmore & Worrell, 2007; Whiteside et al., in press). Research regarding cognitive strategies for child anxiety is likely complicated by the developmental variability in cognitive ability between young children and adolescents, as
well as by the variety of strategies that fall within this category of interventions.
These challenges notwithstanding, the negative findings regarding the efficacy of
cognitive strategies have contributed to a new wave of theories for therapeutic
improvement that are not ostensibly predicated upon cognition.

Acceptance and Commitment Therapy

Acceptance and commitment therapy (ACT) diverges from the other models
presented here through its focus on accepting, rather than changing, anxiety
responses. Specifically, ACT postulates that improvement with treatment stems
from increased acceptance of inner experiences and commitment to pursue
valued activities despite the potential for unpleasant inner experiences (Arch &
Craske, 2008). The mechanism of change is thought to be an increase in psychological flexibility, or the ability to be present in the moment and separate oneself
from one's inner experiences (Twohig et al., 2015). The goals of reducing anxiety
central to the habituation model and challenging unrealistic expectations central

to the cognitive model are viewed as counterproductive in that they contribute to pre-existing futile and detrimental attempts to suppress unpleasant experiences. Furthermore, consistent with the focus on commitment to one's values, rather than prearranging exposures as contrived opportunities to challenge anxiety or associated beliefs, ACT exposures are more likely to be activities that are inherently important to the patient. Consequently, there is more focus on reducing avoidance of activities despite anxiety, as opposed to purposefully seeking activities to induce anxiety. Moreover, during implementation, rather than tracking a patient's anxiety or strength of beliefs, under an ACT rubric clinicians might measure a patient's willingness to engage in the feared activity (Twohig et al., 2015).

Despite the previously discussed differences, the degree to which the acceptance and commitment paradigm contributes to a novel understanding of the mechanism of change underlying exposure remains to be determined. Acceptance-based strategies may have more in common than not with traditional cognitive–behavioral approaches (Arch & Craske, 2008). For example, cognitive defusion and cognitive restructuring may both be forms of self-talk that can serve as exposure to distressing thoughts or be misused as thought suppression. In addition, acceptance and cognitive–behavioral approaches may both give individuals tools that increase their sense of self-efficacy by decreasing the unpredictability and uncontrollability of anxiety. Perhaps because of a high degree of overlap, acceptance- and commitment-based treatments have not been able to improve upon traditional CBT (Öst, 2014), including for child anxiety (Hancock et al., 2018). Despite these limitations, the success of acceptance and commitment approaches contributes a new and valuable emphasis on accepting, rather than diminishing or correcting, unpleasant emotions and unrealistic thoughts.

Coping Model

The role of exposure in helping children develop more effective coping skills has been a dominant model in the child anxiety treatment literature. Coping skills can include a number of different strategies but generally are active attempts to manage emotions and one's surrounding, often including problem-solving and relaxation strategies (Kendall et al., 2016). This theory has led to CBT protocols that teach children coping skills during the first half of treatment and then guide the implementation of these skills through exposure during the second half (Kendall, 2000). The coping model is based on the assumption that instruction in coping skills is a necessary precursor to exposure, not only to facilitate cognitive change as discussed previously but also to tolerate the unpleasant experience of exposure (Kendall, 1985; Manassis, Russell, & Newton, 2010). Once children have received instruction in coping skills, exposures are viewed as providing repeated opportunities to increase their sense of self-efficacy through successful practice of these skills (Kendall et al., 2005). Support for this model of change derives from the vast literature demonstrating the effectiveness of treatments consistent with this paradigm (Wang et al., 2017) as well as the role of coping efficacy as a potential mediator of outcome (Kendall et al., 2016).

The coping model shares commonalities with some of the models we have previously reviewed. First, both coping and anxiety inhibition models propose replacing the experience of anxiety with relaxation exercises. Second, as mentioned previously, the coping model overlaps with the cognitive change model through its focus on identifying and changing anxiety-provoking cognitions and expectancies. On the other hand, the coping model diverges from habituation/emotional processing theory and ACT through the prescribing of active coping rather than passive attention to either learn corrective information or accept unpleasant inner experiences, respectively. Specifically, the mechanism of change in the coping model is increasing confidence in one's ability to manage stressful situations rather than learning that such situations are not as dangerous as one thought. Enthusiasm for the coping model is dampened by research questioning the added benefit of cognitive or relaxation strategies (Ale, McCarthy, Rothschild, & Whiteside, 2015; Longmore & Worrell, 2007; Whiteside et al., in press). Moreover, to the extent that coping strategies distract individuals from learning that situations are relatively safe or that negative emotions are tolerable, these strategies may hinder the learning processes emphasized in other models of change. Furthermore, the incomplete nature of the empirical support for treatments based on the coping model (i.e., difficulty improving over other credible treatments and underperforming relative to other exposure-based treatments) undercuts the attractiveness of this model (Ale et al., 2015; Whiteside et al., 2015).

Inhibitory Learning

In light of the inability of previous models to adequately explain the mechanism of action underlying exposure and account for the empirical findings regarding the return of fear, inhibitory learning theory was proposed based on basic research into learning and memory (Craske et al., 2008). Inhibitory learning theory differs from previous models in large part through the assertion that exposure therapy does not *degrade existing connections* between stimuli and the fear reactions but, rather, *creates new safety learning that competes* with previous association. As such, the goal of exposure is to create varied learning experiences that make it more likely that safety associations, rather than fear associations, will be accessed by an individual. As a result, inhibitory learning provides a number of specific recommendations for enhancing the implementation of exposure.

Much of the distinction between inhibitory learning theory and emotional processing theory, the previously dominant model, focuses on the role of habituation (Craske et al., 2008). Whereas emotional processing theory views decreases in fear as a reflection of corrective learning, inhibitory learning disconnects the expression of fear from learning and asserts that the continued experience of fear— that is, lack of habituation—is a poor proxy for learning. Instead, the focus is placed on expectancy violations. Exposures are continued for as long as needed for the individual to learn that what he or she expected to happen did not, regardless of fear level (Craske, Treanor, Conway, Zbozinek, & Vervliet, 2014). In fact, measuring anxiety levels during exposure raises concerns of inadvertently communicating that the patient should repress rather than tolerate distress. Instead, the therapist should elicit from the patient their feared outcome and likelihood of it occurring and then continue the exposure until the patient's likelihood judgment is sufficiently low (e.g., 5%; Deacon et al., 2013).

Inhibitory learning also differs from the coping model in the approach to preparing for exposures. As reviewed previously, the coping model directs youth to use cognitive and relaxation strategies to manage exposures. In contrast, inhibitory learning theory posits that anxiety and feared beliefs should be high at the beginning of exposures because learning experiences are strongest when the mismatch between the expectancy and the experience is greatest. In addition, some research suggests that heightened anxiety may actually enhance learning (Craske et al., 2008, 2014). As such, efforts to use coping strategies to reduce expectations of harm or physiological anxiety may actually be detrimental. In another departure from the traditional approach to exposure, inhibitory learning theory hypothesizes that conducting exposures in an unpredictable order, rather than progressing linearly up a graduated fear ladder, may enhance the accessibility of new safety learning. Other practical implications from the learning and memory literature include combining two feared stimuli together, removal of safety signals, varying the content of exposures, and maintaining attention during exposures.

To date, there has been relatively little criticism or empirical documentation of inhibitory learning theory, possibly because the theory is relatively new. However, inhibitory learning, as with all theories, should be evaluated critically. First, the superiority of learning theory over emotional processing lies in the latter's inability to account for empirical findings, specifically regarding habituation. As such, research supporting the importance of habituation (Benito et al., 2018) has theoretical implications regarding the relative adequacy of each theory, as well as practical implication regarding the appropriateness of tracking anxiety levels. However, research supporting the importance of habituation could be consistent with both theories because this process is acknowledged to potentially play a role in extinction learning (Craske et al., 2014). Second, as with other models, the adequacy of inhibitory learning theory lies in its ability to account for empirical findings. However, to date a number of specific predictions made by inhibitory learning theory have not been empirically confirmed. For instance, the literature does not clearly support the predictions regarding the deleterious effect of distraction or the benefits of compound exposures, cognitive enhancers, spaced practice, shifting contexts, retrieval cues, and reconsolidation (Weisman & Rodebaugh, 2018). Because the existing literature is small, each of these predictions may eventually be supported by empirical findings. However, we recommend caution when discarding previous theories that have guided the successful development of exposure therapy, based on inconsistent basic research, when the replacement theory also has inconsistent basic research support without the history of clinical support.

A CLINICAL MODEL OF EXPOSURE'S MECHANISM OF ACTION TO GUIDE IMPLEMENTATION

As the previous review demonstrates, important questions remain unanswered about how exposure brings about change and thus what implementation or augmentation strategies are likely to maximize improvement. Fortunately, sufficient commonalities exist to assemble a working model regarding the mechanism of action underlying exposure to guide clinical implementation. In presenting this model, we endeavor to be consistent with basic research supporting existing theories, clinical research documenting the efficacy of exposure therapy, and the realities of clinical practice based on our experience. By considering clinical practice, we attempt to provide a framework that is understandable and practical. Moreover, we believe it would be irresponsible to recommend in a practitioner-oriented resource volume such as this new strategies that have not been field tested in our own clinical practice or research studies. Overall, our goal is not to contribute to the theoretical debates regarding how exposures works but, rather, to translate our understanding of these theories and empirical support into a clinical framework to guide the use of exposure for childhood anxiety and OCD. The framework discussed next is summarized in Table 2.1.

Overview

We begin by specifying our objective with exposure therapy. Namely, the goal of treatment is to *decrease the degree to which anxiety regarding acceptably safe*

Table 2.1 A CLINIC THEORY OF EXPOSURE'S MECHANISM OF ACTION

Goal of treatment
Decrease the degree to which anxiety regarding acceptably safe situations contributes to excessive distress and dysfunction
Principle 1: Exposures should be intentional and frequent.
Exposure therapy should include repeatedly and intentionally seeking out life-like experiences, frequently for no other purpose than to elicit and challenge the anxiety response.
Principle 2: Exposures should provoke a fear response.
Exposures should engage both the emotional and cognitive aspects of anxiety, without efforts to attenuate the anxiety response prior to beginning the exposure (with children, the emotional components are frequently more accessible).
Principle 3: Exposures should disconfirm fears.
An exposure should be continued until the child's fears of negative events or intolerability of anxiety has been disproven (with children, such changes are often most accessible through anxiety ratings).

situations contributes to excessive distress and dysfunction. This definition is consistent with the focus on distress and dysfunction as hallmarks for psychiatric disorders in common diagnostic systems (American Psychiatric Association, 2013). Accordingly, treatment must alleviate distress and improve functioning. In addition, our definition emphasizes the difference between anxiety regarding reasonably safe situations, for which exposure is indicated, and reactions to environmental stress, for which exposure is not indicated. As such, treatment must focus on learning that the world is less dangerous than the patient currently believes, as opposed to learning to cope with adverse circumstances. Finally, the definition emphasizes *decreasing* excessive anxiety, as opposed to completely *removing* anxiety, a goal that would be impossible and undesirable. Accordingly, treatment must also include learning that anxiety is tolerable and even good for us. In summary, we propose that exposures promote symptom improvement by providing youth the opportunity to learn that their fears are unlikely to come true and that their anxious feelings are tolerable, as well as by directly decreasing the avoidance that contributes to dysfunction and replacing it with approach behaviors. Next, we outline important principles for conducting exposures based on this clinical model and how it relates to existing theories.

Exposures Should Be Intentional and Frequent

Treatment must include frequent attempts to face ones' fears that are designed to optimize learning. All the theories reviewed previously emphasize the importance of individuals engaging with feared stimuli long enough to determine that the stimulus does not need to be avoided in the future. As such, our first principle is that exposure works through experiential learning, and so these experiences need to be repeated, intentional, and life-like. To some extent, this is an unsurprising conclusion based on a review of exposure models in a book on exposures. However, this principle strays from straight cognitive therapy in which "behavioral experiments" are one of multiple change strategies, from some versions of the coping model that do not include in-session exposures (Whiteside et al., in press), and from ACT in which exposure consists more of eliminating avoidance during daily life rather than planned experiments. Instead our proposal is more consistent with the other theories in which exposures are sought out explicitly to challenge anxiety and so may frequently include engaging in activities with no purpose other than eliciting the anxiety response.

Exposures Should Provoke a Fear Response

To be effective, the exposure activities that are intentionally sought out or created need to evoke the youth's fear response. Although each theory of exposure's mechanism of action operationalizes the construct differently, they all emphasize the importance of engaging in activities that have elicited anxiety. The anxiety inhibition and coping models necessitate the experience of fear to have the opportunity to replace that feeling or cope with the situation, respectively. The habituation and emotional processing model posits that the elicitation of anxious feelings is a prerequisite for learning, whereas the inhibitory learning and cognitive models focus on the engagement of fear-provoking beliefs or expectancies. Finally, the ACT model prescribes engaging in valued activities regardless of immediate emotional distress. As such, there is consensus that experiencing the fear response, emotional and/or cognitive, is a necessary aspect of successful exposure. Thus, in our clinical model, we propose that it is necessary to engage both emotional and cognitive aspects of anxiety. However, it has been our experience that it is more clinically feasible with youth, especially younger children, to identify situations that provoke *feeling* anxious rather than specific cognitions. Specifically, many children are unable to verbalize specific fears. Thus, we recommend that exposures be designed to evoke the feelings of anxiety and that the clinician, to the extent possible, also attempts to identify the beliefs that cause that anxiety.

Moreover, we recommend that clinicians include exposure exercises that evoke high levels of anxiety without efforts to attenuate the anxiety prior to beginning the exposure. This recommendation is consistent with the emotional processing theory that fear structures need to be activated in exposures. Although the connection between higher fear activation and better outcome has not be established, inhibitory learning theory also postulates that higher fear expectancies pre-exposure lead to more impactful learning experiences and that heightened arousal may improve learning. Given our perception of the clinical challenges to measuring fear expectancies in youth, we recommend using child-reported (and parent-reported) fear levels as a practical guide to ensuring that exposures elicit sufficient fear responses, while incorporating fear expectancies as possible.

Exposures Should Disconfirm Fears

All the theories of exposure's mechanism of action again converge upon the necessity of learning corrective information, although the theories diverge on the nature of that information. Habituation/emotional processing, cognitive change, and inhibitory learning theories emphasize learning that feared consequences do not occur (i.e., that the world is less dangerous than previously believed). In contrast, anxiety inhibition, ACT, and the coping model focus more on learning that one can handle the situation through replacing anxiety, accepting unpleasant emotions, or increasing coping efficacy (i.e., that one is more capable than previously believed). In keeping with our definition of anxiety disorders and treatment goals (addressing unrealistic anxiety in reasonably safe situations), we believe that helping patients learn that situations are not as dangerous as they thought is an essential therapeutic task. Thus, our framework is consistent with the habituation/emotional processing, cognitive change, and inhibitory learning models. However, we do not disregard the role of self-efficacy because this likely is an important step in first engaging patients in exposure and is compatible with inhibitory learning theory (Craske et al., 2008).

As reviewed previously, theories of habituation/emotional processing, cognitive change, and inhibitory learning diverge on how best to assess and optimize the learning that occurs with exposure about the threat posed by the environment. Habituation/emotional processing theory postulates that a decrease in anxiety indicates that the previously feared stimulus is no longer associated with anxiety. Cognitive change theories propose that patients disconfirm exaggerated beliefs of danger and develop new, more realistic beliefs regarding safety. Inhibitory learning theory proposes that new associations that harm is unlikely to occur begin to outcompete danger associations. The differences between these theories potentially have implications for how exposures are set up, conducted, and ended. Specifically, whereas the habituation/emotional processing theory sets a decrease in anxiety as the goal of exposure, the latter two focus on disconfirming beliefs or expectations. Despite important conceptual differences, each approach relies on the patient reporting their internal experience, whether it be feelings, beliefs, or likelihood expectancies. Reference back to our goal of therapy, as well as the tripartite theory of anxiety, suggests that successful treatment needs to address the emotional and cognitive aspects of anxiety disorders, in addition to the behavioral component inherently addressed through exposure. As such, the approach we outline attempts to be consistent with the tenets of the habituation/emotional processing as well as the inhibitory learning/cognitive models.

In practice, this translates into setting up exposures to test both cognitive and emotional aspects of fear. To address the former, we ask patients to identify their feared outcome prior to exposure and then review whether it came true after completing the exposure. To address the latter, we ask patients to rate severity of their anxiety throughout the exposure. Measuring anxiety during exposure has become a contentious topic because of concerns that it may encourage attempts to suppress anxiety rather than learn to tolerate it. Our reasons for continuing to assess anxiety ratings are multiple. First, this procedure has been used successfully for decades and should not be abandoned until empirical evidence supports a more successful approach. Second, many children have difficulty articulating a feared outcome beyond experiencing anxiety. For them, observing that anxiety dissipates, as it often does, or at least plateaus is the most important disconfirmation. Third, it remains to be seen to what degree ratings of likelihood and anxiety differ from each other (Benito & Walther, 2015), particularly in children. Finally, as we have discussed previously, fear habituation, when carefully studied, may indeed be an important component of successful treatment (Benito et al., 2018).

Along a more practical vein, our goal in writing this book is not only to promote the use of exposure as an effective therapeutic technique but also to promote the competent implementation of this technique. Unfortunately, many therapists implement exposure in a timid fashion that undercuts its effectiveness (Farrell, Deacon, Dixon, & Lickel, 2013). It is our concern that modifications to exposure that allow therapists to decrease the emotional valence of an exposure (i.e., focusing on expectations rather than emotions) or to discontinue an exposure earlier (i.e., when a patient professes to realize their fear is unlikely, even though they remain anxious and would rather avoid) run the risk of diluting exposure.

SUMMARY

In this chapter, we reviewed the theories of how exposure leads to symptom relief. We attempted to synthesize these theories into a practical framework to guide the clinical implementation of exposure. In Section 2, we turn our attention to the empirical support for exposure.

ACKNOWLEDGMENT

We thank Dr. Chelsea Ale for her assistance in preparing this chapter.

REFERENCES

Ale, C. M., McCarthy, D. M., Rothschild, L., & Whiteside, S. (2015). Components of cognitive behavioral therapy related to outcome in childhood anxiety disorders. *Clinical Child and Family Psychology Review, 18*, 240–251. doi:10.1007/s10567-015-0184-8

Arch, J. A., & Craske, M. G. (2008). Acceptance and commitment therapy and cognitive behavioral therapy for anxiety disorders: Different treatments, similar mechanisms? *Clinical Psychology: Science and Practice, 15*, 263–279.

American Psychiatric Association. (2013). *Diagnostic and statistical manual of mental disorders* (5th ed.). Arlington, VA: American Psychiatric Publishing.

Benito, K. G., Machan, J., Freeman, J. B., Garcia, A. M., Walther, M., Frank, H., . . . Franklin, M. (2018). Measuring fear change within exposures: Functionally-defined habituation predicts outcome in three randomized controlled trials for pediatric OCD. *Journal of Consulting and Clinical Psychology, 86*(7), 615–630. doi:10.1037/ccp0000315

Benito, K. G., & Walther, M. (2015). Therapeutic process during exposure: Habituation model. *Journal of Obsessive-Compulsive and Related Disorders, 6*, 147–157. doi: 10.1016/j.jocrd.2015.01.006

Berman, N. C., Fang, A., Hansen, N., & Wilhelm, S. (2015). Cognitive-based therapy for OCD: Role of behavior experiments and exposure processes. *Journal of Obsessive-Compulsive and Related Disorders, 6*, 158–166. doi:http://dx.doi.org/10.1016/j.jocrd.2015.01.001

Craske, M. G., Kircanski, K., Zelikowsky, M., Mystkowski, J., Chowdhury, N., & Baker, A. (2008). Optimizing inhibitory learning during exposure therapy. *Behaviour Research and Therapy, 46*(1), 5–27. doi:10.1016/j.brat.2007.10.003

Craske, M. G., Treanor, M., Conway, C. C., Zbozinek, T., & Vervliet, B. (2014). Maximizing exposure therapy: An inhibitory learning approach. *Behaviour Research and Therapy, 58*, 10–23. doi:10.1016/j.brat.2014.04.006

Deacon, B., Kemp, J. J., Dixon, L. J., Sy, J. T., Farrell, N. R., & Zhang, A. R. (2013). Maximizing the efficacy of interoceptive exposure by optimizing inhibitory learning: A randomized controlled trial. *Behaviour Research and Therapy, 51*(9), 588–596.

Farrell, N. R., Deacon, B. J., Dixon, L. J., & Lickel, J. J. (2013). Theory-based training strategies for modifying practitioner concerns about exposure therapy. *Journal of Anxiety Disorders, 27*(8), 781–787.

Foa, E. B., Huppert, J. D., & Cahill, S. P. (2006). Emotional processing theory: An update. In B. O. Rothbaum (Ed.), *Pathological anxiety: Emotional processing in etiology and treatment* (pp. 3–24). New York, NY: Guildford.

Foa, E. B., & Kozak, M. J. (1986). Emotional processing of fear: Exposure to corrective information. *Psychological Bulletin, 99*, 20–35.

Hancock, K. M., Swain, J., Hainsworth, C. J., Dixon, A. L., Koo, S., & Munro, K. (2018). Acceptance and commitment therapy versus cognitive behavior therapy for children with anxiety: Outcomes of a randomized controlled trial. *Journal of Clinical Child and Adolescent Psychology, 47*(2), 296–311. doi:10.1080/15374416.2015.1110822

Jones, M. C. (1924). The elimination of children's fears. *Journal of Experimental Psychology, 7*, 383–390.

Kendall, P. C. (1985). Toward a cognitive–behavioral model of child psychopathology and a critique of related interventions. *Journal of Abnormal Child Psychology, 13*, 357–372.

Kendall, P. C. (2000). *Cognitive-behavioral therapy for anxious children: Therapist manual* (2nd ed.). Ardmore, PA: Workbook.

Kendall, P. C., Cummings, C. M., Villabo, M. A., Narayanan, M. K., Treadwell, K., Birmaher, B., . . . Albano, A. M. (2016). Mediators of change in the Child/Adolescent Anxiety Multimodal Treatment Study. *Journal of Consulting and Clinical Psychology, 84*(1), 1–14. doi:10.1037/a0039773

Kendall, P. C., Robin, J. A., Hedtke, K. A., Suveg, C., Flannery-Schroeder, E., & Gosch, E. (2005). Considering CBT with anxious youth? Think exposures. *Cognitive and Behavioral Practice, 12*(1), 136–150.

Longmore, R. J., & Worrell, M. (2007). Do we need to challenge thoughts in cognitive behavior therapy? *Clinical Psychology Review, 27*(2), 173–187. doi:10.1016/j.cpr.2006.08.001

Manassis, K., Russell, K., & Newton, A. S. (2010). The Cochrane Library and the treatment of childhood and adolescent anxiety disorders: An overview of reviews. *Evidence-Base Child Health, 5*, 541–554.

McGlynn, F. D., Smitherman, T. A., & Gothard, K. D. (2004). Comment on the status of systematic desensitization. *Behavior Modification, 28*(2), 194–205. doi:10.1177/0145445503259414

McMillan, D., & Lee, R. (2010). A systematic review of behavioral experiments vs. exposure alone in the treatment of anxiety disorders: A case of exposure while wearing the emperor's new clothes? *Clinical Psychology Review, 30*(5), 467–478. doi:10.1016/j.cpr.2010.01.003

Miller, L. C., Barrett, C. L., Hampe, E., & Noble, H. (1972). Comparison of reciprocal inhibition, psychotherapy, and waiting list control for phobic children. *Journal of Abnormal Psychology, 79*(3), 269–279.

Obler, M., & Terwilliger, R. F. (1970). Pilot study on the effectiveness of systematic desensitization with neurologically impaired children with phobic disorders. *Journal of Consulting and Clinical Psychology, 34*(3), 314–318.

Ollendick, T., & Cerny, J. A. (1981). *Clinical behavior therapy with children*. New York, NY: Plenum.

Ollendick, T. H., Öst, L. G., Ryan, S. M., Capriola, N. N., & Reuterskiold, L. (2017). Harm beliefs and coping expectancies in youth with specific phobias. *Behaviour Research and Therapy, 91*, 51–57. doi:10.1016/j.brat.2017.01.007

Ollendick, T. H., Ryan, S. M., Capriola-Hall, N. N., Reuterskiold, L., & Öst, L. G. (2017). The mediating role of changes in harm beliefs and coping efficacy in youth with specific phobias. *Behaviour Research and Therapy, 99*, 131–137. doi:10.1016/j.brat.2017.10.007

Öst, L. G. (2014). The efficacy of acceptance and commitment therapy: An updated systematic review and meta-analysis. *Behaviour Research and Therapy, 61*, 105–121. doi: 10.1016/j.brat.2014.07.018

Rachman, S. (1980). Emotional processing. *Behaviour Research and Therapy, 18*(1), 51–60.

Rankin, C. H., Abrams, T., Barry, R. J., Bhatnagar, S., Clayton, D. F., Colombo, J., . . . Thompson, R. F. (2009). Habituation revisited: An updated and revised description of the behavioral characteristics of habituation. *Neurobiology of Learning and Memory, 92*(2), 135–138. doi:10.1016/j.nlm.2008.09.012

Rozenman, M., Vreeland, A., & Piacentini, J. (2017). Thinking anxious, feeling anxious, or both? Cognitive bias moderates the relationship between anxiety disorder status and sympathetic arousal in youth. *Journal of Anxiety Disorders, 45*, 34–42. doi: 10.1016/j.janxdis.2016.11.004

Salkovskis, P. M., Hackmann, A., Wells, A., Gelder, M. G., & Clark, D. A. (2006). Belief disconfirmation versus habituation approaches to situational exposure in panic disorder with agoraphobia: A pilot study. *Behaviour Research and Therapy, 45*, 877–885. doi: http://dx.doi.org/10.1016/j.brat.2006.02.008.

Twohig, M. P., Abramowitz, J. S., Bluett, E. J., Fabricant, L. E., Jacoby, R. J., Morrison, K. L., . . . Smith, B. M. (2015). Exposure therapy for OCD from an acceptance and commitment therapy (ACT) framework. *Journal of Obsessive–Compulsive and Related Disorders, 6*, 167–173. doi:http://dx.doi.org/10.1016/j.jocrd.2014.12.007

Wang, Z., Whiteside, S. P. H., Sim, L., Farah, W., Morrow, A. S., Alsawas, M., . . . Murad, M. H. (2017). Comparative effectiveness and safety of cognitive behavioral therapy and pharmacotherapy for childhood anxiety disorders: A systematic review and meta-analysis. *JAMA Pediatrics, 171*(11), 1049–1056. doi:10.1001/jamapediatrics.2017.3036

Weisman, J. S., & Rodebaugh, T. L. (2018). Exposure therapy augmentation: A review and extension of techniques informed by an inhibitory learning approach. *Clinical Psychology Review, 59*, 41–51. doi:10.1016/j.cpr.2017.10.010

Whiteside, S. P. H., Ale, C. M., Young, B., Dammann, J., Tiede, M. S., & Biggs, B. K. (2015). The feasibility of improving CBT for childhood anxiety disorders through a dismantling study. *Behaviour Research and Therapy, 73*, 83–89. doi:10.1016/j.brat.2015.07.011

Whiteside, S. P. H., Sim, L. A., Morrow, A. S., Farah, W. H., Hilliker, D. R., Murad, M. H., & Wang, Z. (in press). A meta-analysis to guide the enhancement of CBT for childhood anxiety: Exposure over Anxiety Management. *Clinical Child and Family Psychology Review.*

Wolpe, J. (1958). *Psychotherapy by reciprocal inhibition*. Stanford, CA: Stanford University Press.

Empirical Support

3

Review of Evidence

Adult Literature

In Chapter 1, we suggested that one of the major reasons for engaging in exposure therapy, whether you are a clinician or a patient, is that it enjoys the most empirical support of any treatment for anxiety and obsessive–compulsive disorder (OCD). In Section 2, we review the research supporting the efficacy of exposure therapy for these disorders. We begin this chapter with a brief commentary on the importance of using research to guide clinical practice. Then we review the evidence supporting exposure therapy for adult anxiety disorders. As with many areas of health care, the adult anxiety disorder research literature is larger than that for childhood anxiety disorders. As such, the former can provide answers to broad questions and includes more explorations of specific questions than the latter. Of course, children are not simply little adults, and conclusions from adult studies do not necessarily apply to childhood disorders. As such, in Chapter 4 we review the empirical support for exposure therapy in children with anxiety disorders and OCD.

AN INTRODUCTION TO RESEARCH

For some readers, the relevance of research to clinical practice is self-evident and the current section may seem unnecessary. However, many clinicians continue to wrestle with the challenge of combining the art and science of psychotherapy (Lucock, Hall, & Noble, 2006; Seligman et al., 2016). For many of us, the lure of experience as a guide is powerful. It is easy to believe that after years of providing therapy to hundreds of patients, clinicians develop a clear understanding of what works well and what does not work well. Although clinical experience is undoubtedly valuable for the art of conducting therapy, it is not sufficient for understanding which interventions work best for a given condition. Personal clinical experience can provide information only on what happened given what a clinician chose to do and does not provide any information on what would have happened if an alternative intervention had been used. Under these circumstances, it is

Exposure Therapy for Child and Adolescent Anxiety and OCD. Stephen P. H. Whiteside, Thomas H. Ollendick, and Bridget K. Biggs, Oxford University Press (2020). © Oxford University Press.
DOI: 10.1093/med/9780190862992.001.0001

impossible to know if a clinician has helped a patient as fully as possible, even if she improved, because a different treatment could have potentially been more powerful and potentially delivered in less time.

Well-controlled clinical research provides essential information about effective treatment that no amount of clinical wisdom, insight, or natural talent can provide. In the gold standard of research, the randomized clinical trial (RCT), comparable groups of patients are randomly assigned to receive one intervention or another. If successful, this process tells two sides of the story for a hypothetical patient: specifically, how much would she improve with Treatment A versus Treatment B. Of course, research is not immune to errors, bias, and chance. If different researchers conduct multiple RCTs with the same treatments, the results of each study will differ somewhat. To make sense of multiple individual studies, researchers have a second tool, meta-analysis. Meta-analysis is an objective method for averaging the results of multiple studies into a single value called an effect size (ES). The ES attempts to separate meaningful differences between the benefits of two treatments from the noise and confusion created by chance and error. To help understand our review of the literature that follows, effect sizes of 0.8 or more are typically interpreted as being large, whereas those greater than 0.5 and 0.2 are interpreted as being medium and small, respectively (Cohen, 1988). Meta-analyses and RCTs are the best tools we have to answer the deceptively complicated question of "Which treatments work best?" Consequently, the remainder of this chapter and the next review what the research tells us about exposure therapy.

CONTRIBUTIONS FROM THE ADULT LITERATURE

Beginning our review of the empirical support for exposure with the adult treatment literature has a number of advantages. First, RCTs with anxious adults have examined treatments for each of the anxiety disorders separately, whereas the child literature has typically combined disorders together. Although the high comorbidity of anxiety disorders implies that transdiagnostic treatments may more accurately match the needs of real-world patients, combining diagnostic samples limits our ability to determine the effectiveness of exposure therapy for each disorder. The second advantage of the adult literature is its size. A comprehensive meta-analysis of the child literature included 22 studies of exposure therapy for combined anxiety disorders, 9 for social phobia, 3 for specific phobia, 9 for posttraumatic stress disorder (PTSD), and 5 for OCD (Reynolds, Wilson, Austin, & Hooper, 2012). In contrast, RCTs of the adult literature have included 40 studies for generalized anxiety disorder (GAD; Cuijpers et al., 2014), 37 for Öst OCD (Öst, Havnen, Hansen, & Kvale, 2015), 29 for social phobia (Acarturk, Cuijpers, van Straten, & de Graaf, 2009), 33 for specific phobia (Wolitzky-Taylor, Horowitz, Powers, & Telch, 2008), and 37 for OCD (Öst et al., 2015).

A third advantage of the adult literature is the existence of dismantling studies. As we introduced in Chapter 1, exposure is often delivered in combination with other strategies under a broader category of cognitive–behavioral therapy (CBT). As a result, much of the evidence supporting the use of exposure therapy derives from studies of CBT more generally. As such, we at times use the term *exposure-based treatment* to refer to studies of treatments that include exposure as a central component of CBT. Combining multiple techniques together may be wise if one is unsure how effective each individual component is by itself. However, once the combined package has been found useful, further research is needed to determine which components are necessary and/or sufficient and which can be discarded. Given that this book focuses on the use of exposure and that clinicians have been much more reluctant to adopt exposure compared to other CBT components (Whiteside, Deacon, Benito, & Stewart, 2016; Whiteside, Sattler, et al., 2016), we need to examine the smaller and more nuanced literature examining the relative value of exposure as a stand-alone treatment. Fortunately, the adult treatment literature includes such comparisons, often referred to as *dismantling studies*.

The final advantage of the adult scientific literature compared with the child literature is the frequent inclusion of active control groups. As previously mentioned, RCTs allow one to compare a representative patient's improvement under two conditions. Ideally, each condition would represent two viable choices available to the clinician—that is, Treatment A versus Treatment B. Understandably, research typically begins with answering the question whether Treatment A is better than doing nothing at all—that is, the wait list condition. Although this comparison provides an entry level of support for the value of a treatment, it does not inform the clinician whether the experimental treatment is better than other available treatment options. As such, studies demonstrating that Treatment A is better than an alternative treatment provide substantially more convincing evidence to the clinician. Comparisons with alternative treatments can take various forms, such as an active placebo that controls for nonspecific therapeutic features, treatment typically provided in non-research settings (sometimes referred to as "treatment as usual"), or, even better, another established treatment. For instance, if Treatment A is better than a comparison treatment that is similar to what a clinician has been doing, that clinician would be wise to consider adopting Treatment A. Given that such comparisons represent more stringent tests, they are generally limited to more developed research literatures, such as that for adult, as opposed to child, anxiety disorders.

Now that we have examined the value of research and the applicability of knowledge gained from studying the treatment of adults, let us turn our attention to reviewing the empirical support for exposure therapy in adult anxiety disorders. The effect sizes and levels of support are summarized in Table 3.1 and Figure 3.1, respectively.

Table 3.1 LEVELS OF SUPPORT FOR EXPOSURE BY DISORDER

Disorder	Package[a]	Placebo[b]	Other Tx[c]	Augmentation[d]	Stand-Alone[e]
Social anxiety disorder	✓	✓	✓	Inconclusive	✓
OCD	✓	✓	✓	No gain	✓
Specific phobia	✓	✓	✓	No gain	✓
GAD	✓	✓	✓	No gain	✓
PTSD	✓	✓	✓	Decrease	✓
Panic disorder	✓	✓	✓	Decrease	✓

[a]More effective than no treatment when delivered with other strategies (e.g., cognitive–behavioral therapy).

[b]More effective than a placebo treatment (e.g., educational support).

[c]More effective than other credible treatment (e.g., cognitive therapy, relaxation therapy, and medication).

[d]Studies suggesting adding other components decreases or does not increase effectiveness (or literature is inconclusive).

[e]Effective treatment without other components.

GAD, generalized anxiety disorder; OCD, obsessive–compulsive disorder; PTSD, post-traumatic stress disorder.

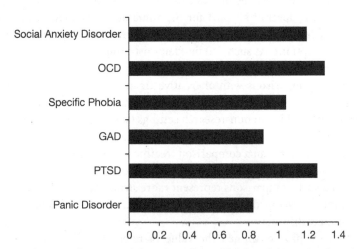

Figure 3.1 Effect sizes for exposure-based treatments for the adult anxiety disorders. *X* axis = effect size: 0.8 or more, large; 0.5, medium; and 0.2, small (Cohen, 1988). SOURCES: Social anxiety disorder, Mayo-Wilson et al. (2014); obsessive–compulsive disorder (OCD), Öst et al. (2015); specific phobia, Wolitzky-Taylor et al. (2015); generalized anxiety disorder (GAD), Cuijpers et al. (2014); post-traumatic stress disorder (PTSD), Bradley et al. (2005); and panic disorder, Pompoli et al. (2016).

EMPIRICAL SUPPORT FOR EXPOSURE THERAPY IN ADULT ANXIETY DISORDERS

Social Anxiety Disorder

The literature on social anxiety disorder provides a good starting point for the value of reviewing studies conducted with adults. As with many of the anxiety disorders, exposure for social anxiety in adults is typically combined with cognitive restructuring, social skills training, and relaxation exercises in a CBT protocol. The literature examining social anxiety disorder is extensive, including a meta-analysis of 101 studies of psychological and pharmacological treatments (Mayo-Wilson et al., 2014). In addition, the literature allows for comparisons of the effectiveness of CBT compared to active treatments and an examination of the separate components.

Multiple meta-analyses across decades have concluded that exposure-based CBT is effective for social anxiety disorder in adults with large effect sizes (Feske & Chambless, 1995; Gould, Buckminster, Pollack, Otto, & Yap, 1997; Mayo-Wilson et al., 2014). The most recent of these reviews found large effect sizes for multiple exposure-based interventions, including individual CBT (ES = 1.19), group CBT (ES = 0.92), and exposure with social skills (ES = 0.86), compared to no treatment (Mayo-Wilson et al., 2014). Furthermore, this review found CBT to be more effective than other credible psychotherapies, such as psychodynamic therapy (ES = 0.56), and a combined grouping of interpersonal, mindfulness, and supportive therapies (ES = 0.82). CBT was the only psychotherapy found to be more effective than psychological placebo (ES = 0.56). Results from previous meta-analyses further suggest that the effectiveness of CBT results from exposure as opposed to other techniques, including cognitive restructuring (Feske & Chambless, 1995; Gould et al., 1997). For example, ESs comparing post-treatment to pretreatment scores within a given treatment (which are generally larger than ESs comparing treatment changes in one group to changes in another group) were 0.89 for exposure alone, 0.80 for exposure plus cognitive restructuring, and 0.60 for cognitive restructuring alone (Gould et al., 1997). However, this pattern has not always been found, with other meta-analyses suggesting a benefit to adding cognitive strategies to exposure (Mayo-Wilson et al., 2014; Taylor, 1996). Finally, Feske and Chambless found that more exposure sessions were related to greater improvement in treatment.

In summary, the literature examining psychotherapy for social anxiety provides fairly convincing evidence that therapists should be using exposure. Exposure-based CBT is not only more effective than no treatment but also more effective than other approaches that therapists might use, including nonspecific psychological strategies and other credible therapeutic paradigms.

Obsessive–Compulsive Disorder

Similar to social anxiety disorder, the adult literature provides clear support for exposure-based treatments for OCD. Such treatments historically have been referred to as exposure and response prevention (ERP) to emphasize the importance of decreasing ritualizing, but they have also been referred to as CBT. Multiple meta-analyses during the past 20 years support the effectiveness of ERP (or CBT) for the treatment of OCD (Abramowitz, 1996; Olatunji, Davis, Powers, & Smits, 2013; Öst et al., 2015; van Balkom et al., 1994). For example, Öst and colleagues examined 37 RCTs of psychotherapy and pharmacotherapy and found that CBT was more effective than no treatment (ES = 1.31) and non-specific psychological control treatments (ES = 1.29). In addition, an earlier review found that ERP was more effective than relaxation therapy (ES = 1.18; Abramowitz, 1997). However, meta-analyses have not found a difference between ERP and cognitive therapy without exposure, partly because cognitive therapy often includes behavioral experiments similar to exposure. Importantly, ERP without cognitive strategies has been found to be effective (ES = 1.47; van Balkom et al., 1994), and in a direct comparison ERP was found to be more effective than non-exposure cognitive therapy (Olatunji, Rosenfield, et al., 2013). It is also noteworthy that ERP has also been found to be more effective than pharmacotherapy and that adding medication does not increase the effectiveness of ERP (Foa et al., 2005; Öst et al., 2015).

Similar to the research on social anxiety disorder, a large body of evidence suggests exposure is an effective treatment for OCD in adults. Moreover, exposure is more effective than other strategies therapists might use (e.g., nonspecific supportive techniques, relaxation, and potentially cognitive techniques) and other available treatments (i.e., medication).

Specific Phobia

In addition to the long history of using exposure therapy to treat childhood phobias described in Chapter 1, there is also a large adult treatment literature. As opposed to treatments for other disorders that integrate exposure into a broader CBT, treatment for specific phobias has been largely exposure in isolation. The single meta-analysis available examined 33 RCTs conducted between 1977 and 2004 (Wolitzky-Taylor et al., 2008). Similar to the disorders discussed previously, exposure therapy was found to be more effective than no treatment (ES = 1.05), active placebo treatments (ES = 0.48), and other credible non-exposure treatments such as relaxation and cognitive therapy (ES = 0.44). Not only was exposure effective as a stand-alone treatment but also the addition of cognitive strategies did not increase its effect. Beyond comparing exposure to other approaches, Wolitzky-Taylor and colleagues also examined the effectiveness of different types of exposures. They found that treatments involving direct contact with the feared stimuli (i.e., in vivo exposure) were more effective than treatments that were limited to imagining having contact with the item (i.e., imaginal exposure).

As with social anxiety disorder and OCD, exposure is a necessary ingredient for effective treatment of specific phobia. Furthermore, the literature on treatment of specific phobia provides strong evidence of the effectiveness of exposure in isolation. Moreover, the specific phobia literature also provides clear evidence that direct in vivo exposure is more effective than indirect, or imaginal, exposure.

Generalized Anxiety Disorder

Compared to the phobia-based disorders, exposure has played a less central role in the treatment of GAD (Siev & Chambless, 2007), perhaps because GAD largely involves diffuse worries rather than tangible triggers of immediate fear. As such, CBT for GAD typically combines a variety of components, including cognitive restructuring, problem-solving, applied relaxation, and biofeedback, in addition to exposure. A meta-analysis of 41 studies examining psychotherapy for GAD defined CBT as consisting of at least one of the associated components, so not all treatments included exposure (Cuijpers et al., 2014). This study found CBT to be highly effective (ES = 0.90). Moreover, an earlier meta-analysis found CBT to be more effective than placebo conditions (ES = 0.57; Mitte, 2005).

Because exposure has not been as integral to CBT for GAD as for other disorders, we need to explore individual studies that have examined the benefit of exposure. Such studies have examined the use of imaginal techniques as a direct exposure to worry, a core component of GAD. One study found that having worriers do exposures to writing their worst fears reduced GAD symptoms more than a neutral writing assignment (Goldman, Dugas, Sexton, & Gervais, 2007). The optimal approach to worry exposure was later clarified in a study of patients with GAD in which those who repeated worry exposures to a single topic experienced more benefit than those who did exposures to multiple topics (Fracalanza, Koerner, & Antony, 2014). Finally, worry exposure as a stand-alone treatment protocol appears to be as effective as a well-supported protocol combining relaxation with imaginal exposure and efforts to reduce avoidance (Hoyer et al., 2009).

Taken together, the research literature supporting the effectiveness of exposure for GAD is not as robust as that for other adult anxiety and related disorders. However, exposure is included in well-supported CBT protocols for GAD, and research is being undertaken to support the use of worry exposure as a stand-alone intervention.

Post-Traumatic Stress Disorder

Although we do not directly address treatment for PTSD in this book, this literature is important because it provides the most direct demonstration of the effectiveness of imaginal exposure. The central component of treatment for PTSD, often called prolonged exposure (PE), is direct exposure to traumatic memories through imaginal (or narrative) exposure accompanied by in vivo exposure to reminders of the event. Not surprisingly, the core exposure techniques are often combined with other strategies, including cognitive restructuring and relaxation techniques. Meta-analyses suggest that exposure therapy by itself is more effective than no treatment (ES = 1.26; Bradley, Greene, Russ, Dutra, & Westen, 2005), which was comparable to the effectiveness of broader CBT (ES = 1.26) and exposure plus cognitive therapy (ES = 1.53). Exposure as a stand-alone treatment was also more effective than supportive therapy (ES = 0.84). In addition, PE has demonstrated superiority over another credible treatment—stress inoculation training (Foa et al., 1999). Finally, based on the fact that the addition of non-exposure techniques have resulted in smaller effect sizes than exposure alone, some experts have cautioned that such augmentation may have a deleterious effect on treatment outcomes (Hembree & Brinen, 2009).

As such, the literature on PTSD continues the theme of demonstrating the effectiveness of exposure. In addition, some research suggests that adding additional techniques may diminish treatment effects.

Panic Disorder

Although panic is relatively rare in youth compared to the other anxiety disorders, the adult literature in this area is particularly important because it demonstrates the benefit of interoceptive exposures (i.e., exposure to internal, bodily sensations associated with anxiety). Multiple meta-analyses during the past two decades or more have demonstrated the effectiveness of exposure-based treatments for panic disorder (Chambless & Gillis, 1993; Pompoli et al., 2016). A recent meta-analysis found that CBT was not only more effective than no treatment (ES = 0.83) but also the most studied and empirically supported psychotherapy for panic disorder (Pompoli et al., 2016). Unfortunately, the use of interoceptive exposures to bodily sensations is a relatively new development that may not be fully represented in meta-analyses that included the early treatment literature. When treatment protocols are limited to those that include interoceptive exposures, these interventions are more effective than relaxation therapy (Siev & Chambless, 2007). In fact, similar to the PTSD literature, some studies have suggested that adding other components—that is, coping strategies or breathing retraining—may diminish the benefit of exposure therapy (Craske et al., 2006; Schmidt et al., 2000).

SUMMARY OF EVIDENCE FROM THE ADULT LITERATURE

Overall, the literature compiled during approximately the past 20 years on the treatment of anxiety and related disorders provides compelling evidence for the effectiveness of exposure therapy. For each of the disorders that we reviewed, exposure-based therapies have been found to be more effective than no treatment, placebo support conditions, and other credible treatments. Furthermore, exposure by itself without other CBT components has been found to be effective, and adding other components to exposure may not be necessary in the treatment of GAD or specific phobia and may be detrimental for PTSD and panic disorder. These specific conclusions are consistent with meta-analyses that have examined the treatment of adult anxiety disorders in general. For example, across disorders, multicomponent CBT interventions are no more effective than exposure alone (Adams, Brady, Lohr, & Jacobs, 2015).

REMAINING QUESTIONS

Despite the value of beginning our evidence review in the adult treatment literature, a number of important questions remain unanswered. As stated at the outset of this chapter, children are not simply little adults. As such, the evidence that we reviewed in this chapter may not necessarily apply to youth. Furthermore, "youth" is a broad category ranging from young children to older adolescents, and developmental changes may affect the delivery and success of exposure over this age span. In addition to differences in treatment response, anxiety may present differently in children compared to adults (Whiteside & Ollendick, 2009). For instance, separation anxiety disorder and school avoidance are common anxiety presentations in children for which there is not a large adult literature to consult. Finally, the context in which anxiety disorders present and are treated is often much different in youth versus adults. Whereas adult patients typically seek treatment for themselves, parents typically initiate youth treatment (Ollendick & Cerny, 1981). The role of parents in therapy, not to mention children's daily lives, presents challenges and opportunities that the scientific literature has not fully addressed (Grills-Taquechel & Ollendick, 2012). Moreover, children's interest and engagement in treatment vary widely, and comorbidities such as disruptive behavior disorders are more common concerns with this population than with adults. With these questions in mind, we turn our attention in Chapter 4 to the literature regarding exposure therapy for anxiety and related disorders in children.

REFERENCES

Abramowitz, J. S. (1996). Variants of exposure and response prevention in the treatment of obsessive–compulsive disorder: A meta-analysis. *Behavior Therapy, 27,* 583–600.

Abramowitz, J. S. (1997). Effectiveness of psychological and pharmacological treatments for obsessive–compulsive disorder: A quantitative review. *Journal of Consulting and Clinical Psychology, 65,* 44–52.

Acarturk, C., Cuijpers, P., van Straten, A., & de Graaf, R. (2009). Psychological treatment of social anxiety disorder: A meta-analysis. *Psychological Medicine, 39*(2), 241–254. doi: 10.1017/S0033291708003590

Adams, T. G., Brady, R. E., Lohr, J. M., & Jacobs, W. J. (2015). A meta-analysis of CBT components for anxiety disorder. *The Behavior Therapist, 38*, 87–97.

Bradley, R., Greene, J., Russ, E., Dutra, L., & Westen, D. (2005). A multidimensional meta-analysis of psychotherapy for PTSD. *American Journal of Psychiatry, 162*(2), 214–227. doi:10.1176/appi.ajp.162.2.214

Chambless, D. L., & Gillis, M. M. (1993). Cognitive therapy of anxiety disorders. *Journal of Consulting and Clinical Psychology, 61*(2), 248–260.

Cohen, J. (1988). *Statistical power analysis for the behavioral sciences.* Hillsdale, NJ: Erlbaum.

Craske, M. G., Roy-Byrne, P., Stein, M. B., Sullivan, G., Hazlett-Stevens, H., Bystritsky, A., & Sherbourne, C. (2006). CBT intensity and outcome for panic disorder in a primary care setting. *Behavior Therapy, 37*(2), 112–119. doi:S0005-7894(06)00013-X

Cuijpers, P., Sijbrandij, M., Koole, S., Huibers, M., Berking, M., & Andersson, G. (2014). Psychological treatment of generalized anxiety disorder: A meta-analysis. *Clinical Psychology Review, 34*(2), 130–140. doi:10.1016/j.cpr.2014.01.002

Feske, U., & Chambless, D. L. (1995). Cognitive behavioral versus exposure only treatment for social phobia: A meta-analysis. *Behavior Therapy, 26*, 695–720.

Foa, E. B., Dancu, C. V., Hembree, E. A., Jaycox, L. H., Meadows, E. A., & Street, G. P. (1999). A comparison of exposure therapy, stress inoculation training, and their combination for reducing posttraumatic stress disorder in female assault victims. *Journal of Consulting and Clinical Psychology, 67*(2), 194–200.

Foa, E. B., Liebowitz, M. R., Kozak, M. J., Davies, S., Campeas, R., Franklin, M. E., . . . Tu, X. (2005). Randomized, placebo-controlled trial of exposure and ritual prevention, clomipramine, and their combination in the treatment of obsessive–compulsive disorder. *American Journal of Psychiatry, 162*(1), 151–161.

Fracalanza, K., Koerner, N., & Antony, M. M. (2014). Testing a procedural variant of written imaginal exposure for generalized anxiety disorder. *Journal of Anxiety Disorders, 28*(6), 559–569. doi:10.1016/j.janxdis.2014.05.011

Goldman, N., Dugas, M. J., Sexton, K. A., & Gervais, N. J. (2007). The impact of written exposure on worry: A preliminary investigation. *Behavior Modification, 31*(4), 512–538. doi:10.1177/0145445506298651

Gould, R. A., Buckminster, S., Pollack, M. H., Otto, M. W., & Yap, L. (1997). Cognitive-behavioral and pharmacological treatment for social phobia: A meta-analysis. *Clinical Psychology: Science and Practice, 4*, 291–306.

Grills-Taquechel, A. E., & Ollendick, T. H. (2012). *Phobic and anxiety disorders in children and adolescents.* Cambridge, MA: Hogrefe.

Hembree, E. A., & Brinen, A. P. (2009). Prolonged exposure (PE) for treatment of childhood sexual abuse-related PTSD: Do we need to augment it? *Pragmatic Case Studies in Psychotherapy, 5*, 35–44.

Hoyer, J., Beesdo, K., Gloster, A. T., Runge, J., Hofler, M., & Becker, E. S. (2009). Worry exposure versus applied relaxation in the treatment of generalized anxiety disorder. *Psychotherapy and Psychosomatics, 78*(2), 106–115. doi:10.1159/000201936

Lucock, M. P., Hall, P., & Noble, R. (2006). A survey of influences on the practice of psychotherapists and clinical psychologists in the UK. *Clinical Psychology & Psychotherapy, 13*, 123–130.

Mayo-Wilson, E., Dias, S., Mavranezouli, I., Kew, K., Clark, D. M., Ades, A. E., & Pilling, S. (2014). Psychological and pharmacological interventions for social anxiety disorder in adults: A systematic review and network meta-analysis. *Lancet Psychiatry, 1*(5), 368–376. doi:10.1016/S2215-0366(14)70329-3

Mitte, K. (2005). Meta-analysis of cognitive–behavioral treatments for generalized anxiety disorder: A comparison with pharmacotherapy. *Psychological Bulletin, 131*(5), 785–795. doi:10.1037/0033-2909.131.5.785

Olatunji, B. O., Davis, M. L., Powers, M. B., & Smits, J. A. (2013). Cognitive–behavioral therapy for obsessive–compulsive disorder: A meta-analysis of treatment outcome and moderators. *Journal of Psychiatric Research, 47*(1), 33–41. doi:10.1016/j.jpsychires.2012.08.020

Olatunji, B. O., Rosenfield, D., Tart, C. D., Cottraux, J., Powers, M. B., & Smits, J. A. (2013). Behavioral versus cognitive treatment of obsessive–compulsive disorder: An examination of outcome and mediators of change. *Journal of Consulting and Clinical Psychology, 81*(3), 415–428. doi:10.1037/a0031865

Ollendick, T., & Cerny, J. A. (1981). *Clinical behavior therapy with children.* New York, NY: Plenum.

Öst, L. G., Havnen, A., Hansen, B., & Kvale, G. (2015). Cognitive behavioral treatments of obsessive–compulsive disorder. A systematic review and meta-analysis of studies published 1993–2014. *Clinical Psychology Review, 40,* 156–169. doi:10.1016/j.cpr.2015.06.003

Pompoli, A., Furukawa, T. A., Imai, H., Tajika, A., Efthimiou, O., & Salanti, G. (2016). Psychological therapies for panic disorder with or without agoraphobia in adults: A network meta-analysis. *Cochrane Database of Systematic Reviews, 2016*(4), CD011004. doi: 10.1002/14651858.CD011004.pub2

Reynolds, S., Wilson, C., Austin, J., & Hooper, L. (2012). Effects of psychotherapy for anxiety in children and adolescents: A meta-analytic review. *Clinical Psychology Review, 32,* 251–262.

Schmidt, N. B., Woolaway-Bickel, K., Trakowski, J., Santiago, H., Storey, J., Koselka, M., & Cook, J. (2000). Dismantling cognitive–behavioral treatment for panic disorder: Questioning the utility of breathing retraining. *Journal of Consulting and Clinical Psychology, 68*(3), 417–424.

Seligman, L. D., Hovey, J. D., Hurtado, G., Swedish, E. F., Roley, M. E., Geers, A. L., . . . Ollendick, T. H. (2016). Social cognitive correlates of attitudes toward empirically supported treatments. *Professional Psychology: Research and Practice, 47,* 215–223.

Siev, J., & Chambless, D. L. (2007). Specificity of treatment effects: Cognitive therapy and relaxation for generalized anxiety and panic disorders. *Journal of Consulting and Clinical Psychology, 75*(4), 513–522. doi:10.1037/0022-006X.75.4.513

Taylor, S. (1996). Meta-analysis of cognitive–behavioral treatments for social phobia. *Journal of Behavior Therapy and Experimental Psychiatry, 27*(1), 1–9. doi: 0005791695000585

van Balkom, A. J. L. M., van Oppen, P., Vermeulen, A. W. A., van Dyck, R., Nauta, M. C. E., & Vorst, H. C. M. (1994). A meta-analysis of the treatment of obsessive compulsive disorder: A comparison of antidepressants, behavior, and cognitive therapy. *Clinical Psychology Review, 14,* 359–381.

Whiteside, S. P., & Ollendick, T. H. (2009). Developmental perspectives on anxiety classification. In D. McKay, J. S. Abramowitz, & S. Taylor (Eds.), *Current perspectives on the anxiety disorders: Implications for DSM-V and beyond* (pp. 303–325). New York, NY: Springer.

Whiteside, S. P. H., Deacon, B. J., Benito, K., & Stewart, E. (2016). Factors associated with practitioners' use of exposure therapy for childhood anxiety disorders. *Journal of Anxiety Disorders, 40*, 29–36. doi:http://dx.doi.org/10.1016/j.janxdis.2016.04.001

Whiteside, S. P. H., Sattler, A., Ale, C. M., Young, B., Hillson Jensen, A., Gregg, M. S., & Geske, J. R. (2016). The use of exposure therapy for child anxiety disorders in a medical center. *Professional Psychology: Research and Practice, 47*, 206–214. doi:http://dx.doi.org/10.1037/pro0000077

Wolitzky-Taylor, K., Zimmermann, M., Arch, J. J., De Guzman, E., & Lagomasino, I. (2015). Has evidence-based psychosocial treatment for anxiety disorders permeated usual care in community mental health settings? *Behaviour Research and Therapy, 72*, 9–17.

Wolitzky-Taylor, K. B., Horowitz, J. D., Powers, M. B., & Telch, M. J. (2008). Psychological approaches in the treatment of specific phobias: A meta-analysis. *Clinical Psychology Review, 28*(6), 1021–1037.

4

Review of Evidence

Child Literature

Now that we have reviewed the empirical support for exposure in the treatment of adult anxiety disorders, we turn our attention to the child treatment literature. As will be shown, research examining the treatment of anxiety in children often combines multiple diagnoses (i.e., transdiagnostic) and/or multiple treatment components. Such an approach has important benefits. Combining diagnoses together in the same studies likely builds upon commonalities underlying the various anxiety disorders and increases the speed of recruitment, allowing the literature to expand more quickly. The results of transdiagnostic treatment studies are also applicable to a larger group of diverse patients compared to those limited to a single diagnosis. Moreover, in the early stages of research, combining multiple therapeutic components increases the chance that treatment packages will include at least one technique that is effective. However, for our purposes of understanding the value of exposure for specific anxiety disorders, broad inclusive studies are more difficult to interpret. In this chapter, we begin with a review of the large literature base supporting cognitive–behavioral therapy (CBT) for anxiety disorders and then focus on the smaller literature examining specific diagnoses and the use of exposure per se. We also review the outcome literature for other components of treatment to help readers evaluate the empirical support for exposure relative to these other components. Finally, we discuss the research pertaining to developmental and contextual factors that are unique to children.

OVERVIEW OF COGNITIVE–BEHAVIORAL THERAPY STUDIES

As noted in Chapter 1, the most substantial amount of empirical support for the value of exposure in child anxiety treatment derives from studies of CBT for combined samples of children with social anxiety disorder, generalized anxiety disorder (GAD), and separation anxiety disorder. Although the emphasis on, and delivery of, components in CBT protocols varies, they generally begin exposure

Exposure Therapy for Child and Adolescent Anxiety and OCD. Stephen P. H. Whiteside, Thomas H. Ollendick, and Bridget K. Biggs, Oxford University Press (2020). © Oxford University Press.
DOI: 10.1093/med/9780190862992.001.0001

after introducing anxiety management strategies (AMS), including emotion identification, relaxation strategies, problem-solving, and cognitive restructuring.
AMS are typically presented first based on the assumption that children need
AMS before exposure to address their anxiety-maintaining beliefs and to tolerate
the distress associated with exposure (Crawley et al., 2013; Hirshfeld-Becker et al.,
2010; Kendall, 1985; Kendall et al., 1997; Manassis, Russell, & Newton, 2010).
AMS are often delivered during the first 4–9 sessions depending on the length
of the treatment protocol. The remaining 6–8 sessions then focus on exposure to
feared stimuli typically in session and/or assigned as homework. Exposure is included in virtually all CBT approaches to combined childhood anxiety disorders
and typically constitutes approximately one-third to one-half of the treatment
protocol, although some protocols have minimal in-session exposures (Ale,
McCarthy, Rothschild, & Whiteside, 2015; Whiteside et al., in press). The ubiq-
uity of the AMS followed by exposure model is demonstrated by its use in more
than 90% of the studies included in a meta-analysis (Reynolds, Wilson, Austin,
& Hooper, 2012), including the seminal Child/Adolescent Anxiety Multimodal
Study trial (Walkup et al., 2008).

EMPIRICAL SUPPORT FOR EXPOSURE THERAPY
IN CHILDHOOD ANXIETY DISORDERS

Cognitive–Behavioral Therapy for Combined Anxiety Disorders

A large body of research supports the efficacy of CBT for childhood anxiety
disorders. The most recent meta-analysis included 7,719 patients with separation
anxiety disorder, GAD, social anxiety disorder, specific phobia, or panic disorder
from 115 studies of medication and psychotherapy trials (Wang et al., 2017). The
results from 41 randomized controlled trials indicated that CBT was more effective than no treatment with large effect sizes (ESs) based on reports from independent evaluators (ES = 1.36), parents (ES = 0.88), and children (ES = 0.77)
(Figure 4.1). The support for CBT over no treatment is consistent with numerous
other meta-analyses conducted during the past decade or more (Cartwright-
Hatton, Roberts, Chitsabesan, Fothergill, & Harrington, 2004; James, James,
Codrey, Soler, & Choke, 2013). For example, a meta-analysis of 48 studies that
included obsessive–compulsive disorder (OCD) and post-traumatic stress disorder (PTSD) as well as the other anxiety disorders found an effect size of 0.77
(Reynolds et al., 2012). However, the most recent meta-analysis was the first to
find evidence supporting CBT's superiority over control interventions that provided supportive contact (ES for child report = 0.36; Wang et al., 2017). Moreover,
Wang and colleagues found limited but important evidence that CBT led to more
symptom reduction than medications without CBT.
   As mentioned previously, treatment studies of childhood anxiety disorder
most frequently combine social anxiety disorder, GAD, and separation anxiety disorder. As such, the support for these treatments derives primarily from

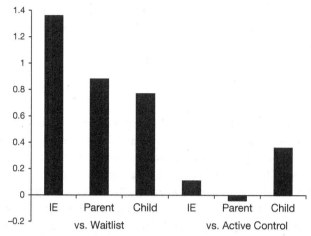

Figure 4.1 Effect sizes for CBT for combined childhood anxiety disorders. Child, child report; IE, independent evaluator rating; Parent, parent report.
SOURCE: Wang, Z., Whiteside, S. P. H., Sim, L., Farah, W., Morrow, A. S., Alsawas, M., . . . Murad, M. H. (2017). Comparative effectiveness and safety of cognitive behavioral therapy and pharmacotherapy for childhood anxiety disorders: A systematic review and meta-analysis. *JAMA Pediatrics*, *171*(11), 1049–1056. doi:10.1001/jamapediatrics.2017.3036

these transdiagnostic studies. However, to varying degrees, there is a literature examining each disorder independently.

Social Anxiety Disorder

Of the three disorders that have been historically combined together, social anxiety disorder has been most frequently examined independently. In addition to the previously described treatment components (i.e., exposure and AMS), protocols for childhood social anxiety frequently include social skills training. Of note, treatments for social anxiety frequently do not include relaxation strategies (Beidel et al., 2007). Moreover, given the nature of the disorder and importance of having peers available for exposure and social skills training, these approaches frequently are conducted in group formats. A recent meta-analysis including 13 studies of CBT treatment for social anxiety disorder in children found a large effect size compared to control groups (ES = 0.71), with improvement continuing after the completion of treatment (Scaini, Belotti, Ogliari, & Battaglia, 2016). Of particular importance to our review, one of the few CBT protocols to demonstrate superiority over medication was a treatment for social anxiety disorder that consisted solely of exposure and social skills training (Beidel et al., 2007). Relatedly, some children with social anxiety disorder also meet criteria for selective mutism because they do not speak in certain settings, such as schools or other public places. Although the treatment literature for selective mutism is small, an early review supported the use of behavioral interventions, including exposure (Pionek Stone, Kratochwill, Sladezcek, & Serlin, 2002), as did a more recent review (Muris & Ollendick, 2015).

Separation Anxiety Disorder

To our knowledge, the study of separation anxiety disorder treatment, independent of other diagnoses, has been fairly limited and has not been reviewed through meta-analysis. However, the available studies have been promising and typically include the basic CBT components, including exposure. In addition, given the relational aspect of separation anxiety disorder, these treatment protocols often involve parents. For example, an early trial found that 76% of children no longer met diagnostic criteria following a 16-session CBT program that included both children and parents (Schneider et al., 2011). Moreover, a novel 1-week intensive treatment for separation anxiety disorder began exposure on the first day and was found to be more effective than wait list (Santucci & Ehrenreich-May, 2013). Finally, the importance of exposure in treating separation anxiety disorder is underscored by the need to train parents as exposure coaches in addition to standard behavior management techniques (Pincus, Santucci, Ehrenreich, & Eyberg, 2008).

Generalized Anxiety Disorder

Research on the independent treatment of GAD in children is sparse. However, when applying the standard CBT protocol for GAD, it is recommended to include imaginal exposures to worry thoughts (Kendall et al., 2005). Similarly, a pilot study examined an approach to treatment that specifically uses exposures to uncertainty as well as unpleasant images and worries (Payne, Bolton, & Perrin, 2011). All of the patients completed the treatment, and 81% were diagnosis-free at post-treatment. Although the use of exposure is not as well developed for GAD as it is for the other anxiety diagnoses, the emerging literature on treatment specific to childhood GAD supports the use of imaginal and in vivo exposures.

In addition to the evidence supporting the effectiveness of exposure-based CBT for the "combined" anxiety disorders, literatures are developing examining treatment of the remaining diagnoses.

Obsessive–Compulsive Disorder

We begin our review of treatment for the remaining disorders with OCD, which is typically studied separately from the anxiety disorders. As mentioned in Chapter 3, treatment for OCD is typically referred to as exposure and response prevention (ERP), although the term CBT is used more frequently in the child than the adult literature. Multiple meta-analyses clearly demonstrate the efficacy of CBT/ERP for childhood OCD, although they differ on the strengths of their conclusions (Abramowitz, Whiteside, & Deacon, 2005; O'Kearney, Anstey, von Sanden, & Hunt, 2009; Skarphedinsson et al., 2015). For instance, a meta-analysis of ERP and medication for pediatric OCD concluded that ERP (ES = 1.98) was more effective than medication (ES = 1.13) or pill placebo (ES = 0.48) (Abramowitz et al., 2005), and a more recent meta-analysis concluded that ERP was more effective than psychotherapy placebo (Skarphedinsson et al., 2015). Finally, ERP may be effective enough that adding medication does not improve treatment outcome (Storch et al., 2013), although this has not been found consistently (Pediatric OCD Treatment Study Team, 2004; Skarphedinsson et al., 2015). Regardless, the evidence suggests that ERP for childhood OCD is highly effective, leading to large effect sizes. Important to our review, ERP for OCD primarily consists of exposure and typically does not include or emphasize anxiety management strategies (Ale et al., 2015).

Post-Traumatic Stress Disorder

Similar to OCD, PTSD is typically studied separately from the combined anxiety disorders. A review of psychological treatments for PTSD in children and adolescents included multiple approaches, such as CBT, exposure therapy alone, eye movement desensitization and reprocessing, and narrative therapy, all of which include some element of exposure to memories that trigger anxiety (Gillies, Taylor, Gray, O'Brien, & D'Abrew, 2012). When examined as a group, these therapies have been found to be effective at reducing PTSD symptoms with a large effect size (ES = 0.90). In addition, the authors concluded that CBT had the strongest evidence for support and led to improvements in symptoms up to 1 year following treatment. Although we do not directly address treatment for PTSD in this book, this literature supports the use of imaginal exposures, including to distressing memories, in youth.

Specific Phobia

Phobias are a third disorder that is typically excluded from the study of combined anxiety disorders. As with the adult literature, the treatment of specific phobias provides a clear example of the effectiveness, efficiency, and acceptability of exposure as a stand-alone treatment. Specifically, the one-session treatment protocol consists of a single 3-hour session devoted largely to in vivo exposure (Öst & Ollendick, 2001, 2017). Not only has this treatment been found to be superior to wait-list and nonspecific supportive therapy but also its acceptability is supported by the finding that no children asked to end the session early (Öst, Svensson, Hellstrom, & Lindwall, 2001).

Panic Disorder

Although panic disorder was included in the recent meta-analysis by Wang and colleagues (2017), it is typically not included in studies of combined anxiety disorders and is also rarely studied on its own. However, a treatment protocol that includes exposures to the physiological sensations has been found to be more effective than a self-monitoring control group (Pincus, May, Whitton, Mattis, & Barlow, 2010) and also to be effective when delivered once weekly or intensively through daily sessions (Chase, Whitton, & Pincus, 2012). These studies are particularly important to our review because they demonstrate the efficacy of interoceptive exposure (i.e., the purposeful experiencing of physical symptoms of panic) in youth.

School Refusal

Treatment of school refusal in children has received little empirical evaluation and does not have an adult literature for reference. A meta-analytic review found that of the eight treatment studies identified, seven examined CBT. The results were mixed, with significant improvement in school attendance but little or no effect on reductions in anxiety symptoms (Maynard et al., 2015). Treatment of school refusal may be somewhat more complicated to study because it is not clearly defined, is not a diagnosis within the *Diagnostic and Statistical Manual of Mental Disorders* (American Psychiatric Association, 2013), and combines children with different associated anxiety disorders or symptoms (i.e., separation vs. social fears). Furthermore, for some children, school refusal may be unrelated to anxiety and instead result from other factors, such as family systems, school environments, or oppositionality.

Other Interventions

In order to appreciate the relevance of the empirical support for exposure-based therapies, it is helpful to review the evidence supporting other treatments. Medications, particularly selective serotonin reuptake inhibitors, are the most common alternative to CBT in community practice (Whiteside et al., 2016). Although direct comparisons often find medication and CBT to be equally effective, there is some indication that CBT has a slight advantage in the treatment of combined anxiety disorders (Wang et al., 2017) and leads to larger effect sizes in the treatment of OCD (Abramowitz et al., 2005). Moreover, the sheer volume of studies examining CBT outweighs that for medication as well as any other therapies. For example, the literature search for the meta-analyses by Wang and colleagues (2017) included almost 200 conditions examining CBT compared to approximately 50 examining medication monotherapy, 3 examining stand-alone attention bias modification, 2 examining acceptance and commitment therapy, and 2 examining psychodynamic-based therapies.

RELATIVE IMPORTANCE OF EXPOSURE

The bulk of the evidence supporting the use of exposure for childhood anxiety disorders derives from studies of CBT. However, because the format of treatments referred to as CBT varies widely, it is impossible to determine the relative importance of exposure compared to AMS from this literature. In fact, as discussed previously, exposure constitutes only approximately one-third to one-half of frequently used CBT protocols (e.g., Coping Cat; Kendall, 2000), and some protocols do not include any in-session exposure. As such, it is conceivable that the benefits of CBT stem from the exposure, AMS, or the combination of the two. In order to answer the question of which components contribute to the efficacy of CBT for anxiety, we can look to the advice of child anxiety experts who conduct child psychotherapy research. In general, experts agree that exposure to feared stimuli is an essential treatment component (Beidel, Turner, & Morris, 2000; Davis & Ollendick, 2005; Kazdin & Weisz, 1998; Kendall et al., 2005; Silverman & Kurtines, 1996).

There is also a growing body of literature suggesting not only that exposure is the essential ingredient of treatment but also that adding AMS may not be necessary. A recent meta-analysis found that protocols including more in-session exposure had better outcomes, whereas protocols including relaxation had poorer outcomes (Whiteside et al., in press). Moreover, it has long been recognized that symptom improvement only begins after the introduction of exposure in treatment studies (Kendall et al., 1997; Ollendick, 1995; Ollendick, Hagopian, & Huntzinger, 1991) and more recently that more exposure delivered during treatment is related to better outcomes (Tiwari, Kendall, Hoff, Harrison, & Fizur, 2013; Vande Voort, Svecova, Brown Jacobsen, & Whiteside, 2010). Furthermore, a few studies suggest that AMS is no more effective than no treatment (Muris, Meesters, & Gobel, 2002; Muris, Meesters, & van Melick, 2002; Ollendick et al., 2009). Moreover, treatment protocols such as those for combined anxiety disorders that include more AMS, particularly relaxation, and thus less exposure are less effective than protocols with a clearer emphasis on exposure (e.g., ERP for OCD; Ale et al., 2015). Finally, not only are CBT protocols that introduce exposure early effective and acceptable (Baer & Garland, 2005; Ollendick et al., 2009; Storch et al., 2013) but also they may be more effective and efficient than those that introduce AMS first (Whiteside et al., 2015).

CONTEXTUAL ISSUES

As mentioned in Chapter 3, treatment of childhood anxiety disorders presents challenges that are less relevant or not present in adult populations. Most of these issues are related to developmental stages of childhood and adolescence and the degree to which youth are dependent on their parents and other adults, such as school personnel. Although treatment packages are generally adapted for different ages (i.e., children vs. adolescents), effect sizes typically do not differ significantly by age. However, there is evidence that including parents may improve treatment outcome for younger children more so than adolescents (Barrett, Dadds, & Rapee, 1996). Environmental factors, including families and schools, are particularly important with youth. Schools provide an opportunity to bring treatment to an environment in which anxiety might be present, and they have been found to be successful settings for child anxiety treatment (Bernstein, Layne, Egan, & Tennison, 2005; Ginsburg, Becker, Drazdowski, & Tein, 2012). Finally, given the degree to which children are expected to be compliant with adults, comorbid disruptive behavior disorders and attention deficit disorders often decrease the effectiveness of child anxiety treatment (Halldorsdottir & Ollendick, 2014; Storch et al., 2008).

TREATMENT GUIDELINES

Another area of support for exposure-based treatments comes from institutions that provide practice guidelines for clinicians. For example, the guidelines developed by the National Institute for Health and Clinical Excellence (NICE), an independent organization that provides treatment recommendations to the National Health Services in England and Wales, recommend CBT as the first-line treatment for childhood OCD, social anxiety disorder, and PTSD. NICE has more extensive guidelines for adult treatment that designate exposure-based CBT as the treatment with the most empirical support and recommend it as the most appropriate first-line intervention for OCD, social anxiety disorder, PTSD, and GAD. Similarly, the Canadian Anxiety Guidelines Initiative Group recommends CBT as the preferred first-line treatment for childhood anxiety disorders (Katzman et al., 2014).

SUMMARY

A large amount of research has been conducted during the past two decades supporting the use of exposure-based treatments for childhood anxiety and OCD. This research suggests that exposure-based treatments are effective and have some advantages over other interventions. Although more research needs to be conducted to better understand how to best treat childhood anxiety and OCD, no other intervention has close to the amount of empirical support as exposure-based CBT. As such, clinicians who implement exposure with their child anxiety patients can feel confident that their practice is consistent with the latest research and practice guidelines.

Now that we have established the case for using exposure therapy, we turn our attention to learning how to actually do exposure. In Section 3, we introduce the basic structure for applying exposure to childhood anxiety and OCD.

REFERENCES

Abramowitz, J. S., Whiteside, S. P., & Deacon, B. J. (2005). The effectiveness of treatment for pediatric obsessive–compulsive disorder: A meta-analysis. *Behavior Therapy, 36,* 55–63.

Ale, C. M., McCarthy, D. M., Rothschild, L., & Whiteside, S. (2015). Components of cognitive behavioral therapy related to outcome in childhood anxiety disorders. *Clinical Child and Family Psychology Review, 18,* 240–251. doi:10.1007/s10567-015-0184-8

American Psychiatric Association. (2013). *Diagnostic and statistical manual of mental disorders* (5th ed.). Arlington, VA: American Psychiatric Publishing.

Baer, S., & Garland, E. J. (2005). Pilot study of community-based cognitive behavioral group therapy for adolescents with social phobia. *Journal of the American Academy of Child and Adolescent Psychiatry, 44,* 258–264. doi:S0890-8567(09)61471-4

Barrett, P. M., Dadds, M. R., & Rapee, R. M. (1996). Family treatment of childhood anxiety: A controlled trial. *Journal of Consulting and Clinical Psychology, 64*(2), 333–342.

Beidel, D. C., Turner, S. M., & Morris, T. L. (2000). Behavioral treatment of childhood social phobia. *Journal of Consulting and Clinical Psychology, 68,* 1072–1080.

Beidel, D. C., Turner, S. M., Sallee, F. R., Ammerman, R. T., Crosby, L. A., & Pathak, S. (2007). SET-C versus fluoxetine in the treatment of childhood social phobia. *Journal of the American Academy of Child & Adolescent Psychiatry, 46*(12), 1622–1632. doi:10.1097/chi.0b013e318154bb57

Bernstein, G. A., Layne, A. E., Egan, E. A., & Tennison, D. M. (2005). School-based interventions for anxious children. *Journal of the American Academy of Child and Adolescent Psychiatry, 44*(11), 1118–1127. doi:S0890-8567(09)62214-0

Cartwright-Hatton, S., Roberts, C., Chitsabesan, P., Fothergill, C., & Harrington, R. (2004). Systematic review of the efficacy of cognitive behaviour therapies for childhood and adolescent anxiety disorders [see Comment]. *British Journal of Clinical Psychology, 43*(Pt. 4), 421–436.

Chase, R. M., Whitton, S. W., & Pincus, D. B. (2012). Treatment of adolescent panic disorder: A nonrandomized comparison of intensive versus weekly CBT. *Child and Family Behavior Therapy, 34,* 305–323.

Crawley, S. A., Kendall, P. C., Benjamin, C. L., Brodman, D. M., Wei, C., Beidas, R. S., . . . Mauro, C. (2013). Brief cognitive–behavioral therapy for anxious youth: Feasibility and initial outcomes. *Cognitive and Behavioral Practice, 20,* 123–133.

Davis, T. E., III, & Ollendick, T. H. (2005). Empirically supported treatments for specific phobia in children: Do efficacious treatments address the components of a phobic response? *Clinical Psychology: Science and Practice, 12,* 144–160.

Gillies, D., Taylor, F., Gray, C., O'Brien, L., & D'Abrew, N. (2012). Psychological therapies for the treatment of post-traumatic stress disorder in children and adolescents. *Cochrane Database of Systematic Reviews, 2012*(12), CD006726. doi:10.1002/14651858.CD006726.pub2

Ginsburg, G. S., Becker, K. D., Drazdowski, T. K., & Tein, J. Y. (2012). Treating anxiety disorders in inner city schools: Results from a pilot randomized controlled trial comparing CBT and usual care. *Child Youth Care Forum, 41*(1), 1–19. doi:10.1007/s10566-011-9156-4

Halldorsdottir, T., & Ollendick, T. H. (2014). Comorbid ADHD: Implications for the treatment of anxiety disorders in children and adolescents. *Cognitive and Behavioral Practice, 21*, 310–322.

Hirshfeld-Becker, D. R., Masek, B., Henin, A., Blakely, L. R., Pollock-Wurman, R. A., McQuade, J., . . . Biederman, J. (2010). Cognitive behavioral therapy for 4- to 7-year-old children with anxiety disorders: A randomized clinical trial. *Journal of Consulting and Clinical Psychology, 78*(4), 498–510. doi:10.1037/a0019055

James, A., James, G., Codrey, F., Soler, A., & Choke, A. (2013). Cognitive behavioural therapy for anxiety disorders in children and adolescents. *Cochrane Database of Systematic Reviews, 2013*(6), CD004690.

Katzman, M. A., Bleau, P., Blier, P., Chokka, P., Kjernisted, K., Van Ameringen, M., . . . Walker, J. R. (2014). Canadian clinical practice guidelines for the management of anxiety, posttraumatic stress and obsessive–compulsive disorders. *BMC Psychiatry, 14*(Suppl. 1), S1. doi:10.1186/1471-244X-14-S1-S1

Kazdin, A. E., & Weisz, J. R. (1998). Identifying and developing empirically supported child and adolescent treatments. *Journal of Consulting and Clinical Psychology, 66*, 19–36.

Kendall, P. C. (1985). Toward a cognitive–behavioral model of child psychopathology and a critique of related interventions. *Journal of Abnormal Child Psychology, 13*, 357–372.

Kendall, P. C. (2000). *Cognitive–behavioral therapy for anxious children: Therapist manual* (2nd ed.). Ardmore, PA.: Workbook.

Kendall, P. C., Flannery-Schroeder, E., Panichelli-Mindel, S. M., Southam-Gerow, M., Henin, A., & Warman, M. (1997). Therapy for youths with anxiety disorders: A second randomized clinical trial. *Journal of Consulting and Clinical Psychology, 65*(3), 366–380.

Kendall, P. C., Robin, J. A., Hedtke, K. A., Suveg, C., Flannery-Schroeder, E., & Gosch, E. (2005). Considering CBT with anxious youth? Think exposures. *Cognitive and Behavioral Practice, 12*(1), 136–150.

Manassis, K., Russell, K., & Newton, A. S. (2010). The Cochrane Library and the treatment of childhood and adolescent anxiety disorders and overview of reviews. *Evidence-Based Child Health, 5*, 541–554.

Maynard, B. R., Brendel, K. E., Bulanda, J. J., Heyne, D., Thompson, A., & Pigott, T. D. (2015). Psychosocial interventions for school refusal with primary and secondary students: A systematic review. *Campbell Systematic Reviews, 12*. doi:10.4073/csr.2015.12

Muris, P., Meesters, C., & Gobel, M. (2002). Cognitive coping vs. emotional disclosure in the treatment of anxious children: A pilot-study. *Cognitive Behaviour Therapy, 31*, 59–67.

Muris, P., Meesters, C., & van Melick, M. (2002). Treatment of childhood anxiety disorders: A preliminary comparison between cognitive–behavioral group therapy and a psychological placebo intervention. *Journal of Behavioral Therapy and Experimental Psychiatry, 33*(3–4), 143–158. doi:S0005791602000253

Muris, P., & Ollendick, T. H. (2015). Children who are anxious in silence: A review on selective mutism, the new anxiety disorder in DSM-5. *Clinical Child and Family Psychology Review, 18*(2), 151–169. doi:10.1007/s10567-015-0181-y

O'Kearney, R. T., Anstey, K., von Sanden, C., & Hunt, A. (2009). Behavioural and cognitive behavioural therapy for obsessive compulsive disorder in children and adolescents. *Cochrane Database of Systematic Reviews 2009*(1), CD004856.

Ollendick, T. (1995). Cognitive behavioral treatment of panic disorder with agoraphobia in adolescents: A multiple baseline design analysis. *Behavior Therapy, 26,* 517–531.

Ollendick, T. H., Hagopian, L. P., & Huntzinger, R. M. (1991). Cognitive–behavior therapy with nighttime fearful children. *Journal of Behavioral Therapy and Experimental Psychiatry, 22*(2), 113–121. doi:0005-7916(91)90006-Q

Ollendick, T. H., Öst, L.-G., Reuterskiold, L., Costa, N., Cederlund, R., Sirbu, C., . . . Jarrett, M. A. (2009). One-session treatment of specific phobias in youth: A randomized clinical trial in the United States and Sweden. *Journal of Consulting and Clinical Psychology, 77*(3), 504–516.

Öst, L. G., & Ollendick, T. H. (2001). *Manual for one-session treatment of specific phobias.* Unpublished manuscript.

Öst, L. G., & Ollendick, T. H. (2017). Brief, intensive and concentrated cognitive behavioral treatments for anxiety disorders in children: A systematic review and meta-analysis. *Behaviour Research and Therapy, 97,* 134–145. doi:10.1016/j.brat.2017.07.008

Öst, L. G., Svensson, L., Hellstrom, K., & Lindwall, R. (2001). One-session treatment of specific phobias in youths: A randomized clinical trial. *Journal of Consulting and Clinical Psychology, 69,* 814–824.

Payne, S., Bolton, D., & Perrin, S. (2011). A pilot investigation of cognitive therapy for generalized anxiety disorder in children aged 7–17 years. *Cognitive Therapy & Research, 35,* 171–178.

Pediatric OCD Treatment Study Team. (2004). Cognitive–behavior therapy, sertraline, and their combination for children and adolescents with obsessive–compulsive disorder: The Pediatric OCD Treatment Study (POTS) randomized controlled trial. *JAMA, 292,* 1969–1976.

Pincus, D., Santucci, L. C., Ehrenreich, J. T., & Eyberg, S. M. (2008). The implementation of modified parent–child interaction therapy for youth with separation anxiety disorder. *Cognitive and Behavioral Practice, 15,* 118–125.

Pincus, D. B., May, J. E., Whitton, S. W., Mattis, S. G., & Barlow, D. H. (2010). Cognitive–behavioral treatment of panic disorder in adolescence. *Journal of Clinical Child and Adolescent Psychology, 39*(5), 638–649. doi:10.1080/15374416.2010.501288

Pionek Stone, B., Kratochwill, T. R., Sladezcek, I., & Serlin, R. C. (2002). Treatment of selective mutism: A best-evidence synthesis. *School Psychology Quarterly, 17,* 168–190. doi:http://dx.doi.org/10.1521/scpq.17.2.168.20857

Reynolds, S., Wilson, C., Austin, J., & Hooper, L. (2012). Effects of psychotherapy for anxiety in children and adolescents: A meta-analytic review. *Clinical Psychology Review, 32,* 251–262.

Santucci, L. C., & Ehrenreich-May, J. (2013). A randomized controlled trial of the Child Anxiety Multi-Day Program (CAMP) for separation anxiety disorder. *Child Psychiatry and Human Development, 44,* 439–451.

Scaini, S., Belotti, R., Ogliari, A., & Battaglia, M. (2016). A comprehensive meta-analysis of cognitive–behavioral interventions for social anxiety disorder in children and adolescents. *Journal of Anxiety Disorders, 42,* 105–112. doi:10.1016/j.janxdis.2016.05.008

Schneider, S., Blatter-Meunier, J., Herren, C., Adornetto, C., In-Albon, T., & Lavallee, K. (2011). Disorder-specific cognitive–behavioral therapy for separation anxiety disorder in young children: A randomized waiting-list-controlled trial. *Psychotherapy and Psychosomatics, 80*(4), 206–215. doi:10.1159/000323444

Silverman, W. K., & Kurtines, W. M. (1996). Transfer of control: A psychosocial intervention model for internalizing disorders in youth. In E. D. Hibbs & P. S. Jensen (Eds.), *Psychosocial treatments for child and adolescent disorders: Empirically based strategies for clinical practice* (pp. 63–81). Washington, DC: American Psychological Association.

Skarphedinsson, G., Hanssen-Bauer, K., Kornor, H., Heiervang, E. R., Landro, N. I., Axelsdottir, B., . . . Ivarsson, T. (2015). Standard individual cognitive behaviour therapy for paediatric obsessive–compulsive disorder: A systematic review of effect estimates across comparisons. *Nordic Journal of Psychiatry, 69*(2), 81–92. doi:10.3109/08039488.2014.941395

Storch, E., Bussing, R., Small, B., Geffken, G., McNamara, J., Rahman, O., . . . Murphy, T. (2013). Randomized, placebo-controlled trial of cognitive–behavioral therapy alone or combined with sertraline in the treatment of pediatric obsessive–compulsive disorder. *Behavior Research and Therapy, 51*, 823–829.

Storch, E. A., Merlo, L. J., Larson, M. J., Geffken, G. R., Lehmkuhl, H. D., Jacob, M. L., . . . Goodman, W. K. (2008). Impact of comorbidity on cognitive–behavioral therapy response in pediatric obsessive–compulsive disorder. *Journal of the American Academy of Child and Adolescent Psychiatry, 47*(5), 583–592. doi:10.1097/CHI.0b013e31816774b1

Tiwari, S., Kendall, P. C., Hoff, A. L., Harrison, J. P., & Fizur, P. (2013). Characteristics of exposure sessions as predictors of treatment response in anxious youth. *Journal of Clinical Child and Adolescent Psychology, 42*, 34–43.

Vande Voort, J. L., Svecova, J., Brown Jacobsen, A., & Whiteside, S. P. (2010). A retrospective examination of the similarity between clinical practice and manualized treatment of childhood anxiety disorders. *Cognitive and Behavioral Practice, 17*, 322–328.

Walkup, J. T., Albano, A. M., Piacentini, J. C., Birmaher, B., Compton, S. N., Sherrill, J. T., . . . Kendall, P. C. (2008). Cognitive behavioral therapy, sertraline, or a combination in childhood anxiety. *New England Journal of Medicine, 359*, 2753–2766.

Wang, Z., Whiteside, S. P. H., Sim, L., Farah, W., Morrow, A. S., Alsawas, M., . . . Murad, M. H. (2017). Comparative effectiveness and safety of cognitive behavioral therapy and pharmacotherapy for childhood anxiety disorders: A systematic review and meta-analysis. *JAMA Pediatrics, 171*(11), 1049–1056. doi:10.1001/jamapediatrics.2017.3036

Whiteside, S. P., Ale, C. M., Young, B., Olsen, M. W., Biggs, B. K., Gregg, M. S., . . . Homan, K. (2016). The length of child anxiety treatment in a regional health system. *Child Psychiatry and Human Development, 47*(6), 985–992. doi:10.1007/s10578-016-0628-5

Whiteside, S. P. H., Ale, C. M., Young, B., Dammann, J., Tiede, M. S., & Biggs, B. K. (2015). The feasibility of improving CBT for childhood anxiety disorders through a dismantling study. *Behaviour Research and Therapy, 73*, 83–89. doi:10.1016/j.brat.2015.07.011

Whiteside, S. P. H., Sim, L. A., Morrow, A. S., Farah, W. H., Hilliker, D. R., Murad, M. H., & Wang, Z. (in press). A meta-analysis to guide the enhancement of CBT for childhood anxiety: Exposure over Anxiety Management. *Clinical Child and Family Psychology Review.*

Clinical Application

5

Preparing for Exposure

In Sections 1 and 2, we provided the rationale for emphasizing exposure in the treatment of childhood anxiety and obsessive–compulsive disorder (OCD) by introducing its history, theoretical underpinnings, and extensive empirical support. With the justification for exposure therapy in place, we dive into the specifics of how to implement exposure therapy in Section 3. The chapters in this section explain how to prepare the family for exposure therapy (this chapter) and how to conduct different forms of exposures (Chapter 6). After we introduce the basic mechanics of implementation, we further illustrate these procedures through several case examples in Section 4.

Exposure therapy is a learning process, and to be successful, patients and their parents need to understand how exposure works and why it can be helpful to them. Although the setup is an important stage of therapy, it need not be overly lengthy or cumbersome. Some therapists seem to spend so much time preparing their patients for exposure through rapport building, relaxation training, and cognitive restructuring or problem-solving exercises that they never begin the actual exposures or leave little time for doing so in an efficacious manner (Whiteside, Deacon, Benito, & Stewart, 2016). Based on the literature we reviewed in Section 2 indicating that neither relaxation nor cognitive restructuring is necessary for exposure to be successful, we recommend that therapists plan to begin exposure as soon as possible (Whiteside et al., 2015). Preparation for exposure typically requires completion of three fundamental tasks (Table 5.1): (1) teaching the patient and family the cognitive behavioral conceptualization of anxiety maintenance through avoidance and applying it to the child's specific symptoms, (2) learning how to "do" exposures, and (3) building a fear ladder based on the child's symptoms. Implementation of exposure activities is the next step, and it is discussed in Chapter 6. The speed with which these three tasks can be completed varies by patient, depending on child and family readiness; symptom complexity and severity; as well as other potential complicating factors, such as the presence of comorbidities and situational/contextual constraints. However, in our experience, the majority of families can progress through these steps in 1 or 2 hours with an experienced clinician. As such, most patients can begin exposure therapy by the third session of standard once-weekly 50-minute individual therapy following

Exposure Therapy for Child and Adolescent Anxiety and OCD. Stephen P. H. Whiteside, Thomas H. Ollendick, and Bridget K. Biggs, Oxford University Press (2020). © Oxford University Press.
DOI: 10.1093/med/9780190862992.001.0001

Table 5.1 PREPARING FOR EXPOSURE

Why? Teach the family the cognitive–behavioral conceptualization of how anxiety/OCD is maintained through avoidance and use it to conceptualize to the child's specific symptoms.
How? Teach the family how to conduct exposures.
What? Help the family build a fear ladder to guide exposures.

an initial assessment (Whiteside et al., 2015). We discuss how to complete these tasks next.

LEARNING AND APPLYING THE COGNITIVE– BEHAVIORAL CONCEPTUALIZATION OF SYMPTOM MAINTENANCE

Preparing a child for exposure therapy requires coming to a shared under-standing of how anxiety and OCD function over time. The cognitive–behav-ioral conceptualization of the maintenance of these disorders can take different forms with varying degrees of complexity. However, in order to initiate expo-sure therapy, children and their families need to be able to identify the norma-tively safe stimuli that set off the child's reaction, the beliefs or expectations that lead the child to interpret the situation as dangerous (Ollendick, Öst, Ryan, Capriola, & Reuterskiold, 2017; Ollendick, Ryan, Capriola-Hall, Reuterskiold, & Ost, 2017), and the child's avoidance behaviors that lead to short-term re-lief and prevent learning. We refer to these components and their interplay as the anxiety cycle (or OCD cycle depending on the patient's symptoms). It is often helpful to begin psychoeducation with an overview of the cycle and then to explain each of the three components in detail. We find that the use of a straightforward example, such as a fear of dogs, and a visual aid assists in the presentation of the anxiety cycle.

Overview

To introduce a child and parents to the anxiety or OCD cycle, a therapist could use an illustration such as Figure 5.1. The therapist could begin by saying,

> It turns out that all fears, worries, obsessions, and compulsions work the same way. Because some fears are easier to understand than others, we are going to use a boy's fear of dogs as an example. Once we learn how a fear of

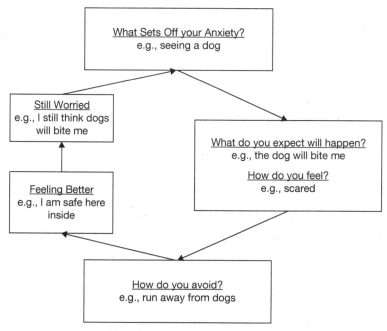

Figure 5.1 The anxiety/OCD cycle overview.

dogs works and how to treat it, we can use that to understand your experience and how to help you with your particular fears or worries.

The therapist could then explain the anxiety cycle of a boy with fear of dogs:

The anxiety cycle starts when the boy sees the dog. And then he reacts. Because he expects the dog will bite him, he feels scared. He then runs away. Once he gets away from the dog, he feels safe and his anxiety goes down. However, because he still believes that dogs will bite him, he continues to worry about them, and the next time he sees a dog, the cycle repeats itself. There are three important points that we want to learn and fully understand from this cycle. First is the importance of expectations, or beliefs. The boy is afraid of the dog [even though dogs are generally safe], because he believes it will bite him. In order to stop feeling scared he needs to learn that dogs are generally safe. However, our beliefs and expectations are based strongly on our experiences. Which brings us to the second point, avoidance. If the boy always avoids dogs by running away, he will never have the chance to learn that dogs are relatively safe. So, if running away doesn't work, why does he keep doing it? That brings us to point number three, reinforcement, which is another word for reward. The boy doesn't like to feel scared. So, anything he does that makes him feel better, like running away, is automatically rewarded, or reinforced. This means that he is more likely to run away the next time he sees a dog.

After the family indicates that they understand the cognitive–behavioral cycle of anxiety, the therapist then explains each of the key components in more detail. If they do not seen to understand, we suggest using a second example, such as a fear of talking to other kids. Usually, however, the first example is sufficient.

Stimuli That Set Off Anxiety and OCD

The anxiety cycle begins when the child is confronted with the feared stimuli, something that is generally safe and/or tolerable to most other children. The therapist's goal in presenting this item is to help families understand that there are a variety of stimuli that set off anxiety. It is not uncommon for families to state that the child is "always nervous" or "afraid of everything." Although some children have frequent fears or worries in many situations (such as with generalized anxiety disorder), a successful exposure plan requires an understanding of the specific feared stimuli that the child needs to confront (see the example anxiety cycle for general anxiety and worry in Figure 5.2). It can be helpful to explain that anxiety and OCD reactions can be set off by things from three broad categories of items. The therapist might introduce this as follows:

> There are three groups of things that are generally safe, but can set off anxiety or OCD in some kids and teenagers. The first is "Things Out There in the World." This includes places you have to go, activities you have to do, or

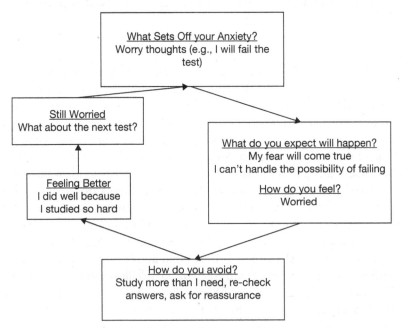

Figure 5.2 The anxiety/OCD cycle—general anxiety and worry example.

items you have to be around. For example, some kids' anxiety is set off by being around dogs, riding elevators, having to take tests, talking to people, touching doorknobs, or being away from their parents. The second group is "Thoughts in Our Heads." Sometimes kids are not in a scary place, but they start to worry about the future, have scary memories about the past, or have strange unpleasant thoughts pop into their heads. The third group is "Feelings in Our Body." Sometimes kids are not in a scary place and are not worrying about anything, but it is the feelings in their body that frighten them. For example, their heart might start beating fast, or they feel dizzy, like they can't breathe, that they might throw-up, or like they are having a panic attack. Oftentimes, the symptoms that kids experience are set off by different things from two or all three of these groups.

This explanation helps families start to broaden their ideas of what sets off anxiety to include thoughts and bodily feelings in addition to external items that are more readily observable. After the therapist has described the different stimuli, she can help the family identify the items that set off the child's fears, worries, or distress. We discuss the process for mapping the cognitive–behavioral cycle onto the child's symptoms in more detail after we review each component of the cycle.

Expectations That Cause Distress

After explaining the variety of stimuli that set off the anxiety cycle, the therapist then begins to explain the different reactions children have to those stimuli that lead to anxiety or distress. Recall that in Chapter 2 we explained the role of expectations or beliefs in the development and maintenance of anxiety disorders and OCD. These expectations or beliefs can become greatly exaggerated and even catastrophic in scope. Understanding how a child's expectations turn a nonthreatening situation into a feared one and how these expectations can become "blown out of proportion" is essential for laying the groundwork for exposure therapy. It can be helpful to simplify these expectations into two groups: expecting something bad to happen versus expecting the experience to be unbearable. The therapist might introduce this topic as follows.

There are two types of expectations or beliefs kids have that make them anxious in relatively safe situations. First, kids feel afraid when they expect something bad will happen to them or someone else. For example, believing that the dog will bite them, or people will laugh at them, or the germs from the doorknob will make them sick. Other times, kids don't have a specific fear of something bad happening. Rather, they expect that the situation will be so uncomfortable that they can't possibly handle it. For example, they think if they get germs on them they will feel gross unless they wash them off. Or feelings of panic or nervousness talking to people will spiral out of control.

After introducing the importance of expectations in eliciting an anxious re-sponse to neutral stimuli, the therapist helps the family identify the child's expec-tations associated with each of the stimuli identified previously. It is also helpful to have the child label the feeling that results from these beliefs, such as scared, worried, dirty, or just-not-right.

Avoidance That Prevents Learning

After the family understands the role of beliefs or expectations, the therapist introduces the concept of avoidance. Avoidance includes any actions, physical or mental, that a child takes to avoid the situation or prevent the expected feared outcomes from occurring or that parents take to accommodate for the child's anxiety. Importantly, these actions also prevent the child from learning that their expectations are inaccurate, thus maintaining the cycle of anxiety or OCD. The therapist can introduce this topic in the following way:

> There are many different ways that kids avoid things that make them anxious or upset. Sometimes they simply don't go near those items, or get away as soon as possible, like running away from dogs, or not going to social activi-ties. Sometimes, however, kids can't avoid the situations altogether, but they do things to partially avoid while they are there, like not asking questions in class and not making eye contact, or not touching doorknobs and using their sleeve to open doors. Rituals, like hand washing, checking, re-reading, or repeating, are other ways of avoiding. Sometimes kids rely on others, such as their parents, to avoid by frequently asking for reassurance, having parents order for them at restaurants, or clinging to parents when it is time to separate. Other times kids might use what we call "safety behaviors" like holding a favorite doll or a good luck charm to help them avoid the anxiety. Finally, overpreparing, such as studying much more than is needed, is a way of avoiding worries about the possibility of failure. Avoidance is a problem, because it prevents kids from learning that their fear is unlikely to come true because the thing they are afraid of is generally safe.

As with the other components of the anxiety cycle, the therapist helps the family identify overt (i.e., clearly observable) and covert (e.g., mental actions that are not observable) methods that the child and parents use to avoid fear stimuli and prevent feared outcomes. It is particularly important to include the actions and responses engaged in by the parents on this list.

Exposure

The final step of psychoeducation is to introduce the concept of replacing avoid-ance with exposure. This involves explaining the basic outline for how facing one's fears reduces anxiety or fear and builds confidence, as well as how the exposure exercises relate to the components of the anxiety or OCD cycle that the family now understands. Using a diagram such as Figure 5.3, the therapist could introduce exposure as follows:

The way we treat anxiety or OCD is to help children break the cycle that keeps them stuck in fear and worry. Here is an example for how the boy who is afraid of dogs would break his cycle. We start in the same place. The boy sees a dog, believes that it will bite him and he feels scared. However, this time he faces his fears by approaching and petting the dog to test whether dogs are likely to bite him. This is called an exposure. Because approaching and petting dogs is generally safe, the exposure goes well and he begins to believe that he can handle dogs and to feel more confident. It is very important to notice that the boy changes his behavior and faces his fear, even though he still feels scared and worries that the dog might bite him. It would be easier if we could turn off his scary thoughts and feelings like a light switch or a water faucet, but we can't. Instead, when he faces his fear, the boy needs to initially expect the dog to bite him and to feel nervous. This allows him to learn that these thoughts and feelings are misleading him. In this way, exposures are like experiments that test our beliefs and help us learn that we can handle things better than we thought. Fortunately, the more we learn what we can do by facing our fears, the more confident and less nervous we will feel. It is also important to realize

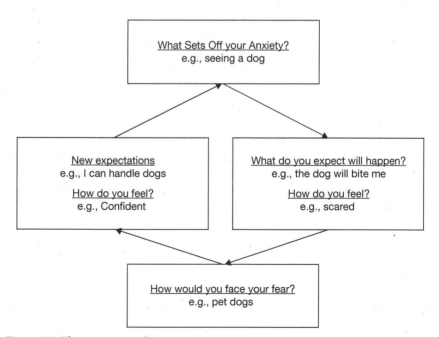

Figure 5.3 The exposure cycle.

that facing our fears starts a new cycle. It is not a onetime thing. The boy can't just pet one dog, he has to pet many dogs in many places, until he believes he can handle most dogs, most of the time.

After the therapist introduces the general concept of exposure, it can be helpful to provide more detail about how exposure exercises are set up. Specifically, exposures need to involve confronting the feared stimuli as directly as possible. In addition, the therapist should emphasize that exposures need to be designed as experiments to test the child's expectations that either something bad will happen or that she cannot handle the situation. Finally, exposures are not merely the cessation of avoidance but, rather, an active attempt to bring on anxiety. For example, social anxiety exposures are not limited to answering a question when called upon but, rather, actively raising one's hand. Similarly, exposures to OCD germs include actively touching many doorknobs and wiping one's hands on one's clothes and face. The therapists should end the psychoeducation by introducing the different types of exposure with the following description:

> Just like there are three categories of things that make kids scared, there are three ways to do exposures. If a child's anxiety is set off by something out in the world, the child needs to go there and do it. Children who are nervous in social situations need to practice talking to people, those with OCD fears of germs need to touch contaminated doorknobs, and those afraid to be away from their parents need to practice being in a room alone. If a child's anxiety is set off by thoughts, she needs to repeat those scary thoughts until they get boring. For example, a child might repeat "I am going to fail my test" over and over until she learns that thinking something doesn't mean it is true and that she can feel calm even while having an unpleasant thought. And finally, if a child is afraid of feelings in his body, he needs to bring on those feelings until he learns that even though those feelings are uncomfortable, they are not dangerous and they go away over time. For example, a boy might run in place until he realizes that his heart pounding doesn't mean he is having a heart attack.

As with the components of the anxiety (or OCD) cycle, after explaining the various approaches to exposure, the therapist works with the family to identify, in general terms, what activities the child will need to engage in to face his fears. In the next section, we provide some additional discussion of how to use the information about avoidance and exposure to frame the child's symptoms.

APPLYING THE COGNITIVE–BEHAVIORAL MODEL TO THE CHILD'S SYMPTOMS

The cognitive–behavioral model of anxiety and OCD provides a framework for the therapist and the family to reach a shared understanding of the child's symptoms and treatment plan. We find that it works well to first present the general overview of the model as described previously and ensure the family has a basic under-standing of how it works. Then, as the therapist describes the details of each of the four components (stimuli, expectations, avoidance, and exposure), she works with the family to identify how the child's experience fits into each component in the cycle. For example, after introducing the types of stimuli that set off anxiety, the therapists might work with the family as follows:

> THERAPIST: Okay. So now that we know about the different things that can start kids feeling anxious, let's figure out how this works for you. What makes you anxious?
>
> CHILD: School.
>
> THERAPIST: Okay, good. Let's get more specific. What about school makes you nervous?
>
> MOTHER: She does get nervous at school, but she also isn't going to other places that she used to, like dance class or to her friend's house.
>
> CHILD: I am scared to be around people.
>
> THERAPIST: I see. What are you afraid of when you are around other people?
>
> CHILD: I am too scared to talk because they might not like me.
>
> THERAPIST: That is very helpful. Let's write down that your anxiety is set off by having to talk to people. Does that sound right?
>
> MOTHER AND CHILD: Yes.
>
> THERAPIST: Great. Now let's talk about the beliefs some kids have that make talking to people scary. Let's see if they are true for you as well.

The process of applying the cognitive–behavioral model to the child's symptoms is crucial for developing an effective treatment plan. The anxiety cycle provides a frame-work for conducting a behavioral analysis that helps the therapist and the family identify the factors that precipitate and maintain the child's symptoms. Specifically, applying the cognitive–behavioral conceptualization to the child's symptoms identifies the stimuli to be used for exposures, the expectations and beliefs that need to be tested, and the avoidance behaviors that need to be prevented. Moreover, this is a good opportunity for the therapist to ensure that the child's symptoms are con-sistent with an exaggerated fear response to neutral stimuli rather than an expected stress response to an environmental hardship. Once the therapist and family have a shared understanding of the child's symptoms and feel confident that they involve exaggerated anxiety, the therapist can introduce how to implement exposures.

LEARNING HOW TO DO EXPOSURE

Overview

Exposures are experiments designed to test the child's anxiety-provoking beliefs and lead to new learning when those expectations do not come true. Once the family understands the importance of replacing avoidance with exposure, and the therapist understands the child's symptoms, it is time to teach the family how to implement exposures. Treatment usually begins with highly planned and structured exposures, simply called planned exposures. Planned exposures involve doing an activity to test anxious beliefs and prove that the child can handle them. These exposures are typically completed with the therapist, who serves as a coach, often in the therapy room; are recorded with paper and pencil (Figure 5.4); and include clearly defined setup, execution, and debriefing activities. Planned exposures are designed to build the child's confidence that she can handle unplanned situations when they occur in real life, which we call *everyday exposures*. Teaching families how to do exposure often begins with a general overview, followed by a discussion

Setting up an Exposure:
What are you going to do for an exposure? _____
                                                        (exposure activity)

What do you fear will happen? _____
                                        (anxiety-causing belief)

How afraid are you that this will happen? _____
                                              (0 to 10 rating of fear/distress)

Doing an exposure.
Record fear rating every few minutes. Focus on whether your fear is coming true and whether you can handle the situation. Do not avoid, do rituals, ask for reassurance, or other safety behaviors.

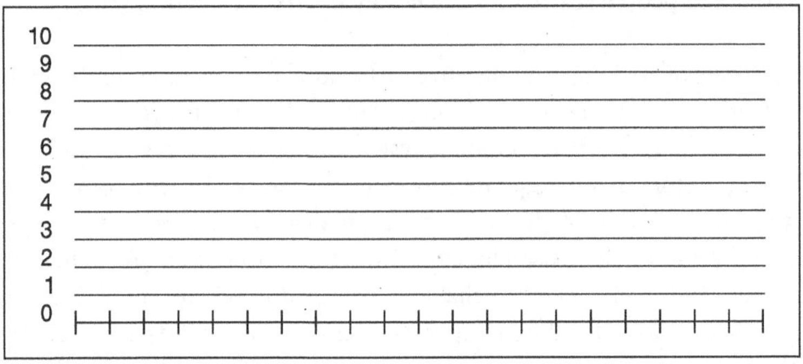

Learning from the exposure.
Stick with it until you believe you could do this again. Lowering your fear that something bad will happen by half suggests that you have been successful.

Did your fear come true?
    No
    Yes, but it wasn't bad
    Other: _____ (if other, review the exposure to see what happened)

What happened to your anxiety?
    It went down
    It stayed high, but I handled it
    Other: _____ (if other, review the exposure to see what happened)

Figure 5.4 Exposure record form.

of the essential principles for setting up, doing, and learning from successful exposures exercises. A therapist might introduce these concepts as follows:

> We want to set up exposures as experiments to test the beliefs you have that make you scared or nervous. In other words, we do exposures to test the belief that "something bad is likely to happen." To do this we need to think about what you are afraid will happen, how likely you think it is to happen, and how bad you think it would be if it actually happened. We already know that the boy with the dog phobia is afraid that dogs will bite him. If he goes around petting a lot of dogs, and none of them bite him, the boy will learn that it is unlikely that dogs will bite and he will become less nervous. But sometimes our fears come true, which is why we also need to think about how bad it would be if our fears came true. For example, if the boy does exposures to playing with puppies, they might bite him gently like puppies tend to do. Or, the boy might be most concerned about feeling very nervous when he is around dogs, which also will probably happen. In both of these examples, the boy can learn that even if his fear of being nipped by the puppy or feeling very nervous comes true, he can still handle it.

Setting Up an Exposure

Once the family members understand the general concept of exposures as experiments, the therapist should instruct them on how to start planned exposures. There are two principles regarding setting up exposures. First, *be consistent*. Quite simply, exposures need to be completed, ideally every day. The major challenge with exposure therapy is ensuring that the child, parent, and therapist engage in exposure frequently enough to improve the child's symptoms. This responsibility rests first with the therapist to lead the family through in-session exposures, second with the parent to guide the child through between-session exposures, and finally with the child to cooperate and gradually become more independent with doing exposures on a daily basis. If exposures are not being done in session, the therapist needs to re-evaluate the treatment plan. If exposures are not being completed outside the treatment session, the therapist needs to talk with the parent about what is interfering with the plans made during the session. If the child is being uncooperative, the therapist needs to make a plan to increase motivation.

The second principle for starting exposures is to *set them up as an experiment* to violate the child's anxiety-provoking expectations. To do so, the child must specifically identify what she fears will happen. Initially, this often requires significant assistance from the therapist, over time it requires assistance from the family, and finally the child can do this independently. The information gathered while framing the child's symptoms within the anxiety or OCD cycle can inform the identification of specific beliefs for a given exposure. These beliefs may involve the likelihood of a negative event occurring (e.g., being bit by a dog) or the severity of an event (e.g., it is terrible to make a mistake). Once the anxiety-provoking belief is identified, the child is asked to rate how afraid she is that it will happen. The therapist, parents, and child should not attempt to lower the child's ratings through relaxation or cognitive restructuring because such efforts may reduce the impact of the corrective learning experience (see Chapter 2, this volume).

Because the goal of the exposure is to confront and disprove the child's misperceptions of danger, the therapist should take steps to ensure that the exposure is appropriate and likely to turn out well. Recall from Chapter 1 that exposure is appropriate for addressing exaggerated expectations of threat, not for helping a child manage environmental stress. As such, when setting up an exposure, therapists must ensure that it is unlikely that anything bad will happen. For example, a social anxiety exposure to talking to kids at school is appropriate when the child is overly shy, but it is not appropriate to an aggressor who is bullying a child. Similarly, thought exposures to previous traumatic events are appropriate, whereas thought exposures to ongoing abuse or mistreatment are not. However, this should not be construed to suggest that therapists should prevent patients from experiencing distress or unpleasant outcomes. To the contrary, anxiety and OCD are most thoroughly treated when patients experience what have been called "desirable difficulties." As such, appropriate exposures involve activities that may, and sometimes do, result in the feared outcomes occurring. Moreover, exposures by design must involve experiencing emotional distress. This may involve engaging in unusual activities that highlight or exaggerate the feared activity, such as purposely stumbling over one's words, repeating scary thoughts, or touching a public toilet seat. In summary, the therapist should ensure that exposures involve a level of risk, uncertainty, and distress similar to everyday life events but do not place the child in situations that it would be unreasonable to expect her to handle or will confirm her anxious beliefs.

Doing an Exposure

There are also two main principles to keep in mind while a child is conducting an exposure. First, *stay positive*. Exposure therapy is difficult work, and children need support and encouragement. So, the first job of the exposure coach, whether therapist or parent, during exposure is to be a coach and even a cheerleader. If the child is trying, the coach should give lots of positive attention, cheer her on, and generally be warm and supportive. Statements such as "You are doing a great job, keep going" or a simple pat on the back and a smile reinforce the child's effort to face her fears. In contrast, the exposure coach should ignore anxious behavior, as well as whining and arguing, and focus attention on brave behavior. Finally, children should be encouraged to maintain a positive, open attitude. If they approach exposures with a negative resistant attitude such as "This is dumb, it won't work," they will probably have less success.

The second guiding principle during exposure is to *pay attention*. The exposure coach should help the child pay attention to what is happening and what she is learning. The goal of an exposure is for the child to learn that she can handle the feared activity without any safety behaviors, simply because the activity is reasonably safe. To learn this, the child needs to pay attention to the fact that nothing is happening that she cannot handle. The exposure coach can encourage focus and learning by asking the child throughout the exposure to rate how afraid she is that her fear will come true. We typically use a scale from 0 (not at all afraid my fear will come true) to 10 (as scared as possibly could be that my fear will come true). If the child's fear of a negative outcome decreases, the exposure coach prompts the child to explain why and guides her answer to focus on the lack of an adverse outcome despite the fact that she continues to engage in the exposure. An exchange with the boy from our example who is doing an exposure to petting a dog might proceed as follows:

THERAPIST: You are doing a great job staying with the dog. How afraid are you now that the dog will bite you?

CHILD: Umm, a three I think.

THERAPIST: That's great. It was a five before. What brought it down?

CHILD: I don't think he will bite me.

THERAPIST: That's good. What changed your mind?

CHILD: I don't know.

THERAPIST: What have you been doing since the last time I asked about your anxiety?

CHILD: Just petting him.

THERAPIST: That's right. You are facing your fears and your anxiety is coming down, because nothing bad is happening.

CHILD: I guess so.

THERAPIST: Are you doing anything else to make yourself feel better. Are you distracting yourself, taking deep breaths, or thinking about something fun?

CHILD: No.

THERAPIST: Great. You are facing your fears head on. Good for you. Keep going.

As the therapist indicated at the end, in order to pay attention, children cannot engage in avoidance, including distraction, not making eye contact, or ritualizing. Similarly, although exposure coaches should provide encouragement for effort, they must refrain from providing reassurance of safety. Statements such as "You are fine, everything is going to be okay" signal safety and prevent the child from learning that he can handle the exposure independently. Direct and subtle avoidance, rituals, distraction, and reassurance seeking are often called safety behaviors and prevent children from learning during the exposure. This can occur by leading kids to believe that the action (e.g., handwashing) prevented the feared outcome (e.g., getting sick) rather than that the exposure (e.g., touching doorknobs) was safe. Alternatively, distraction or receiving reassurance from a parent prevents youth from learning they can handle their distress independently and maintains the belief that the exposure object is overwhelming. As such, coaches should monitor for avoidance and refrain from providing reassurance during exposures. If they suspect the child is avoiding or ritualizing, they should gently raise that possibility and encourage the child to stop the safety behavior and re-engage directly with the exposure object. More generally, coaches can encourage youth to focus on the exposure stimuli, such as having them describe all the germs they suspect are on a doorknob.

As reviewed in Chapter 2, the role of habituation (i.e., decreases in anxiety during exposure) in eventual symptom improvement is uncertain. Because most patients experience habituation during exposures and habituation-focused treatment has decades of demonstrated success, we continue to use anxiety ratings during exposure to help children focus on their experience. However, it is important for exposure coaches (therapists or parents) to avoid suggesting that feelings of anxiety should be avoided or forced to dissipate. As such, if the child's anxiety increases or remains the same, the exposure coach replies by complementing her for sticking with a challenging exposure and pointing out that she is proving that she can handle experiencing anxiety. Asking the child to rate how afraid she is that her fear will come true has two potential advantages. First, it keeps her focused on the anxiety related to the current activity rather than on other items that may cause more anxiety but are not being addressed at the moment. Second, it combines subjective feelings with expectancies of negative outcomes. The differences between these constructs is important, but asking for a single rating simplifies the exposure process by combining concepts that are likely difficult to distinguish, especially for young children.

Ending and Learning from an Exposure

There are two principles to consider when ending an exposure to maximize learning. First, children need to continue an exposure until they have disconfirmed their fear expectancy: *Disprove your fear.* Simply stated, they need to learn that their fear is unlikely to come true or that if it did come true, it was not that bad. When wrapping up an exposure, the exposure coach (therapist or parent) should ask, "Did your fear come true?" If the child is able to say that her fear did not come true, then the exposure has been successful. However, as discussed previously, life involves risk, and some fears, especially social embarrassment, frequently (or intentionally) come true. In this case, the child's answer may be "My fear came true, but it was not so bad." In either case, the goal is for the child to realize that the anticipated threat was exaggerated and for the child to be willing to do the activity again.

The second principle is *Stick with it!* The exposures should continue until the child learns that her anxiety or OCD-related distress is manageable. The exposure coach can help accomplish this task by asking, "What happened to your anxiety?" We recommend using a decrease in anxiety by at least 50% to suggest that exposure has been sufficiently successful. It is our experience that this is a straightforward and time-tested method for gauging a child's response during an exposure (see discussion in Chapter 2, this volume). For many children, feeling anxious in the situation is the most salient experience, more so than misperceptions of danger, that leads to avoidance. As such, rating anxiety is the most straightforward measure of their experience. Moreover, it is our perception that setting a goal of a 50% decrease in anxiety provides a tangible guideline to reduce the likelihood that children discontinue exposure prematurely, before they have a chance to learn from the experience. However, as mentioned previously, it is perfectly acceptable (and at times desirable) for the child's anxiety to remain high. In these situations, the child may respond, "My anxiety stayed high but I handled it." Therefore, the 50% decrease should be used as a guide that therapists implement flexibly.

In general, children need to continue the exposure long enough to learn from it. Exposure coaches can help the child determine when the exposure has been engaged in for a sufficient duration and can be discontinued. Because the role of exposures is to prepare the child to approach rather than avoid everyday activities, from a practical perspective, an exposure can be considered complete when the child is willing to do it again in the routine of daily life. From a theoretical perspective, an exposure is complete when the child's anxiety-provoking expectancy has been violated. A therapist might instruct families about ending an exposure as follows:

One way to know that you have successfully completed an exposure is to continue until your child says "That wasn't so bad, I can do that again." This suggests that your child has learned that the activity is not as dangerous as she thought and that she can handle it. One way to make this a little more concrete is to continue the exposure until your child's rating of how afraid she is that her fear will happen drops in half, by at least 50%. So, if her anxiety starts at a 6 out of 10, keep going until it gets to a 3 or less. If possible, stick with the exposure until her anxiety goes all the way down to a 0 or 1. However, remember that exposures can be successful even if anxiety stays high. So, if your child's anxiety stays high, which is not unusual with more challenging exposures, it can still be successful if your child learns that the activity and anxiety were manageable. Most important, try to avoid ending an exposure while anxiety is increasing and feels like it is spiraling out of control. If your child believes ending the exposure was necessary to avoid something bad happening, the exercise will not be helpful.

Sometimes exposures do not go as well as planned. If at the end the child responds that her fear came true and was bad or that her anxiety remained high and was not manageable, this suggests that the exposure was not successful and that the therapist needs to determine what went wrong. Such an experience could reflect that the exposure activity was inappropriate because it involved an environmental stress (e.g., exposure to taking a test without recognition of a learning disability). As such, the therapist should reconceptualize the presenting problem. However, if the activity was appropriate, the lack of disconfirmation may reflect insufficient time to learn from the exercise (e.g., discontinuing exposure after 2 minutes) or inadequately defined feared beliefs. In this case, the therapist should help the child (and parent) continue with the exposure for a longer time period; more clearly design the exposure as a testable experiment; or break the exposure down into a smaller, more manageable activity.

Everyday Exposures

Planned exposures are essentially practice for the big game of everyday life. A goal of therapy is to transition from highly structured in-session planned exposures to everyday exposures completed independently by the child during normal daily activities. Everyday exposures involve taking advantage of naturally occurring situations to challenge the child to face his fears. This might mean simply per-forming previously feared activities, such as ordering food at a restaurant. Alternatively, it might consist of creating an extra-challenging task to manage "desirable difficulties," such as asking the waiter for something that is clearly not on the menu. Due to the nature of the context in which everyday exposures are completed, the family typically will not be able to complete a record form in the moment or continue/repeat the activity multiple times to ensure the feared belief is disproven. Rather, parents are encouraged to follow the steps for setting up, doing, and learning from planned exposures more informally. For example, the parent may simply help the child identify her feared belief before the activity and then review whether it came true afterwards. The therapist should encourage the family to complete an exposure form afterwards (perhaps in the evening after they return home) to have a record of the child's success transferring her in-session exposures to real-world achievements.

Everyone involved in conducting exposures (therapists, parents, and youth) needs to learn the steps for setting up, doing, and learning from exposures. We intend for therapists to read the information in this book as they develop their expertise in delivering exposure. However, the goal of parent-coached exposure therapy is to teach the parents how to deliver exposure, so all the information here can, and should, be presented to the parents. Moreover, because the final goal is for youth to independently challenge their fears, they also need to understand how to set up, do, and learn from exposures. As such, we recommend that therapists pre-sent the these steps and principles to the child and parent(s) together. Figure 5.5 presents the steps for conducting exposures and can be provided to families as a summary of the content covered in session. We further discuss the role of parents as exposure coaches later.

Staying Motivated

To varying degrees, youth need support staying motivated to engage in exposure during the course of therapy. The following strategies are summarized in Figure 5.5.

Setting-up an exposure:

- **Be Consistent.** Do exposures every day. It is the therapist's job to make sure exposures are done during the session. It is the parents' job to make sure exposures are done between sessions. It is the child's job to cooperate with exposures and to start doing them independently over time.
- **Exposures are Experiments.** Set exposures up as an experiment by deciding what you are afraid will happen and rating how afraid you are it will happen. The goal is to learn that what you are afraid of probably won't happen, and that if it does you can handle it and handle feeling nervous.

Doing an Exposure:

- **Stay Positive.** Exposures work best with a positive, open attitude. When kids are cooperating, coaches should give praise to warmly support brave behavior (Be a cheerleader!). Kids should limit, and coaches should ignore, complaining or other anxious behavior.
- **Pay Attention.** Notice that anxiety about the fear coming true decreases because the situation is not as dangerous as thought by rating anxiety every few minutes. If anxiety stay high, focus on success managing emotions. Do **not** avoid through distraction, ritualizing, or giving reassurance.

Ending and Learning from an Exposure:

- **Disprove Your Fear.** Continue each exposure until it is clear that the fears are unlikely to come true. Ask "Did your fear come true?" The answer should be "No" or "Yes, but it wasn't bad." If the child believes his fear came true and was bad, the exposure needs to be adjusted.
- **Stick with it!** Continue each exposure until it is clear that the child's anxiety has gone down or is manageable. A 50% decrease in anxiety ratings is not required, but suggests that the child has stuck with it long enough to learn she can handle the situation. Ask "What happened to your anxiety?" The answer should be "It went down" or "I handled it."

Every Day Exposures

- After doing "Planned Exposures", shift the focus to "Everyday Exposures" where kids face their fears when they pop-up in everyday life.
- If you don't have time to plan and record the exposure, follow the same steps: 1) set the exposure up as an experiment, 2) stay positive, warm, and supportive, and 3) pay attention to whether the fear came true and if the situation was manageable.

Staying Motivated

- **Small Steps.** Break fears into small steps and limit expectations for Everyday Exposures to situations that have been practiced with Planned Exposures.
- **Attention and Support.** Parents should use praise and attention when kids are trying to face their fears. When kids are letting anxiety win, acting angry, or refusing to cooperate, it is best for parents to walk away.
- **Rewards.** Set a goal for the number of exposures you want to complete each week, pick a reward for meeting that goal, and then make a chart to keep track of progress.
- **Mild Consequences.** Make a plan for no fun activities (like electronics or playing with friends) until exposure practices have been completed for the day.

Figure 5.5 Steps for completing exposures.

Many children are motivated to feel better, and as long as the treatment plan expects them to complete small, manageable steps, they will be generally compliant. Parents can use differential attention (e.g., praise for cooperation, while ignoring anxious complaining) to encourage cooperation. However, the prospect of feeling better in a few months is often insufficient motivation to complete challenging activities in the moment. As such, it is often helpful to establish short-term goals and rewards. A simple plan of making a list of rewards—objects or activities—that the child can earn by completing a reasonable number of exposures (e.g., five) can be helpful, especially with younger children. Rewards should be tied to effort that is under the child's control (i.e., cooperating with and engaging in exposures) and not factors out of his or her control (e.g., decrease in anxiety). Despite the appropriateness of the expected goals and the attractiveness of rewards, there will be times when the child refuses to complete a planned exposure. As such, it is helpful for a family to identify mild consequences, such as loss of privileges, for noncompliance.

In addition, parents can use "therapeutic consequences," in which refusing to do an exposure results in the child being expected to complete two exposures later. For example, if a child refuses to order his food at a restaurant and chooses for his parents do it for him, he will be required to complete two additional exposures to speaking to people in public. Therapeutic consequences serve two purposes. First, if the situation is indeed overwhelming, the child needs additional exposure practice to reduce anxiety. Second, if the child is simply deciding to be resistant, then the prospect of two exposures rather than one exposure can help the child make a better choice. Once a motivation plan is in place, if children are reluctant to complete an exposure, parents can remind them of their progress toward their next reward and that they will lose electronics (or other privileges) until the exposure (and possible additional ones) is (are) completed. This allows parents to remove attention from resistant/avoidant behavior rather than arguing or pleading with their child and to let the prospect of consequence convince the child to cooperate. For children who have more difficulty complying with treatment, we discuss additional strategies in Chapter 9.

BUILDING FEAR LADDERS

Once the family understands why and how to do exposures, and the therapist understands the child's symptoms, it is time to make a specific plan to guide the implementation of exposure therapy. Historically, this plan has been called a fear ladder. A fear ladder is a list of specific activities that a child will complete to learn that a certain feared stimulus is not as dangerous as the child thought. An example fear ladder for a dog phobia is presented in Table 5.2. Fear ladders generally include activities that all address a single fear category with a variety of levels of difficulty that cover all instances of how that fear occurs. If a child has multiple sources of anxiety, such as social anxiety and a fear of the dark, she will likely need multiple fear ladders to organize her exposures for each area separately. A therapist might introduce building a fear ladder as follows:

When building your fear ladder keep three things in mind. First, start with something easy, to build your confidence. Second, make sure you include items that work on your fear in all the places, ways, and times it happens. And third, have the top item on your fear ladder be something really challenging, even harder than things you usually have to do in real life. Because once you have completed that exposure, other situations will seem easier in comparison. For example, the boy with a fear of dogs might start easy by watching videos of dogs barking. He then needs to work on his fear with different kinds of dogs in different places. He might end by going to a dog park where there are lots of dogs all over the place.

Table 5.2 SAMPLE FEAR LADDER FOR A DOG PHOBIA

1.	Watch dog videos.
2.	Stand outside the room and watch therapist pet dog.
3.	Pet dog while therapist is holding it.
4.	Play with dog in office.
5.	Play with bigger (or more active) dog in office.
6.	Pet neighbor's dog.
7.	Ask strangers if I can pet their dog.
8.	Go to humane society and pet dogs.
9.	Go to dog park.

The goal is to master all of the exposures on the fear ladder. As noted previously, fear ladders usually begin with easier items and progress to more difficult ones. However, it is not necessary, and likely not always desirable, to proceed in this structured order. At times, exposure therapy can be successful, and more efficient, when patients face their most difficult fears first. However, for obvious reasons, most children are understandably reluctant to begin this way, as illustrated through the case examples in Chapter 7. Moreover, as reviewed in Chapter 2, learning theory suggests that unpredictability leads to more generalizable safety learning. As such, therapy may be more effective when patients intermingle difficult, easy, and medium exposures rather than strictly progressing up the fear ladder. Consistent with this philosophy, the sample fear ladder in Table 5.2 does not include anxiety ratings because adding this information does not appear to be necessary and may inadvertently focus too much attention on proceeding in a defined order. Given that exposure therapy rarely proceeds in a predictable manner in real-world practice, the take-home message for therapists is that they should not invest inordinate time or effort ensuring that items on the fear ladder are in an exact order. In addition, easier items do not need to be mastered before more difficult items are attempted.

Most important, the fear ladder provides structure for treatment and serves as a treatment plan. A well-designed fear ladder facilitates selecting activities at the time of planned exposures, helps ensure that exposures are targeting the inaccurate fear beliefs driving the anxiety, and keeps treatment consistent with the initial goals. Without a fear ladder, therapy is at risk of straying off task, not sufficiently targeting the child's worries, and getting repeatedly bogged down during each session trying to generate ideas about what to do for an exposure. The speed with which the child progresses through the fear ladder is often a compromise between the parents, who want to see their child better as soon as possible, and the child, who prefers to move slowly, brokered by the therapist. Additional examples of fear ladder items are discussed in Section 4.

PARENT INVOLVEMENT

We recommend including parents in the child's exposure therapy for a variety of reasons. First, many parents want to be involved and to learn how to help their child. Second, the full benefit of therapy will only be realized if the exposures that are conducted in-session are practiced in real-world situations (everyday exposures). It seems safe to assume that anyone, particularly children, would benefit from having someone supporting these efforts between sessions as long as they do not rescue the child or help the child avoid what he or she is afraid of. Third, parents are often involved in their child's anxiety or OCD symptoms in ways that maintain avoidance, and parents need assistance replacing accommodation with encouraging approach. However, rather than increasing the burden of therapy by adding parent-only sessions to address these issues, we recommend working with the child and parent together to teach them how to engage in exposure as a team. In this approach, parents are taught to be exposure coaches.

Treatment Planning

Parents are typically responsible for children entering therapy and provide valuable information during the initial assessment. The prominent role of parents should continue throughout the psychoeducation and fear ladder-building components described previously. Input from the parents will be essential to accurately identify the stimuli that set off a child's distress, the child's fear-provoking expectancies, and avoidance behaviors. Gathering this information, as well as identifying exposure targets and constructing fear ladders, is best approached collaboratively with the child and parent together. If needed, the therapist may find it helpful to meet with the child and/or parent separately to more freely discuss certain symptoms, such as a child's embarrassing intrusive thoughts or a parent's frustration with tantrums as avoidance behavior. In addition, the therapist should be sensitive to the developmental level of the child. For example, an adolescent may be able to fully describe his experience with social anxiety during peer activities, whereas the description of a 7-year-old's separation anxiety may come primarily from parents. Regardless of the child's age, parents are extremely helpful recalling anxiety-causing situations that can serve as the basis for exposures during fear ladder building.

Exposure Coaching

Given the importance of generalizing learning from in-session exposures to real-world situations, parents are a considerable asset to the therapist. The more often parents help their child engage in exposure outside the office, the more likely the child is to improve and the more prepared the family is to maintain these gains after the end of treatment. Training parents to be exposure coaches begins with teaching them how to set-up, do, and end an exposure following the steps outlined previously. The parent can then observe the therapist doing exposures during the session. The therapist can then quickly enlist the parent in directing exposure during the sessions by having the parent record information on the exposure form and lead portions of the exposure. As the parent becomes more proficient, the therapist shifts to advising the parent's exposure coaching rather than directly leading the exposure. By completing hands-on practice and receiving instructive feedback, parents can learn how to successfully direct their children through exposures outside of the therapy session. Moreover, parents have strong emotional responses to their child's anxiety. Directly observing their child successfully manage her fears while completing challenging exposures can reduce the parents' own anxiety about their child and make it easier for them to expect brave behavior outside the session.

Decreasing Accommodation

Parents should also be encouraged to apply the parent coaching strategies they practiced during planned exposures to all situations in which the child has problematic anxiety. This includes responding to their child's efforts to calmly face their fears with warm attention, cheerleading, support, and recording progress (e.g., points and tally marks) toward a reward. Parents should be encouraged to reinforce (with attention or rewards) any effort by the child to replace avoidance with approach. Conversely, anytime the child is giving into anxiety and choosing to avoid a situation that the parent believes she is prepared to handle based on her progress in therapy, the parent should remove attention and, if necessary, remind the child of the consequences of choosing to avoid (e.g., extra exposures and loss of privilege). Moreover, parents should be encouraged to eliminate their participation in accommodation. Specifically, during planned exposures, parents should refrain from providing reassurance, allowing rituals and safety behaviors, and generally discourage any efforts at avoidance. Once a child has successfully completed planned exposures to an item, parents should stop any reassurance or accommodation regarding that item. In general, removing safety behaviors, rituals, and accommodation should proceed in a gradual process that allows the child to practice managing the situation during planned exposure before being expected to handle it independently during daily life. However, this should be approached in a reasonable manner, and it is appropriate (and desirable) to expect the child to handle certain stimuli before planned exposures, if those items are similar to others that have been worked on. In this manner, the child's own self-efficacy for handling their fears and overcoming them will be enhanced (Lebowitz, 2019; Ollendick et al., 2015).

SUMMARY

In this chapter, we presented the steps for preparing the family to engage in exposure therapy. The activities outlined here are designed to help the family understand the rationale for the therapeutic value of exposure, develop a shared understanding with the therapist of the function of the child's symptoms, and understand what they will be expected to do during therapy. It is important to note that the therapist should not expect family members to feel confident that they fully understand how to do exposures at this point. Rather, mastering the art of exposure therapy requires hands-on practice, and families will develop confidence as they progress. The same can be said for therapists new to exposure therapy. Now that the stage has been set for exposure, we turn our attention to implementing the three forms of exposure exercises.

REFERENCES

Lebowitz, E. R. (2019). *Addressing Parental Accommodation when Treating Anxiety in Children*. New York: Oxford University Press.

Ollendick, T. H., Halldorsdottir, T., Fraire, M. G., Austin, K. E., Noguchi, R. J., Lewis, K. M., . . . Whitmore, M. J. (2015). Specific phobias in youth: A randomized controlled trial comparing one-session treatment to a parent-augmented one-session treatment. *Behavior Therapy, 46*(2), 141–155. doi:10.1016/j.beth.2014.09.004

Ollendick, T. H., Öst, L. G., Ryan, S. M., Capriola, N. N., & Reuterskiold, L. (2017). Harm beliefs and coping expectancies in youth with specific phobias. *Behaviour Research and Therapy, 91*, 51–57. doi:10.1016/j.brat.2017.01.007

Ollendick, T. H., Ryan, S. M., Capriola-Hall, N. N., Reuterskiold, L., & Ost, L. G. (2017). The mediating role of changes in harm beliefs and coping efficacy in youth with specific phobias. *Behaviour Research and Therapy, 99*, 131–137. doi:10.1016/j.brat.2017.10.007

Whiteside, S. P. H., Ale, C. M., Young, B., Dammann, J., Tiede, M. S., & Biggs, B. K. (2015). The feasibility of improving CBT for childhood anxiety disorders through a dismantling study. *Behaviour Research and Therapy, 73*, 83–89. doi:10.1016/j.brat.2015.07.011

Whiteside, S. P. H., Deacon, B. J., Benito, K., & Stewart, E. (2016). Factors associated with practitioners' use of exposure therapy for childhood anxiety disorders. *Journal of Anxiety Disorders, 40*, 29–36. doi:http://dx.doi.org/10.1016/j.janxdis.2016.04.001

6

Implementing Exposure

In Chapter 5, we covered how to prepare families for exposure therapy, including how to set up, do, and learn from exposures. We also introduced the three broad categories of exposure to activities, thoughts, and bodily sensations. Here, in one of the most important chapters of the book, we present the mechanics for how to implement exposure therapy for the broad spectrum of anxiety- and distress-provoking stimuli. We begin with descriptions of the categories of exposures (in vivo, imaginal, and interoceptive), the symptoms for which they are best utilized, and the goals for their use. We then turn our attention to important considerations for the optimal implementation of exposure, including identifying symptoms, titrating level of difficulty, and monitoring response. Finally, we present the procedures for implementing exposure for common clinical presentations. In the chapters in Section 4, we present specific case examples to further illustrate these exposure techniques with various disorders.

OVERVIEW

In Vivo Exposure

In vivo exposures are the most straightforward form of exposures and what most people likely think of as "facing your fears." The Latin origin of in vivo is "in the living," and it signifies that these exposures are done in real-life situations. In Chapter 5, we introduced the notion that when children are afraid of "things out there in the world," they need to "go out there and do it." This is the essence of in vivo exposure. In vivo exposure involves putting yourself in a situation that makes you nervous until you learn it is not dangerous and you can handle it. Because most presentations of anxiety or obsessive–compulsive disorder (OCD) involve some level of behavioral avoidance, most anxious patients benefit from including in vivo exposures in their treatment plan. As such, in vivo exposure should be one of the most common techniques used by therapists when treating children with anxiety or OCD. If that is not the case, therapists should likely review their

Exposure Therapy for Child and Adolescent Anxiety and OCD. Stephen P. H. Whiteside, Thomas H. Ollendick, and Bridget K. Biggs, Oxford University Press (2020). © Oxford University Press.
DOI: 10.1093/med/9780190862992.001.0001

approach and consider whether they are inadvertently accommodating their patients' avoidance.

In vivo exposures can be subdivided into three related, and at times overlapping, categories. These categories and the diagnoses of the fifth edition of the *Diagnostic and Statistical Manual of Mental Disorders* (American Psychiatric Association, 2013) to which they frequently correspond are presented in Table 6.1. One category is *situations*. Situational exposures involve the patient going to and staying in a place that makes her nervous. This type of exposure is appropriate for many fears that would fall under a diagnosis of specific phobia, such as a fear of heights, elevators, doctor and dentist appointments, or flying. Furthermore, one of the most common uses of situational exposure in children is with separation anxiety disorder, during which children stay in a room without their parents for increasing lengths of time. Situational exposure can also involve having patients with agoraphobia and/or panic disorder go to public situations, such as crowded shopping malls or restaurants. The goal of situational exposures is to learn that

Table 6.1 EXAMPLES OF IN VIVO EXPOSURES AND ASSOCIATED DIAGNOSES

Exposure Item	Diagnosis
SITUATIONS	
Heights	Specific phobia
Small spaces	Specific phobia
Medical appointments	Specific phobia
Crowds	Agoraphobia
Separation from parents	Separation anxiety disorder
Location of previous trauma	PTSD
OBJECTS	
Contamination	OCD
Asymmetry	OCD
Needles	Specific phobia
Animals/insects	Specific phobia
ACTIVITIES	
Talking to people	Social anxiety disorder
Giving presentations	Social anxiety disorder
Being observed in public	Social anxiety disorder
Making mistakes	GAD
Spreading contamination	OCD
Doing something "not just right"	OCD

GAD, generalized anxiety disorder; OCD, obsessive–compulsive disorder; PTSD, post-traumatic stress disorder.

(1) it is unlikely anything bad will happen in that situation; (2) one can handle feeling anxious, uncomfortable, or distressed in that situation; and (3) feelings of anxiety, discomfort, or distress will likely decrease over time as one stays in the situation.

Confrontation of *objects* is another form of in vivo exposure. The goal of such exposures is for the patient to learn that contact, or at least proximity, to the object will not result in harm or unmanageable distress. Objects might include contaminated doorknobs, chairs, belongings, toilets, or school supplies. Additional OCD exposures in this category could include items being "not-just-right," such as the volume being on the wrong number, desk items being out of order, or stray marks on a homework page. Many exposures for specific phobias can involve objects, such as being near dogs, spiders, blood, or needles.

The third category of in vivo exposures is to *activities*. These exposures are designed to teach patients that it is unlikely that committing some act will result in harm occurring to themselves or others. For instance, activity exposures for social anxiety might include starting conversations, giving presentations, or making a mistake (e.g., dropping coins) in public. Patients with more general worries about the need to be perfect might purposely make mistakes on a homework assignment, when telling a story, or when pushing the button to select a floor in the elevator. Exposure for OCD intrusive thoughts about hurting others might involve spreading contamination by hugging loved ones or walking through a doorway while thinking of harm coming to a friend.

The three categories of in vivo exposures (situations, objects, and activities) are not mutually exclusive and often have considerable overlap. For example, many object exposures involve some action, such as petting a dog, touching a contaminated doorknob, or messing up the order of papers. Similarly, an exposure to a single dog might best be conceptualized as an object, whereas a similar exposure to multiple dogs at once, such as in a dog park or a kennel, would more naturally be considered a situational exposure. Finally, an exposure to talking about personal information in a restaurant may only produce the desired anxiety because the correct activity and situation are present to elicit the necessary fear-provoking expectation. The value of these categories derives from drawing the therapist's attention to variables that must be properly manipulated to test the patient's fear-precipitating beliefs. Specifically, the therapist must consider what the patient will be doing, where, and with what. The relative importance of each variable will depend on the nature of the child's fears, which we discuss later.

Imaginal Exposure

The second type of exposure is imaginal, thought, worry, or narrative exposures. Imaginal exposures are used to address the second category of feared stimuli: "thoughts in our head." As discussed in Chapter 5, for some patients, a mental event sets off their anxiety or OCD cycle. In these cases, the most direct form of exposure is to the thought, image, or urge. Used in this manner, imaginal exposure is a powerful therapeutic tool that is unfortunately often underutilized by clinicians.

Exposure to mental activities can be accomplished in a number of ways. The most straightforward approach is to write down the thoughts and read them aloud repeatedly. Content of the exposure could be very brief, such as a single swear word to address scrupulosity OCD. Future-based worry thoughts may be longer but typically can be expressed in two or three sentences. Traumatic narratives may be longer still. Alternate approaches to thought exposures include repeating the thought aloud without writing it, writing and rewriting the thought, repeating the thought silently in one's head, having another person repeat the thought aloud, or audio recording the thought and playing it back repeatedly. Similarly, imaginal exposures can focus on images rather than words through having the child visualize the scene in her head or draw a picture. No approach is inherently better than another, and patients should typically try different methods to identify those most appropriate to their fears. For example, some patients fear that others will react negatively to their thoughts, and so saying them aloud is very difficult and challenging. For others, repeating a thought out loud quickly becomes tiresome and is an efficient way to lower their anxiety. However, this approach may not engage their fear as fully as quietly immersing themselves in images of the situation. On the other hand, when a child is quietly thinking a thought, it is difficult for the therapist (or parent) to know what he is doing. Therefore, alternating between silent and aloud repetition may be preferable.

Imaginal exposures are used for presenting concerns in which the mental event itself is the fear-provoking stimulus. Examples and corresponding diagnoses are presented in Table 6.2. This includes patients with OCD who are bothered by intrusive thoughts of causing harm, doing something inappropriate, or doing something of a blasphemous nature. The goals of these exposures are for the child to learn that repeating a thought will not make it come true. For example, a child might repeat "I am going to hurt my mother" until she learns that thoughts do not control actions and her anxiety decreases. Similarly, distressing memories, including of trauma, are addressed through narrative exposure in which the patient recounts the events. Through this process, the child learns that painful memories are manageable and that remembering the incident does not equate to reliving it. Finally, thought exposures can be used to address worries about future events, whether realistic or improbable (e.g., someone who worries about tests can repeat "I will fail and never get into college" until his anxiety decreases). Likewise, a child who fears that monsters will take her away from her parents could repeat "Monsters will get me." The goals of such exposures are for the child to learn that thoughts of bad, even horrible, events are unpleasant but in and of themselves cannot hurt him and that he can handle these thoughts independently.

Imaginal exposures can also be used to prepare for another form of exposure, such as in vivo. Theoretically, if a patient is not yet willing to engage in an in vivo exposure or the in vivo exposure cannot feasibly be implemented, the therapist might begin with imaginal exposure to the activity. For example, if a child with OCD is not yet willing to touch a contaminated doorknob, the therapist

Table 6.2 EXAMPLES OF IMAGINAL AND INTEROCEPTIVE EXPOSURES AND ASSOCIATED
DIAGNOSES

Exposure Item	Diagnosis
IMAGINAL: PRIMARY	
Intrusive thoughts	OCD
Distressing memories	PTSD
Future worries	GAD
Thoughts of being kidnapped	Separation anxiety disorder
Thoughts of choking and dying	Specific phobia
IMAGINAL: PREPARATORY	
Imagining a conversation	Social anxiety disorder
Picturing contamination	OCD
INTEROCEPTIVE	
Racing heart	Panic disorder
Shortness of breath	Panic disorder

GAD, generalized anxiety disorder; OCD, obsessive–compulsive disorder; PTSD, post-traumatic stress disorder.

might have her imagine touching the doorknob and spreading the germs over herself. Alternatively, because there are no stores accessible during an appointment, a therapist might have a patient do an imaginal exposure to receiving a rude response from a store clerk. However, clinicians should be careful not to use imaginal exposure as a less stressful, easier-to-implement replacement for in vivo exposures. If in vivo exposures are indicated, but the child is reluctant to begin them, the therapist should make every effort to design easier real-life activities before resorting to imaginal exposures. For example, role playing, use of assistants or confederates, and leaving the office are more active alternatives that approximate challenging in vivo exposures, rather than imaginal exposure. *In our experience, preparatory imaginal exposures are rarely needed, and their use should be kept to a minimum.*

Determining whether a certain thought exposure is appropriate can be challenging. Therapists (and parents) often feel uncomfortable having a child repeat thoughts that are graphic and/or either socially or developmentally inappropriate. Typically, if the frequency with which the child is having a thought is distressing, then it is appropriate for exposure regardless of the content. As such, even when the content of the thought is objectionable and not something children would typically be thinking about (e.g., curse words, explicit sexual thoughts, and violent thoughts), if the child is already having the thought, it needs to be addressed. On the other hand, therapists should use restraint when suggesting thoughts for exposures that are designed to be extra challenging, such as more graphic or violent acts for a child with intrusive thoughts of causing harm. It is unnecessary, and not advisable, to introduce new content that is developmentally inappropriate.

Interoceptive Exposures

The third category of exposures, interoceptive, addresses the "feelings in our body" stimuli introduced in Chapter 5. During these exposures, the therapist guides the patient through an exercise, such as hyperventilating, that induces the feared physical sensations. Interoceptive exposures were developed for, and are most commonly used with, panic disorder (see Table 6.2). The goal is for the patient to learn that although panic attacks are uncomfortable, they are not inherently dangerous, because he is unlikely to pass out, collapse, lose control, break down, or die. This goal is accomplished by having the patient experience physical symptoms as similar as possible to those he experiences during a panic attack. Because symptoms of anxiety and panic differ across individuals, the therapist begins by progressing through a series of exercises that induce various panic symptoms, such as shortness of breath, racing heart, dizziness, and shakiness. Such exposure exercises often include hyperventilation, breathing through a cocktail straw, or running up and down stairs. After the therapist identifies exercises that mimic the patient's panic attacks, exposures consist of repeating those exercises until the patient is convinced that nothing bad will happen from prolonged panic and that he can manage the discomfort. As the role of anxiety sensitivity in anxiety disorders beyond panic has been increasingly understood, interoceptive exposures have been applied more broadly.

In our experience, hyperventilation is a good interoceptive exposure to begin with for many youth. Hyperventilation involves steadily breathing overly deeply without pauses between breathes. The pace should be somewhat quicker than normal but not fast. Although harmless, hyperventilation induces a variety of symptoms commonly experienced in panic or anxiety attacks, including dizziness, tingling, lightheadedness, warmth, and rapid heartbeat. It is helpful for the therapist to first describe how to hyperventilate and then demonstrate hyperventilating for 5–10 seconds. Next, the therapist asks the child to hyperventilate with the therapist for 5–10 seconds. The therapist then pauses and inquires how the child is feeling. At this point, the therapist is interested primarily in a verbal description of how the child feels as well as a rating of how similar those feelings are to the child's panic symptoms. As with other exposures, the therapist is also interested in how anxious the child is about the physical sensation she is experiencing. After only a few seconds of hyperventilation, many children will have only a minimal response that may not feel like the panic they experience nor induce anxiety. However, some children are very sensitive to their physiological reactions, and it is advisable to begin with a short duration. Next, the therapist has the child hyperventilate for increasing amounts of time, progressing as quickly as the child will tolerate, up to 1 minute. After each trial, the therapist receives feedback from the child about physical symptoms, ratings of similarity to panic attacks, and ratings of anxiety level. If hyperventilation induces symptoms similar to the child's panic attack and causes the child to feel anxious, the therapist continues with the exposure by having the child hyperventilate for 1 minute, pause to rate her anxiety, hyperventilate for another minute, pause to rate her anxiety, and repeat. This process continues until the child learns that panic attacks are not dangerous and her fear that something bad will happen has decreased.

If hyperventilating for 1 minute fails to induce symptoms similar to a panic attack or anxiety, then the therapist moves on to another exercise. We frequently turn next to breathing through a cocktail straw as another option that is likely to induce panic and anxiety. Following the same steps as outlined for hyperventilation, the therapist instructs the child to breathe through a small cocktail straw while holding his nose. The therapist should monitor to ensure that the child is not breathing around (as opposed to through) the straw or through his nose. Using a very narrow straw can successfully induce the sensation that one is not getting enough air, although in reality one is receiving sufficient air and one can breathe through the straw for a considerable time. Other interoceptive exercises include spinning in a chair to feel dizzy, running up and down stairs to feel a rapid heartbeat, wearing multiple layers and jackets to feel hot, and squeezing muscles until feeling shaky. Sometimes, the therapist may find it helpful to allow the child to rate how uncomfortable she feels in addition to how anxious she feels. This can help children differentiate between discomfort, which is unlikely to decrease during the exposure, and anxiety, which is expected to decrease.

Combining Exposures

For the best results, it is often helpful to combine different forms of exposure. As discussed previously, anxiety disorders are highly comorbid, so it is likely that patients in treatment for social anxiety, for example, may also have other generalized worries that require a different approach to exposure. Moreover, fear stimuli in a given circumstance are often multifaceted and include both internal and external stimuli. For example, a child's anxiety may be activated by the combination of being by herself and having the thought that her parents will never return. As such, her treatment plan likely needs to include thought exposures to "My parents will never return," in vivo exposures to sitting in a room by herself, and then exposures that combine both exercises together—that is, repeating "My parents will never return" while sitting alone in a dark room. Imaginal exposures can frequently be used to augment or heighten the effect of in vivo or interoceptive exposures, also referred to as secondary imaginal exposures. For example, while touching a contaminated door handle, a child could repeat, "These germs will make me sick." Similarly, an adolescent could silently repeat "I am choking" while breathing through a cocktail straw. In all three examples, adding the imaginal exposure more thoroughly addresses the internal and external stimuli that cause anxiety. The child then has the opportunity to learn that he or she can handle this situation and the associated worry thoughts.

Adding interoceptive exercises to imaginal and in vivo exposures can help address the fear of fear that is often associated with anxiety disorders. This can be particularly important when children fear that an object, activity, or thought will lead to uncontrollable anxiety. For example, to address a child's fear of vomiting, the therapist might have her watch videos of someone vomiting and have her hyperventilate to create the physical anxiety response that she fears will lead to vomiting. Alternatively, a therapist might have a child hyperventilate before beginning a conversation to learn that he can function socially despite high levels of anxiety. Occasionally, a therapist may combine all three forms of exposures. For example, to address test anxiety, a child might complete an exposure to taking a test while hyperventilating and repeating "I am going to fail." In each case, the goal of the exposure is for the child to learn that not only are their feared situations and thoughts not as dangerous as they believed but also that the high levels of anxiety that accompany these situations are manageable.

IMPLEMENTATION

In Chapter 5, we introduced the basic structure for planning, doing, and ending exposures. We then opened this chapter with a description of the different types of exposure. Now, we discuss general concepts for implementing exposure. This section covers designing the appropriate exposure, titrating the level of difficulty, and monitoring the child's response.

Designing an Exposure

Designing an appropriate exposure requires an understanding of the child's symptoms. This process began with the creation of the child's anxiety (or OCD) cycle using the cognitive–behavioral model to understand his or her experience. The anxiety cycle includes the items that set off the child's anxiety, the expectations he has that lead reasonably safe situations to be viewed as dangerous, how the child avoids the situations, and general ideas for exposure. Each of these items is important for designing an effective exposure plan. Specifically, the exposure needs to include confronting the stimulus that sets off the cycle in a manner that challenges the child's fear-provoking expectations while refraining from the avoidance actions. As such, the therapist must understand each of these components whenever planning an exposure.

As introduced previously, the type of exposure needs to match the category of stimuli that sets off the cycle. For example, if the child is nervous in social situations, the exposure will need to be in vivo. Tangible locations, objects, and activities are typically the most straightforward to identify. A key point here is for the clinician to identify internal stimuli, thoughts and feelings, that also need to be directly targeted through exposure. Once the method has been matched to the stimuli, the therapist needs to design the exposure to test the patient's fear-provoking expectations. The exposure must be designed so that when completed, the patient learns through her experience that even though she did activity X, focused on thought Y, or experienced feeling Z, nothing bad happened that she could not handle. For this to be effective, the therapist needs to be aware of any avoidance behaviors that would prevent the child's safety learning.

Titration

Although it is not necessary to progress orderly from the easiest to the most difficult exposure, as noted previously, successful treatment requires the ability to titrate the degree of difficulty within exposures to a given stimulus. First, children typically will not engage in treatment unless the therapist can design an exposure that seems manageable from the beginning. Moreover, for the best results at the end of treatment, the therapist needs to be able to design exposures that ratchet up anxiety levels to exceed those of daily life. In between, the therapist needs the flexibility to continuously present the child with increasingly challenging exposures without overshooting what the child is ready to consider.

The first titration variable that can be adjusted is the content of exposure. For many presentations, the fear ladder will have multiple examples of the feared items that can be ordered in terms of difficulty. For example, dog exposures might include small, medium, and large dogs as well as lethargic, active, and excitable dogs. Contamination exposures might progress from an office chair to an elevator button to a public restroom faucet. Imaginal exposures might begin with repeating thoughts of a parent getting sick and end with thoughts of a parent dying. The level of the child's independence can also be manipulated with most exposures. In vivo, imaginal, and interoceptive exposures can all begin in the office with the parent and therapist present and then occur outside the office with just the parent, alone with the therapist/parent nearby, by oneself, and then by oneself in the real anxiety-provoking situation. For in vivo exposures to objects, proximity can be adjusted by beginning at a distance, gradually approaching, and ending with direct contact. For in vivo activity exposures, aspects of the act as well as the setting can be varied. Social exposures can be made more difficult by increasing the length of interaction or the degree of embarrassing mistakes. In addition, the number of people (small vs. large audience; individual vs. group conversation) or other characteristics (known vs. unknown; friendly vs. stern) can be titrated. In some circumstances, the therapist may consider titrating the duration of the exposure. For instance, a patient could begin by repeatedly hyperventilating for 15 seconds with a brief pause to rate anxiety during one exposure, and then repeat 30-second episodes and then longer still. It is also possible to titrate the duration of in vivo exposures, such as separation from parents. However, predetermined end times can lead children to fend off anxiety until time has expired rather than accepting the separation as manageable. As such, it is preferable to alter other variables, such as distance separated from parents, to encourage cooperation. If time increments are unavoidable, it can be helpful to use nonspecific durations—that is, staying home while parents run a short errand—and progress to other titration strategies as soon as possible. A final option for titration is the combination of multiple stimuli within a single method (i.e., contamination from two sources) or from combining multiple methodologies (i.e., taking a test after hyperventilating and imaging failure).

Monitoring Response

During exposures, therapists need to monitor the child's response, emphasize new learning, and discourage use of safety behaviors. Although the rationale behind these actions is consistent across methods of exposures, the manner in which they are implemented varies. As introduced in Chapter 5, during exposures the therapist helps draw the child's attention to new safety learning by periodically asking for her anxiety ratings and thoughts about why the anxiety is decreasing. Ideally, the therapist requests ratings frequently enough so as not to miss meaningful changes in anxiety without being overly intrusive or disruptive. For continuous exposure, such as sitting with a contaminated item in one's lap or repeating an intrusive thought, the check-ins can be on a time schedule—for example, every 2 minutes. For episodic exposures, including hyperventilating for 1 minute or asking questions in public places, the therapist should inquire about anxiety after each round. However, after the patient completes one activity in a series during an episodic exposure, it is important for the therapist to ensure that the post rating represents the child's anxiety about the *upcoming repetition* of the exposure and not their current relief at being done with the last one. For instance, after a child asks a store clerk a question, the therapist could inquire "How nervous are you to do it again?" By doing so, the therapist can gauge if the child's anxiety about speaking in public is decreasing with practice rather than observing that anxiety is relieved after the interaction has been completed.

Therapists also need to monitor for the presence of avoidance, rituals, or safety behaviors. Any efforts by the child to avoid the feared stimuli, prevent a feared outcome, or reduce anxiety will likely interfere with the new safety learning value of the exposure. Specifically, the child is likely to attribute the lack of feared outcome to the use of the safety behavior rather than to the benign nature of the target stimuli. As a straightforward example, if a child washes his hands during an exposure to contaminated door handles, he is likely to attribute the fact that he did not get sick to the protective properties of handwashing rather than the lack of initial threat from the doorknob. Handwashing and other physical rituals are relatively straightforward to identify, although they can sometimes be subtle, such as quickly "wiping off" germs or lightly tapping the left hand to even out the exposure activity of tapping with the right hand. Mental rituals to "undo" an exposure, such as picturing a healthy person to counteract thoughts of getting a disease, are more difficult to recognize and require cooperation from the child to identify when they occur. Although complete avoidance will prevent an exposure from beginning, children at times engage in partial avoidance during an exposure. For example, a child might avoid making eye contact during a social anxiety exposure, stay close to the wall during an exposure to crowds, leave out frightening details of a thought exposure, or write only one minor spelling error during an exposure to making mistakes on an assignment. Partial avoidance is typically not as detrimental as rituals because it tends to lessen, rather than negate, the perceived threat. As such, partial avoidance can at times be gradually phased out as a form of titration rather than immediately banned. Finally, the therapist should be watchful for other safety behaviors by the child, such as clinging to a railing during an exposure to heights, quickly saying "see you soon" to parents before a separation exposure, drinking from a water bottle during a hyperventilation exposure, or informing the audience that the speech includes practicing making mistakes. Each of these behaviors is intended to provide relief from the fear that something bad will happen and diminishes the opportunity for the child to learn that he or she can handle the situation independently.

EXPOSURE PLANS

In the second half of this chapter, we present exposure plans for common presentations of childhood anxiety and OCD. For each presenting problem, we outline how in vivo, imaginal, and interoceptive exposures or their combination can be applied using the implementation concepts discussed previously.

Social Anxiety

PRECIPITATING STIMULI

Social anxiety is primarily set off by external situations, namely those that require interaction with others. Some children with social anxiety have difficulty in multiple social situations; for others, their fears are limited to certain settings and they may be able to manage other situations with little or no difficulty. For instance, a given child may have different levels of anxiety in performance situations, peer social interactions, and adult-based public interactions. Performance situations involve engaging in at least semistructured activities in front of an audience and include speaking in class, presentations, athletic practice and games, dance or music rehearsals and performances, or interviewing for a job. Peer social interactions are generally unstructured times that involve informal interactions, such as joining or starting conversations, initiating a social plan, greeting classmates in the hallway, having conversations over lunch, and handling disagreements. Finally, public interactions involve functioning in public settings, often with adults, and include ordering food at a restaurant, talking to sales clerks, meeting a parent's friend, asking for directions, or being observed walking or eating. Social anxiety can also be set off by mental stimuli, particularly worries after social interactions during which the child perceived she did something wrong.

ANXIETY-PROVOKING EXPECTATIONS

Routine social interactions are typically transformed into anxious ordeals by the child's expectations that she will be judged negatively. Often, children fear that they will do something wrong, say something silly, make a mistake, or appear overly anxious, which will lead others to judge them. Fears about being perceived as dumb or incompetent often underlie anxiety about performance-related situations. Anxiety in peer interactions is often associated with fears of doing something embarrassing and being deemed unlikeable or unworthy of friendship. Concern about being a burden to others or eliciting anger or annoyance often provokes anxiety about interacting in public settings. Of course, there is significant overlap between categories, and anxiety in each type of situation can result from any of the previously mentioned expectations. Moreover, some children, particularly younger ones, do not have or cannot articulate the feared consequence other than "I am scared to talk to people."

AVOIDANCE

Children most commonly respond to social anxiety with complete or partial avoidance. For instance, socially anxious children often will not join activities, rely on others to initiate social plans, decline invitations, or refuse to give presentations. Partial avoidance may occur in situations that are difficult to get out of and may include providing short answers when called upon, not making eye contact, only talking to familiar peers, or asking the teacher questions after class when other students have left. Parental accommodation occurs frequently with social anxiety when parents (and sometimes peers and siblings) order food for the child, email questions to teachers, or answer for the child in conversations.

EXPOSURES

There is a handful of considerations for the therapist to keep in mind when working with families to design exposure plans for social anxiety. The first is the importance of in vivo exposures. Because social anxiety is precipitated by external stimuli, the exposure exercises must almost exclusively include interacting with others. This can often present a challenge for in-session exposures and typically necessitates leaving the office. Exposures to speaking in public situations are often the easiest to plan, especially if the therapist has access to other therapists, support staff, local stores, restaurants, other businesses, or at least a phone to place calls. These exposures are also fairly straightforward for families to execute between sessions with trips to a local mall or dinner out. Peer interactions are considerably more challenging. If possible, treating children with social anxiety in a group setting or arranging social groups provides an excellent opportunity to conduct peer-based exposures. Groups, or office colleagues, can also provide audiences for presentation exposures. Peer-based exposures can also be more difficult for parents to actively coach, especially parents of adolescents. However, parents can encourage and monitor exposures to initiate social get-togethers and participating in group activities.

Second, because social anxiety often involves an overestimation of the likelihood of making mistakes and the severity of such mistakes, exposures need to address both fears. Exposures involving asking routine questions or giving a competent presentation help children learn that they are less likely to make mistakes than they expected. However, because fears of making mistakes often come true in the course of daily interactions, it is perhaps even more important for children to learn that making mistakes and feeling embarrassed is tolerable. As such, exposure plans should include social mishap exposures such as stumbling over one's words, asking to see dresses in a men's clothing store, or pausing awkwardly during a presentation. Similarly, because socially anxious children often fear that physical symptoms of anxiety will overwhelm them or embarrass them, it can be helpful to combine interoceptive exposures with social interactions. Moreover, anxious thoughts following in vivo exposures about one's poor performance or other's negative reactions can be addressed through thought exposures.

When designing exposure plans, practical considerations frequently affect identifying exposures that are manageable enough to begin with. Role playing, either with the therapist or with the parent, is an option for beginning in a less-threatening manner. For presentations especially, anxious children are generally comfortable speaking in front of their parents. Walking in public places and making eye contact is another less threatening exposure that many children are willing to start with. From there, the therapist has at least three variables she can manipulate to titrate the intensity of the exposures: length, audience, and content. Early exposures are often short (asking a single question or briefly introducing oneself), and over time the therapist can make the exposures more challenging by asking the child to say more (e.g., three questions with responses or present a report). The degree of challenge presented by the audience can be increased in number (e.g., join an ongoing conversation between two people or read in front of three people and then a group) as well as other characteristics. It is often easier to ask questions to people who are working (i.e., desk staff), who appear friendly, or whom one is unlikely to see again. Thus, social exposures should include interacting with people whom the child believes are most likely to respond negatively. Finally, the degree of difficulty can be increased by changing the content of the interaction, such as by having more personal conversations, presenting on topics the child is less familiar with, expressing a differing opinion, or asking questions likely to elicit a "no" answer.

Many social anxiety exposures involve short activities (e.g., asking someone for the time) that are insufficient for safety learning if completed only once. Therefore, a single exposure should involve repeating that activity multiple times. For instance, an exposure to speaking with store clerks may involve approaching several clerks in the same store or entering multiple stores in order to interact with 5–10 employees. Similarly, exposures to public speaking may involve repeating a presentation two or three times (depending on the length) to the same audience. As mentioned previously, because the patient's goal is to learn that they can handle the social interaction, after each social interaction, the therapist should ask, for example, "How nervous are you to speak to the next person?" This helps the therapist identify when they can end the exposures because asking questions no longer elicits as much anxiety, as opposed to stopping when the child's anxiety is low because the perceived threat has passed.

A note of caution: The therapist should feel confident encouraging children to do challenging social exposures that involve social mishaps. However, the child should be prepared beforehand that she may receive rejection in response to her efforts to initiate social interactions or curt responses to unusual questions. Exposures are not designed to learn that social interactions always go smoothly but, rather, that the child can handle them when they do but also when they do not. However, unusual social behavior with one's peer group at school can have negative ramifications, and the therapist should avoid having the child perform behaviors with his peer group that could lead to social ostracism.

Separation Anxiety

PRECIPITATING STIMULI
Separation anxiety is set off by external stimuli with associated internal stimuli. Children with these symptoms feel anxious in situations in which they are alone or are in the act of separating from their parents. Presentations vary, with some children fearful whenever they are away from their parents, whereas others are fearful only when they are alone but feel comfortable when in the presence of other adults or even siblings. Children also differ in the degree of desired proximity, with some children becoming fearful when a parent is out of sight (but in the next room), whereas other children are content until it is time to leave the house. Internal stimuli that can contribute to separation anxiety include thoughts about upcoming separation and scary thoughts about monsters or being kidnapped during separation. When identifying the precipitating stimuli, the therapist should take care to determine if the child's anxiety is set off by being away from the parent (i.e., separation anxiety) or by the environment to which the child is going, which might indicate that the fear is related to social anxiety, for example, rather than separation.

ANXIETY-PROVOKING EXPECTATIONS
In general, children with separation anxiety fear that something bad will happen when they are away from their parents. Some children simply worry that their parents will not return, whereas others have more specific fears, such as their parents getting into a car accident. Alternatively, some children are more concerned that something bad will happen to them, such as someone breaking in and hurting them. Again, identifying the feared belief can help the therapist understand the nature of the child's concerns, such as differentiating anxiety before school due to separation (e.g., "My parents won't pick me up") from social anxiety (e.g., "Other kids will laugh at me"). However, because separation anxiety often occurs in young children, it is not uncommon for them to have difficulty articulating a specific fear. In such cases, therapists may have to infer feared beliefs

based on the situations in which the anxiety does or does not occur and parent recollections of what the child has said to them previously.

AVOIDANCE

Avoidance in children with separation anxiety typically involves efforts to delay or prevent parents from departing. At the time of separation, children may plead, cry, cling to a parent, or get angry. These behaviors may lead to parental accommodation in the form of limiting demands on the child to separate by not enrolling the child in activities, always bringing the child on errands, or not relying on babysitters. Safety behaviors while separate may include frequent phone calls or text messages to the parent. Avoidance within the home may take the form of only playing in a room if someone else is there, standing by the door when the parent is in the bathroom, or frequently checking in with a parent who is in another room. Bedtime can be a time of increased avoidance behaviors, such as children insisting that parents stay with them, coming out of their room, calling out repeatedly, and going to the parents' bedroom.

EXPOSURES

Exposure plans for separation anxiety generally include three components. First, in vivo exposures to being alone typically need to be included. These can begin with being in the office with the therapist while the parent stands in the hallway with the door open (if necessary). In vivo separation exposures can be titrated by removing people from the room (i.e., alone vs. with the therapist), the location of the parent (close by, farther away, and an unknown location), the location of the child (familiar office, new office, dark office, waiting room, and public places), or, if necessary, duration (short, medium, long, and undetermined). In vivo exposures can be practiced in the office setting, in public (e.g., use public restroom alone or walk into store alone), or at home (i.e., stay home alone while parents walk around the block). Exposures in real-world settings and activities (e.g., in the home, staying with babysitters) are often an essential component of treatment for separation anxiety. The vast majority of the time, exposures in the home will be led be parents without the help of therapists, which emphasizes the benefit of having parents gain experience as exposures coaches in the session. Monitoring anxiety should be approached thoughtfully so as to not interfere with the goal of having the child be alone. In vivo separation exposures are typically long, and anxiety can be measured continuously. Initially, having the therapist (or parent) enter the room periodically to obtain an anxiety rating is appropriate, and it also provides positive attention for the child being brave. As treatment progresses and the goal is an extended time without contact, the anxiety can be rated by the child or limited to a pre- and post-rating.

Thought exposures are the second component of a separation exposure plan. Because thoughts of parents not returning, getting kidnapped, robbers breaking in, and monsters under the bed provoke anxiety, these stimuli should be addressed directly. Thought exposures typically begin with repeating a mildly distressing thought in the office with the parent and the therapist. This introduces the family to the procedure and illustrates that it can be successful. The thought exposures can then be titrated by increasing the difficulty of the thoughts (e.g., "My parents won't come back" to "My parents died in a car accident") and the difficulty of the situation (e.g., in the session, at home with parents, and at night when the thoughts are most distressing). As these steps imply, thought exposures can be combined with in vivo exposures as the child progresses. Anxiety ratings should be monitored continuously during thought exposures, with parental assistance fading out, as mentioned previously.

The third component of a separation exposure plan addresses eliminating avoidance, or safety behaviors. Even after children have successfully completed planned exposures to separation (e.g., sitting in an office alone), they often continue to engage in behaviors to prevent separation in daily situations, such as crying, clinging, and complaining in the morning about being dropped off at school. These responses often need to be specifically addressed through a behavior modification plan with rewards for increasingly successful separation. For example, a child could earn 1 point for separating without clinging and another point for not asking his mother to stay. If the child refused to separate and requires intervention by school personnel, she might lose electronics privileges until she completes an extra exposure that afternoon.

Finally, therapists should keep in mind the child's developmental level. Separation anxiety is most common in younger children, which limits the activities that would be appropriately expected of them in public or the duration of time they would be left home alone (if at all). Therapists should use common sense, but at the same time they should resist being unduly discouraged by the child's (or parents' or therapists') anxiety about what the child can handle. Similarly, thought exposures should follow the guidelines discussed previously. The content of a thought is appropriate for an exposure no matter how upsetting (e.g. "My parents will be killed") if the child is already having that thought often enough to be problematic. However, therapists should not *introduce* more extreme thoughts that are not developmentally appropriate.

Generalized Anxiety

PRECIPITATING STIMULI
The primary stimuli in children with generalized anxiety are "worry" thoughts and the variety of activities and situations that prompt these thoughts. Although children can worry about almost anything, common worries center around the health and safety of themselves or their family, school performance, the future, small mistakes, and getting in trouble. Situations that tend to elicit worry include unexpected events (e.g., parent being late), schoolwork or tests, having limited time between classes, and transitions. When identifying stimuli that precipitate worry, it is important to confirm that the worry thoughts are in fact excessive and unlikely to come true. If the child's worry is a developmentally appropriate reaction to a stressful situation, then exposure therapy is likely not the indicated

treatment. For example, worries about school performance because the child is far behind or doing poorly, anxiety about the well-being of an ill grandparent, or anxiety about the reaction of a volatile parent are accurate reactions to stressful situations. As such, these worries are not likely to be addressed through exposure, assuming they are not excessive or unrealistic.

ANXIETY-PROVOKING EXPECTATIONS

Because we have identified the precipitating stimuli as worry thoughts, we need to conceptualize the anxiety-provoking beliefs as expectations surrounding those worry thoughts. One set of expectations is overestimation of the likelihood of those worries coming true and how problematic it would be if they did come true, such as believing one is likely to fail a test or that it would be horrible to get a B in a class. An alternative expectation involves the belief that one cannot handle worry thoughts independently. For example, a child may believe that she cannot handle the uncertainty that her father has gotten into an accident unless she calls him or her mother reassures her that he is okay.

AVOIDANCE

Children with general worry can engage in a variety of activities to reduce anxiety. As previously suggested, frequently children will seek reassurance from parents by asking if something bad is likely to happen or if something or someone will be okay. If parents begin to resist answering questions, children may seek passive reassurance by informing their parents about their concerns and interpreting a lack of response as a safety signal. Similarly, children may seek reassurance by checking to make sure things are okay, such as by calling one's father, as described previously. Children also can overprepare in an effort to reduce the likelihood of a feared event or consequence. For example, a child with good grades may spend an excessive amount of time on schoolwork in an attempt to eliminate any chance of failure.

EXPOSURES

Exposures for generalized anxiety frequently involve direct imaginal exposures to anxiety-provoking thoughts combined with in vivo exposure to situations that elicit those thoughts. For example, an exposure plan might begin with the child repeating distressing thoughts in the session, starting with easier thoughts, such as "I will fail my next test," and progressing to more upsetting thoughts, such as "I will never get a job because I didn't work hard enough in school." Next, the therapist could help the child do in vivo exposures that bring on worry thoughts, such as completing an assignment quickly or writing notes with errors. Increasing the difficulty of exposures can consist of combining imaginal and in vivo exercises, having the family conduct planned exposures at home without the therapist's assistance, having the child conduct the exposures independently during real-life activities, and increasing the valence of the activity (e.g., making mistakes on notes vs. ungraded homework vs. a graded assignment). Response prevention is an important component of general anxiety exposures. This might include having the child refrain from checking in on a parent (e.g., calling one's father when he is late) or asking for reassurance ("Is this safe to eat?") and instead doing an impromptu imaginal exposure (e.g., repeat "Dad got in an accident"). Response prevention could also include time limits, such as restricting homework time to 60 minutes, and then completing imaginal exposure in response to anxiety about not finishing homework.

Contamination

PRECIPITATING STIMULI
Contamination fears are typically precipitated by contact with objects or situations perceived to be contaminated and/or by the prospect of spreading contamination to items or places perceived to be clean. Contamination often originates from other people, such as surfaces in public (e.g., doorknobs), or from people with certain characteristics, such as having been sick, disabilities, or personality characteristics. Contamination can also stem from substances such as chemicals, food, or medical equipment. Sometimes contamination can stem from situations, ideas, or memories that are distressing. Anxiety may also be precipitated by clean stimuli that "need" to be protected, such as loved ones, the home, one's bedroom or bed, and food/eating utensils.

ANXIETY-PROVOKING EXPECTATIONS
The prototypical expectation is that contact with contamination will cause illness, either mild or severe, or even death. However, children may describe contact with contamination as more disgusting or uncomfortable than frightening, in which case the expectation would be that the disgust will be intolerable and the contamination must be removed to feel better. Children may also be concerned that spreading contamination will hurt others, make them a bad person, or make their environment so contaminated that they cannot handle it. Less frequently, children may be concerned that contamination will change who they are or their personality to include the undesirable characteristics of the person from whom the contamination originated.

AVOIDANCE
Children may exhibit physical attempts to avoid contact, such as not going to certain places, using sleeves or paper towels to open doors, or waiting for others to push an elevator button. When contact is unavoidable, children tend to enlist cleaning rituals, such as handwashing, using hand sanitizer, showering, changing clothes, or cleaning items. Other efforts to "remove" contamination include wiping, blowing, or licking it off. Washing rituals may be excessive in terms of frequency, length, or vigorousness (i.e., "surgical scrub"). Some children may ask for reassurance that something is not contaminated or ask parents to wash or confirm that they themselves washed.

Exposures

Typically, exposures must include contact with, and spreading, contamination. Contact exposures must be thorough, with the child touching the item and then ideally rubbing the contamination on her hands, arms, clothes, hair, face, and tongue, as well as contaminating a piece of food and eating it. Spreading the contamination should be thorough as well, such as hugging a parent, touching a contaminated item to multiple surfaces in the home, rubbing the item all over one's bed and pillow, or touching the utensils that family members will use to eat. The difficulty level of exposures can, if necessary, begin with less thorough contact (e.g., touching with one hand) and then progress to more complete contact as described previously. However, it is preferable to begin with a manageable level of contamination (perhaps the child's own shirt or a parent's phone) with which the child can do a thorough exposure from the outset. Titration can then proceed by contacting items that are perceived as increasingly more contaminated and spreading those "germs" to areas that the child believes are increasingly more necessary to keep clean. Thought exposures, such as "The floor germs are all over me" or "The germs will make me sick," can be added to in vivo exposures to increase the level of difficulty, as well as keep the child focused on the exposures, or help resist mental rituals.

Response prevention (i.e., no washing) is essential to successful contamination exposure. Therapists should be alert for overt washing as well as covert wiping or mental cleansing rituals. In addition, patients should be introduced early to the concept of recontamination. Specifically, when they wash, whether ritualistically or part of normal routine, they should recontaminate with the items that led to washing or another source of contamination. Therapists should refrain from using time until ritualizing occurs as a titration schedule (i.e., wait 15 minutes after the exposure until washing) because it can diminish the effectiveness of the exposure. Specifically, knowing that one will eventually wash typically decreases (and sometimes eliminates) the fear of an adverse consequence occurring, thus preventing the child from learning that the contamination is not dangerous.

Not-Just-Right Experiences

Precipitating Stimuli

Not-just-right experiences (NJREs) occur when a child completes a routine action and has the sense that it is incomplete or incorrect. These actions could include reading, writing, walking through doorways, putting down a cup, tapping a desk, chewing food, or asking a question. These actions may seem incorrect (e.g., the letter "e" is not properly formed or doing something an odd number of times) or incomplete (e.g., chewing with the right side, but not the left side, is perceived as leaving one uneven). Sometimes, when the child does the action, it is accompanied by a vague sense of not being right without a clear definition of what would make it right. Other times, participation in the action is initially connected to a negative thought, such as having the thought "I am going to have a bad day" while one is walking through a doorway.

ANXIETY-PROVOKING EXPECTATIONS

Often, the expectation that causes distress during NJREs is the belief that the uncomfortable feeling will not subside unless the situation is fixed or completed. Less frequently, children have a specific belief that something bad will happen if they do not fix or complete the activity. Finally, children may have the sense that something bad will happen if the action is not corrected, without being able to identify what that bad event would be.

AVOIDANCE

Avoidance most commonly takes the form of rituals to address the NJREs. For example, children may attempt to correct actions by rereading, erasing and rewriting, or asking parents to repeat an answer until it is stated "correctly." Alternatively, children may strive for a sense of completion by chewing evenly with both sides of the mouth, tapping the desk with the other hand, or picking up and putting down a cup until it "feels right." The burden of rituals can lead to avoidance, such as not showering because it takes so long to get it right or using a computer to take notes because writing "just right" is too difficult. Parents can also become involved in avoidance as part of the ritual, as in the question-and-answer example mentioned previously, or doing things for their children, such as transcribing homework for them. Rituals may also include repeating the action with a positive thought—for example, thinking "I will have a great day" while walking through a doorway.

EXPOSURES

Exposures begin with doing the activity "wrong" to elicit the NJRE—for example, writing sloppily, reading quickly, chewing only on the right, and putting something down once. Next, the child remains in the situation and focuses their attention on the fact that it feels wrong. This can be intensified by having the child repeat "This is wrong" or the specific feared thought. For example, the child may stare at the poorly formed letter "e" on the page and repeat "This 'e' is sloppy," "I will get a bad grade," or "This will ruin my day." The degree of challenge can be titrated by: the type of activity, because children often have NJREs around multiple activities (writing incorrectly vs. tapping the wrong number of times); increasing the degree that it is "wrong" (e.g., reading quickly vs. skimming over the content vs. purposely mispronouncing words); or the valence of the content of the repeated thought (e.g., "I will have a bad day" vs. "Someone will die because I did not fix this").

Bodily Sensations

PRECIPITATING STIMULI

Some children present with a fear of physical symptoms. This can be in the context of panic attacks in which the anxiety is focused on having sudden uncontrollable bouts of intense fear, or it can involve concerns that an upset stomach will lead to vomiting or that feeling anxiety in response to separation or taking a test is unmanageable. In these situations, it is the physical symptom itself that precipitates anxiety. It is important to note that the fear of physical symptoms can and frequently does occur in combination with the other presentations discussed in this chapter.

ANXIETY-PROVOKING EXPECTATIONS

As mentioned previously, some children fear specific negative outcomes, such as nausea leading to vomiting or shortness of breath leading to dying. However, frequently children's reactions to physical symptoms involve a less specific belief that the symptoms are intolerable, unpleasant, and unmanageable. Some fear the symptoms will spiral out of control and perhaps be embarrassing (e.g., uncontrollable crying in front of peers).

AVOIDANCE

Children may respond to their fears of physical anxiety by avoiding situations that evoke those symptoms, such as not eating before leaving the house or procrastinating with regard to schoolwork or tests. Children may also avoid situations in which it would be difficult or embarrassing to experience the symptoms, such as not going to school or refusing to leave the house without a parent.

EXPOSURES

An exposure plan must provide the child opportunities to learn that physical symptoms of anxiety and panic may be uncomfortable, but they are not dangerous. The therapist should begin by having the child complete a variety of interoceptive exercises until they can successfully induce sensations similar to those feared by the child. Once the appropriate interoceptive exercises are identified, the therapist then leads the child through repeating those exercises, as described previously, until the child believes they are unlikely to lead to the feared outcome (e.g., vomiting, passing out, or losing control). The therapist then titrates the difficulty of the exposure by having the patient complete the interoceptive exercises in more challenging situations, such as while standing up, watching videos of someone vomiting, walking in public, before giving a presentation, or while taking a test. The therapist can also add imaginal exposures, such as repeating "I will throw up" or "I can't breathe," to increase the difficulty and simulate the child's mental experience.

Specific Fears

PRECIPITATING STIMULI

Specific fears may be precipitated by objects, situations, places, or activities. For example, children may fear bugs or animals, small spaces such as elevators, heights, costumed characters, the dark, being in the basement alone, choking, storms, or needles. Some feared stimuli may be encountered frequently (e.g., bugs, dogs, and eating), whereas others may never or rarely be encountered (e.g., sharks and snakes). For items that are unlikely to be encountered or would evoke anxiety in most people (e.g., bears, sharks, and choking), the precipitating stimuli are situations in which the item might be encountered (i.e., walking in the woods, swimming, and eating). Similarly, some specific fears are set off by thoughts experienced in situations, such as images of monsters when alone in the basement.

ANXIETY-PROVOKING EXPECTATIONS

The beliefs that most commonly evoke fear in response to specific objects, situations, or activities involve immediate harm to oneself. For example, children fear that animals or bugs will bite them, elevators will get stuck or fall, storms will destroy their home, or shots will hurt. For some children, the beliefs are catastrophic. For example, a child might fear that a dog will bite him and he will die or that not only will a storm destroy his home but also his parents might be killed. However, some children react to items, such as bugs and snakes, with disgust and fear that the distress will be overwhelming, rather than fear of harm per se.

AVOIDANCE

Children respond to specific fears most commonly with direct physical avoidance. This may include quickly leaving the presence of a feared item, resisting approaching a feared item, or resisting entering a situation in which there *might* be a feared item. When complete avoidance is impossible, children may rely on other safety behaviors, such as demanding a parent's presence, hiding behind a parent, overchewing food or only eating soft foods to avoid choking, frequently checking the weather, asking for reassurance, or having a parent check the closet for monsters.

EXPOSURES

When children fear an item that is reasonably safe, the treatment plan should include direct in vivo exposure to that item. This may include holding bugs, petting dogs, riding elevators, or holding needles and receiving a shot. When children fear an object or situation that is objectively dangerous, such as sharks or choking, the treatment plan likely will include in vivo exposures to reasonably safe situations in which the children inaccurately believe the feared stimuli will be encountered. For example, a child may swim in the ocean, walk in the forest, eat lumpy food quickly, or eat food just before running errands. In vivo exposures can also be supplemented with imaginal exposures, especially when anxiety is precipitated by a thought that is unrealistic (e.g., monsters in the closet) or unlikely (e.g., robbers breaking in and being kidnapping). The most straightforward approach to titration involves having the child gradually increase physical proximity to the feared object or situation. The difficulty level of exposures can also be increased through fading out safety behaviors (e.g., alone vs. with parent and chewing 5 times vs. 30 times) or the characteristics of the stimuli (e.g., big vs. small dogs and old vs. new elevator). Initial exposures can be virtual, such as watching storm videos, in order to find a tolerable starting point or if the real-life exposures (e.g., storms) are difficult to plan.

Distressing Memories

PRECIPITATING STIMULI

Anxiety surrounding past experiences, including trauma, is elicited by a mental event (memories or flashbacks) or external reminders (questions, statements, objects, pictures, locations, or anniversaries). Distressing events may include serious accidents, illnesses, assaults, or natural disasters. However, upsetting memories can also persist after less injurious experiences, such as bullying, arguments with parents, and medical appointments. In cases in which a child has experienced a traumatic event, it is perhaps even more important than with other anxiety presentations to ensure that the child's symptoms are not a normative response to ongoing stress. For example, if children are currently experiencing continued trauma or significant stressors, or they are in the midst of rebuilding their relationship with a parent involved in neglect, exposure therapy is likely not appropriate or must be integrated into a more comprehensive, post-traumatic stress disorder-specific treatment plan.

ANXIETY-PROVOKING EXPECTATIONS

Distressing memories can become problematic when children interpret them as overwhelming and unmanageable. Children may believe that fear or pain associated with the memories will only decrease if the memories and reminders are avoided. Some children may also view people, places, and objects that remind them of the event as threatening. Again, it is essential for the therapist to determine that the child's expectations are unrealistic exaggerations of threat and not an understandable temporary response to recent trauma or an accurate assessment of ongoing mistreatment.

AVOIDANCE

Avoidance of mental events may include efforts to push memories away, distract oneself (mentally or with activities), or engage in self-harm. Physical attempts to avoid often include refusal to discuss the event, enter safe situations similar to the event (e.g., riding in a car), be around safe people associated with the event, or come in contact with reminders of the event (e.g., not watching television or reading stories).

EXPOSURES

Exposure for distressing memories often begins with imaginal exposures to the memories of the event. These exposures can be titrated by beginning with a general account of the event and then adding more upsetting details over time. At times, it may be therapeutic to have the child share the event details with appropriate people in her life. Treatment plans also typically need to include in vivo exposure to items that the child has avoided. This could include general reminders (e.g., stories about car accidents), specific reminders (e.g., a picture of the car after an accident), objects (e.g., the car itself), locations (e.g., returning to the intersection where an accident occurred), or activities (e.g., riding in cars). The therapist should ensure that exposures are reasonably safe and do not involve placing the child in a situation of heightened risk.

SUMMARY

In this chapter, we introduced how to conduct the three forms of exposure: in vivo, imaginal, and interoceptive. We then reviewed how to use the components of the cognitive–behavioral model of anxiety and OCD (i.e., precipitating stimuli, expectations, avoidance, and exposure) to develop an exposure plan for common symptom presentations. Together with the information presented in Chapter 5 on preparing for exposures, the current chapter should prepare therapists to develop an exposure plan for the majority of patients. In the next section, we present case examples to further illustrate the implementation of exposure therapy.

REFERENCE

American Psychiatric Association. (2013). *Diagnostic and statistical manual of mental disorders* (5th ed.). Arlington, VA: American Psychiatric Publishing.

Case Illustrations

7

In Vivo Exposure Case Examples

In Section 3, we presented a framework for conducting exposure therapy with anxious youth and their parents. In the current section, we use case examples to more fully illustrate how to implement exposure therapy with a variety of presenting problems. This chapter begins with case examples detailing primarily in vivo exposure for social anxiety, specific phobias, and separation anxiety. In Chapter 8, we present case examples illustrating the implementation of imaginal and interoceptive exposure for obsessions and compulsions, general anxiety and worry, as well as panic. For each case, we begin with a brief description of the case and then conceptualize the case using the model presented in Chapter 5. We then describe family involvement, discuss the creation of a fear ladder, present a detailed exposure, and comment on the course of treatment. We selected each case to illustrate a broader point related to the implementation of exposure, which is discussed last. All case examples are based on actual patients, with alterations to protect confidentiality and enhance the educational value.

CASE EXAMPLES: IN VIVO EXPOSURE

Social Anxiety

DESCRIPTION

Jasmine was a 14-year-old Caucasian 10th grader who presented for evaluation and treatment with her parents for what the family termed "extreme shyness." Her parents described a long history of shyness without apparent difficulty until this past year, when anxiety began affecting her performance and enjoyment at school. Although typically a strong student who had loved school, her grades started to drop as she began missing school in 9th grade, accumulated 15 absences in the first 3 months of 10th grade, and refused to contact or speak with teachers to get missing assignments. She also missed extracurricular activities more frequently than usual, including dance and, to a lesser extent, her robotics meetings and competitions. At first, Jasmine shrugged her shoulders when asked what was difficult about attending school and extracurricular activities. Her parents noted

Exposure Therapy for Child and Adolescent Anxiety and OCD. Stephen P. H. Whiteside, Thomas H. Ollendick, and Bridget K. Biggs, Oxford University Press (2020). © Oxford University Press.
DOI: 10.1093/med/9780190862992.001.0001

that Jasmine frequently complained that others did not like her at school and that her teachers would not understand or were sometimes "mean" to her. Jasmine's parents had tried to reassure her, explaining that her mother felt the same way in high school and that if she would "open up," others could see how wonderful she was. Her parents wanted to know how best to help Jasmine, because reassurance and encouragement did not seem to help. They also wanted guidance on parenting Jasmine because they had oscillated during the past 6–12 months between reassuring, comforting, or communicating on Jasmine's behalf, on the one hand, and cajoling, yelling, and telling her to "get over it," on the other hand.

Jasmine started feeling more anxious about going to school when she began high school, where she had a larger class with new peers and had to interact with unfamiliar teachers. Compounding her anxiety, some of her teachers conveyed to Jasmine their frustration that she had missed so many class periods and did not seem interested in picking up missing assignments. Socially, toward the end of 9th grade, a friend of her best friend started monopolizing that best friend's time and influenced her and others to leave Jasmine out of activities. At this point in the assessment, Jasmine became more communicative and began adding to her parents' report and providing further background. She conveyed that during the summer, her relationship with her best friend normalized, the monopolizing peer moved away, and Jasmine was no longer experiencing peer victimization or exclusion in 10th grade. Nonetheless, she continued to worry that her best friend was upset with her, peers would judge her, and that she would say or do something that others would view as weird or unlikable. She would get particularly distressed in social interactions if her heart started beating harder, her body got warm, or her face started to flush. She worried that others would notice or that she would get overwhelmed and would not be able to interact gracefully.

Even when Jasmine had a good time with friends, worries that she had said something wrong or "stupid" with her friends frequently kept her up in the middle of the night, making school attendance even more difficult. Jasmine told the therapist that the most difficult aspect about going to school was having so many eyes on her and having to talk to so many people. In dance class, she felt the same way, especially because classes were recently combined such that she was in a class with many unfamiliar peers. She described worrying that these new kids would think she did not dance well enough for this higher level class. When asked about any feedback she had gotten about her dancing, Jasmine stated that the teacher said she danced beautifully but that the teacher "had to say that." She had not gotten any direct feedback from peers but acknowledged that she did not talk to anybody during class and focused on the upcoming moves so as not to mess up. Robotics was less stressful because her best friend was part of the team, as were several other friends she had known for many years. Her best friend was helpful with keeping conversations going.

Jasmine's parents expressed frustration not only about Jasmine's frequent absences but also about her unwillingness to ask teachers for help. Jasmine often told them that teachers were mean or not understanding; however, as they started advocating for her at school, including asking teachers for missing assignments, they found that most teachers were willing to help and were never dismissive or demeaning in their interactions. In fact, several teachers told Jasmine's parents that they viewed Jasmine as a student with a lot of potential and wanted her to participate more in class. Her written responses on schoolwork (when completed and turned in) were typically accurate and thoughtful, according to her teachers. Jasmine's parents expressed concern that her friendship circle was limited and she was overly dependent on her best friend. They could not remember the last time Jasmine initiated a get-together, even with her best friend. She would not even text peers other than her best friend. Jasmine had told them she was "fine" with her social life and did not want to make new friends, but her parents wondered if that was really the case.

Jasmine had met a few times with her school counselor in the spring of her 9th grade year. Jasmine thought the counselor was friendly and initially helpful to talk with about challenges in her friendships at that time. They discussed ideas for talking with her best friend about how she was feeling, and the counselor taught Jasmine ways to relax her body to deal with stress and difficulties sleeping. Jasmine stated that she never did talk with her best friend about wanting more time together because she was afraid her friend would get upset with her. She used diaphragmatic breathing some but found it did not work when she was really upset or worried. Once the school year ended, the sessions stopped and Jasmine did not seek out the counselor in the fall.

ASSESSMENT AND CONCEPTUALIZATION

Jasmine's family had thought of her difficulties as normal shyness and hoped she would feel better with time or with support to build her self-confidence. The therapist explained that her symptoms fit a diagnosis of social anxiety disorder, which differs from shyness in the level of distress and disruption to daily life. The distinction between shyness and social anxiety became clearer to the family as they reflected on how Jasmine's fear of scrutiny was leading her to avoid many social situations others would not avoid, to be distressed when avoidance was not possible, and to have difficulty engaging in the life activities that she wanted and needed to do. For treatment, the therapist explained that helping Jasmine see her self-worth would not be sufficient because her avoidance of social interactions limited opportunities for building a sense of social competence and confidence through direct experience. The therapist recommended exposure-based cognitive–behavioral therapy as the most appropriate treatment. She explained that Jasmine would need to put herself into social situations that make her nervous in order to learn that (1) negative evaluation and embarrassment are not as likely as she believes; (2) she can handle challenging social encounters, including social mishaps; and (3) she can handle feelings of anxiety, including the physical symptoms she experiences. The therapist normalized Jasmine's uncertainty about her current social skills, acknowledging that avoidance of social situations reduced opportunities for practice. She explained that exposure setup would include planning and practice for what she might say and do. As her skills and confidence improved, she would not need such preparation before social interactions. The therapist enlisted the parents to learn how to coach Jasmine through exposures, particularly so that they could facilitate exposures outside of session. She further recommended participation in a group format of exposure therapy so that Jasmine would have in-session exposure opportunities with peers. Jasmine was reluctant about the group format but agreed to start treatment, hopeful of feeling better eventually.

In the following session, the therapist introduced the anxiety cycle and worked with Jasmine and her parents to apply it to her anxiety. The primary precipitating stimuli they identified were activities at school and during extracurricular activities in which she could potentially be observed by and/or had to communicate with others. These activities included walking the school hallways, being in class, participating in classes at school and the dance studio, responding to and initiating conversations with peers and teachers, texting with peers, electronic communication with teachers, and initiating social activity planning with friends and acquaintances. The family noted that there were times when Jasmine's anxiety was also set off by thoughts in her head, namely worries that she had done something wrong or been negatively perceived by peers, that came on during otherwise calm periods such as nighttime. Finally, her anxiety was at times set off by feelings in her body, namely increased heart rate and feeling hot and flushed during social situations.

Next, Jasmine was able to identify expectations and beliefs that made her anxious in social situations. She believed that when she was in public places, people were watching her and thinking bad things about her. She worried that during social interactions she would mess up or say something wrong and lead others to judge her or not like her. She expected teachers to be mad at her if she requested makeup work or that she would be bothering or annoying them if she asked them questions about the course content or material. She worried that if she were to put herself more frequently into social situations or if negative thoughts about social interactions came up, she would become overwhelmed and not able to handle herself, leading to embarrassment. In addition, she worried that physiological symptoms of anxiety would lead others to judge her or prevent her from being able to function.

As they further applied the anxiety cycle to Jasmine's experience, Jasmine identified that avoidance included the obvious staying away from situations in which she would be around others and/or would have to communicate with peers and authority figures at school, dance, and unstructured social activities. She did not spontaneously identify partial avoidance; however, after the therapist described the concept, Jasmine identified a few ways in which she tried to reduce her anxiety when she could not avoid social situations. For example, while in school, she tended to keep her head down, did not volunteer to participate in class, and responded to direct questions with the minimal response to get through the encounter. She further identified that in dance class, she focused very hard on the moves so that she would not make an embarrassing mistake and avoided looking at her classmates, certain that they were judging her. Jasmine realized that relying on her best friend to be her social "agent" was another safety behavior. Her parents recognized that they were facilitating avoidance by communicating on Jasmine's behalf and helping her collect missing assignments.

Finally, the therapist helped the family identify that to shift the cycle of avoidance to one of facing Jasmine's fears, therapy would focus primarily on in vivo exposures to being in places where she could be observed and would allow more social interactions. In reviewing the other stimuli that set off her anxiety cycle, the family added imaginal exposures for thoughts about previous judgment and embarrassment, as well as interoceptive exposures to fast heart rate and feeling hot and flushed. Finally, the therapist emphasized that because the goal of exposures was for Jasmine to learn not only that her fears about social scrutiny are not likely to come true but also that she could handle everyday mistakes and embarrassments, her treatment plan would also need to include planned exposure to making mistakes and other common social mishaps, such as saying the wrong thing. At this suggestion, Jasmine's eyes widened and her parents looked upon her with concern about whether she would handle those types of exposures.

PARENT INVOLVEMENT

In the initial therapy session, the therapist discussed with the family how her parents' involvement in treatment would be important to her progress. First, like anyone doing challenging work, Jasmine would likely benefit from their encouragement, support, and accountability. Because so much of her anxiety involved interactions with people in her daily life that are not accessible during therapy sessions, parent facilitation of exposures between sessions would be very important, including helping her set up and review exposures in which they would not be directly present. For example, Jasmine's parents could oversee exposures to initiating social plans or correspond with teachers to ensure she asked questions in class.

A second reason for involving the parents in treatment was to address the ways they participated in Jasmine's anxiety cycle by facilitating avoidance, namely by providing reassurance and taking over interactions that she was capable of handling. Like many well-intentioned parents, her parents were also contacting the school to excuse her absences and were encouraged to move toward holding her accountable for absences and facilitate exposures to communicating with teachers to practice meeting these responsibilities. A third reason for including the parents in Jasmine's treatment was to assist with motivation to engage in exposures and refrain from habits of avoidance. In a subsequent therapy session, the family created a motivational plan that included earning desired activities and privileges (extra screen time, a fun activity with family or friends, or an outing to get new crafting supplies) by accumulating points for completing planned exposures, attending school and activities with peers (bonus points if done with cooperation rather than complaining or other avoidance/delay tactics), and interacting with others. The behavior plan also included consequences for refusing to complete exposures and for missing school and other important activities. Specifically, if Jasmine refused to complete a planned exposure, her access to her mobile phone and other electronics would be put on hold until she completed the required exposures. If she missed school (without having a significant fever or other sign of contagious illness), her parents communicated up front that they would implement a positive practice consequence of requiring her to get up on Saturday at the usual school day wakeup time and practice riding to school and walking up to the door. Although her parents rightfully identified this consequence as a "punishment" for them, their follow-through with this consequence the first time she missed school resulted in Jasmine attending school consistently thereafter.

Whereas there were multiple reasons for involving Jasmine's parents in her treatment, there were also reasons for Jasmine to do exposures independently. First, her frequent reliance on them functioned as avoidance and provided an unnecessary signal of safety. Second, developmentally, Jasmine was at an age for assuming greater autonomy in completing tasks and engaging in activities, especially with peers. The therapist discussed with Jasmine and her parents these reasons for including opportunities for autonomy development in her treatment plan. Namely, her parents would learn how to directly coach her through in-session exposures and would practice out of session so that they could support the process. They would also work on facilitating exposures without providing reassurance or communicating on Jasmine's behalf. In addition, Jasmine would do exposures without her parents present as part of her fear ladder. Finally, Jasmine would be expected to complete some exposures entirely on her own, especially planned exposures in school and other settings where parents normally would not be present, and the therapist would help the family develop a process for her parents to provide support with planning and accountability for independent exposures.

FEAR LADDER

The therapist started a fear ladder with Jasmine and her parents during the third appointment (the second therapy session), gave them directions for working on the fear ladder on their own, and finalized the fear ladder with them at the beginning of the fourth appointment. The therapist identified that the goal of the exposures within the fear ladder would be to help Jasmine learn that being observed by, and interacting with, others typically proceeded smoothly and that she could handle social situations, even ones that are uncomfortable or embarrassing. Jasmine would need to put herself into situations in which others could see her and would need to interact with others to learn firsthand that her fears about doing embarrassing things and others responding negatively typically do not come true. To learn that she could handle common embarrassments and evaluation from others, she would also need to do exposures that involve intentional mistakes, social mishaps, and potential evaluations from others.

Because social interactions can be brief and not long enough for anxiety to decrease or for the fear-causing beliefs to be convincingly disconfirmed, she would need to repeat many of the activities multiple times as part of a single exposure until her anxiety decreased or she was confident she could do it again. Jasmine understood that she would need to refrain from relying on others (typically her parents and best friend) for comfort and social facilitation. If through repeated exposures her distress decreased and she observed that she usually did not do embarrassing things nor did others seem to react negatively, she would learn that social interactions typically go well. Furthermore, if she experienced her distress decreasing and no other negative ramifications after she purposely made mistakes and had physical symptoms of anxiety during social exposures, she would learn that she could handle these events if and when they occur. The therapist was careful to communicate to Jasmine and her parents that the social mishap exposures would include things that happen in everyday social interactions that could be embarrassing but not behaviors that would be expected to bring on social ostracism or teasing. For example, giving a wrong answer in class would be a helpful exposure, whereas saying something disrespectful or fantastical in class would not; walking into dance class with her face flushed and heart beating fast as if she were running late for class would be a helpful exposure, whereas walking in with wet pants as if she had incontinence would not.

Because Jasmine had fears related to being observed as well as social interactions, the therapist suggested creating two fear ladders. For the first fear ladder, she asked the family to list places and situations that tended to trigger Jasmine's fears about being observed and scrutinized. For the second, she directed them to list the types of social interactions that tended to trigger Jasmine's fears about being judged for doing something wrong or embarrassing. All family members were encouraged to contribute ideas. Jasmine initially argued with some of her parents' ideas, stating that their suggestions would "freak [her] out" and they were expecting too much from her. The therapist stated it would be understandable if Jasmine felt doubtful about what she could accomplish at this early point in treatment and encouraged these challenging items to be included on the list anyway because they would be taking exposures one step at a time and she would likely find the situations helpful to practice eventually.

Included in the "being observed" list were the school hallway, classrooms (especially if she sat in the front), the dance studio, and public places such as stores and restaurants. They placed these items in general order of difficulty. They titrated the difficulty of being in these settings by specifying what Jasmine would be doing—for example, sitting and observing, walking, dancing, or eating. Jasmine also noted that having more people (especially same-age peers) around made situations more anxiety provoking. This was noted as an additional way to titrate exposure difficulty. Furthermore, they added more challenging items to the bottom of the list, including intentional mistakes (e.g., doing the wrong dance move in dance class), social mishaps (e.g., dropping coins in a public space), and physical symptoms (e.g., walking in a public place flushed and perspiring slightly after running stairs).

The second "social interactions" fear ladder included speaking in class, conversations with peers and teachers, getting together with friends, and initiating social plans. The therapist and family titrated the difficulty of these exposure ideas by specifying the setting and length of interaction. For example, Jasmine noted some classrooms were easier to speak in than others and some people were easier to converse and socialize with than others. Jasmine understood that relying on others was an impediment to her feeling confident about handling social situations on her own, but she was unsure if she would be able to manage many of the fear ladder items without the support of her parents or best friend. The therapist agreed to a parent or friend being present the first time Jasmine completed a difficult exposure and encouraged her to work toward doing things independently because doing so was important to building her self-confidence. The most difficult items for social interactions included intentional mistakes (e.g., giving a wrong answer), social mishaps (e.g., stuttering or asking a question with an obvious answer), and feared physical symptoms (e.g., talking to others with a flushed face after running the stairs).

SAMPLE EXPOSURE

Jasmine started exposures after finalizing her fear ladders during the fourth appointment and continued them during and between every subsequent session. Approximately one-third of the way through treatment, Jasmine completed a series of exposures that exemplified her course of treatment and common issues with social anxiety exposures more generally. For several sessions in a row, Jasmine had completed in-session and between-session exposures around the theme of asking questions. She had asked clinic volunteers for directions and information, store clerks for information about merchandise, and school office staff for information regarding sport teams' schedules. The therapist expressed concern at the next appointment that they were getting stuck on this rung of her social interaction fear ladder and suggested progressing to back-and-forth conversations. Jasmine was reluctant but acknowledged that asking questions was no longer that difficult and that she was avoiding conversations because she did not know what to say. The therapist explained that conversations have a beginning, middle, and an end and helped her identify a few conversation starters. They agreed that for the next exposure, Jasmine would give a compliment and follow up with at least one comment or question. Jasmine agreed that as with previous exposures, she would repeat this process with different people in the clinic until her anxiety decreased by at least 50% or she became confident she could handle brief conversations. At this point, Jasmine could identify several "targets" she would likely encounter in the clinic, such as visitors waiting for or riding elevators, people walking around the main lobby area, and people standing in line at the coffee shop. Because Jasmine had accumulated quite a bit of practice interacting with adults, the therapist encouraged her to include younger people in her exposure.

Prior to starting the exposure, Jasmine identified her fear was that she would stumble over her words or others would "look at [her] funny." Her initial anxiety rating was a 7 out of 10. Jasmine practiced the conversation starter and follow-up statement/question with her mother and the therapist, after which she rated her anxiety about approaching a clinic visitor as a 5 out of 10. The therapist then accompanied Jasmine and her mother around the clinic, reinforcing with her mother the importance of staying at a distance and allowing Jasmine to do the exposure independently, with check-ins only to rate her anxiety between conversations and to assist with identifying the next approach if needed. Jasmine began immediately on the elevator by complimenting a woman on her shoes. The woman appeared pleased and said "thank you." Jasmine followed up with "Can I ask where you found them?" as she had practiced in the therapist's office. The woman replied that she had found them in her hometown, to which Jasmine replied, "Oh thanks."

Jasmine rated her anxiety about approaching the next person as a 6. She completed the conversation process five more times with various people, including someone who appeared to be in high school. By the sixth interaction, Jasmine rated her anxiety about approaching the next person as a 2 and felt confident about doing it on her own. In reviewing the exposure, Jasmine noted nobody reacted negatively and several people seemed pleased by the compliment. The therapist commended Jasmine for keeping her head up and making eye contact so that she could observe people's reactions. Jasmine also reported that she had not stumbled over her words as feared, which she attributed to rehearsing mentally what she would say as she approached people. The therapist gently pointed out that rehearsing could be a safety behavior and noted it would not be practical in many situations. She encouraged Jasmine to identify an exposure to do in the next session that would involve stumbling over her words or saying the wrong thing. Jasmine expressed nervousness about doing an exposure to purposely making a mistake but felt less intimidated than when this type of exposure was first suggested in the second session. They concluded with making plans to practice brief conversations during the week, including with classmates she did not know well.

When Jasmine and her father returned for the next session, she reported completing her planned exposures and even had a positive experience with an acquaintance whom she had complemented on a concert T-shirt. The conversation had progressed easily to shared music interests across genres, and Jasmine was happy to discover it was actually enjoyable to talk to this classmate after she got over her initial anxiety about approaching her. Jasmine had not, however, identified a social mishap exposure to do in this session and acknowledged she was avoiding the task out of fear her anxiety would "spin out of control," her heart would race and her face would flush, and then she would be "super embarrassed." She was not sure she could handle that. The therapist reflected that anxiety was making predictions that made Jasmine nervous. She encouraged Jasmine to reflect on the number of social exposures she had done already and how often anxiety's predictions were accurate. Jasmine acknowledged that each exposure had proved anxiety's predictions wrong or exaggerated.

The therapist suggested that if it seemed too large a step to make a mistake in a conversation, they could start with asking "silly" questions with an obvious answer, such as asking "Where is the restroom?" while standing near the bathroom door or "Do you make lattes here?" at the coffee shop. By now, Jasmine was quite comfortable asking questions and had integrated asking questions into her daily life, so the idea of starting with potentially embarrassing questions in this type of interaction seemed doable. She and the therapist quickly identified where in the clinic she could go and wrote down a few silly questions she could ask. Jasmine identified that this exposure would test her fear that others would react negatively to her or think badly of her (as evidenced by a disapproving stare) if she said something silly apparently by accident. She rated her anxiety as an 8 and proceeded with the exposure similarly to how she had approached the previous in-session exposure, with her mother and therapist tracking her responses from a distance. Her mother did well refraining from providing reassurance and instead complimenting Jasmine on her persistence and audible speech.

After approximately six interactions, Jasmine's anxiety about asking silly questions had decreased to a 1. She reflected that reactions varied: Some simply answered her question; a couple seemed confused by her question, asked for clarification, and eventually gave an answer; and only the barista gave a "judgy" response by shaking her head and stating that *of course* they had lattes, what kind of latte did she want? Jasmine reflected that contrary to her anxious expectations, most people seemed neutral or even oblivious that she had asked a question with an obvious answer; furthermore, she was relieved that even with the barista's response, her anxiety did not spiral out of control. Now that she was calmer, she thought that the barista might have been at the end of a long shift and probably could use more training in customer service.

COURSE OF TREATMENT

As mentioned previously, the therapist initiated exposures with Jasmine in the fourth session following the initial evaluation (session 1) and psychoeducation and fear ladder building (sessions 2 and 3). In total, Jasmine attended 14 sessions over 4 months, including individual- and group-based sessions. Initially, sessions were weekly, with a few missed appointments due to illness or vacations. Toward the end of treatment, as Jasmine and her parents expressed confidence in the exposure process, sessions were spaced apart so that they could practice doing exposures on their own and use sessions for problem-solving and relapse prevention planning.

In the initial exposure sessions, Jasmine was reluctant but compliant, with parent cajoling, completing exposures to being in public places where she could be observed (e.g., sitting and then walking around a busy clinic lobby, and going to the grocery store with her father). After 2 weeks during which the family did not follow through on the therapist's recommendation to attend group exposure therapy sessions, the therapist confirmed with the parents that they believed it would be helpful but were struggling with convincing Jasmine to attend. The therapist worked with the family to create a behavior plan that included incentives and consequences related to group session participation, completion of exposures, and participation in school and extracurricular activities. Knowing that group attendance was necessary to have access to her mobile phone and tablet motivated Jasmine to attend group sessions. The initial expectation was for Jasmine simply to be present and allow her parents to report to the group regarding in-session and between-session exposure practice. Although she reported that her fear of others staring at her and judging her did not appear to come true, her anxiety remained high at an 8 or 9 without lowering for the entirety of the group session.

After 2 weeks of group participation with persistently high anxiety, her parents conveyed to the therapist that Jasmine's hope seemed to be diminishing and it was becoming difficult to get her to sessions. The therapist coached the parents in using the structure of the behavior plan to set expectations and contingencies around her participation and helped the family identify a series of speaking exposures that would gradually build her confidence. After breaking down exposures that were challenging, Jasmine completed in-session and between-session exposures in which her anxiety decreased, and she voiced greater confidence in the process. Her parents also expressed that having clearly defined expectations and a behavior plan not only helped Jasmine do the exposures but also helped them as parents be more predictable and consistent in their responses and interactions with Jasmine. In addition to supporting the parents' use of contingency management to encourage engagement, the therapist worked with the parents early in the treatment process to shift their responses to Jasmine's anxious and avoidant behaviors from accommodating or criticizing to removing attention and re-engaging when Jasmine was ready to face her fears.

As noted in the series of example exposures, Jasmine got stuck as she progressed along her fear ladder but responded to encouragement and eventually proceeded to more challenging exposures, including engaging in intentional social mishaps. This marked a pivotal point in Jasmine's treatment in that doing social mishap exposures in session made doing out-of-session exposures, with and without planned social mishaps, less daunting. Once she completed several of these types of exposures in and out of session, she began to learn that she could tolerate mistakes and embarrassment without catastrophic outcomes. Jasmine integrated thought exposures and interoceptive exposures around this point in treatment to address fears that others had judged her, she would lose physical control, and that others noticed her physical anxiety symptoms. She found the thought exposures particularly helpful when social worry thoughts emerged after exposures, which often happened at night. By focusing on the anxious thoughts that would emerge (e.g., "That person thought what I said was really dumb") and repeating the thoughts either aloud (if alone) or in her head (if around others), she learned that thinking about judgment did not make it come true, and the thoughts lost their anxiety-producing power. When she first completed interoceptive exposures, she did them as stand-alone exposures—for example, running up and down stairs to raise her heart rate or running with a coat on or standing in front of a hand dryer to get herself warm and her face flushed. Through these exposures, she learned that she could tolerate these symptoms, although uncomfortable, and her anxiety did not spiral out of control. She then added these interoceptive exposures into social exposures (e.g., running with her coat on prior to joining dance class so that she would enter class with her heart racing and face flushed). Through these exposures, she learned that others seemed not to notice her symptoms or responded neutrally rather than negatively to her physical presentation and that her anxiety was manageable.

Implications

Jasmine's case illustrates a few key points for engaging children and adolescents in exposure therapy to treat social anxiety. Most striking—and perhaps most challenging for families and therapists—is the importance of integrating social mishap exposures into the fear ladder/treatment plan. By definition, social anxiety involves fear of negative evaluation, embarrassment, and/or judgment, and these types of events are part of everyday life. The beliefs and expectations of individuals with social anxiety typically inflate the likelihood of negative evaluation, embarrassment, and judgment and also catastrophizing the consequences of experiencing these events. If therapists set up exposures to demonstrate that social mishaps and judgment are not likely without integrating social mishap exposures, there are a number of potential risks. First, it is highly likely that some social interaction, even during a carefully crafted exposure, may not go smoothly—people may be rude, or the patient might stumble over words—and the patient might interpret this outcome as evidence for their fears being true, reinforcing the anxious beliefs. Jasmine's therapist addressed this potential pitfall by helping Jasmine identify that part of her fear was about being unable to handle social mishaps and anxious feelings. A second potential outcome of avoiding social mishap exposures is that the patient's symptoms may be only partially treated. Specifically, although she becomes less fearful that unpleasant events will occur, she remains fearful that she could not handle such events if they did occur. Social mishap and interoceptive exposures were important for Jasmine to learn that common socially awkward moments, including experiencing physical symptoms in social settings, are manageable and need not be feared.

Despite the utility of social mishap exposures, individuals with social anxiety and their families are commonly reluctant to engage in these types of exposures because purposely creating a feared outcome is understandably uncomfortable for the individual and the individual's loved ones. These types of exposures can also be uncomfortable for therapists, who commonly enter the profession to help people feel more—not less—comfortable. The case of Jasmine not only illustrates the utility and importance of these exposures but also illustrates that completing easier exposures first can help individuals build confidence in themselves and in the process, which can facilitate integrating social mishap exposures into treatment. This case also illustrates that engaging parents in setting expectations and contingency management can assist with motivation to engage in exposures, especially when the desire to avoid is strong.

A key point related to the use of social mishap exposures is the importance of utilizing exposures that represent commonly occurring embarrassments and evaluations that children and adolescents are likely to encounter in their daily lives. Sometimes families can become overly enthusiastic or misconstrue the concept of social mishap exposures as meaning that the child or adolescent should do something bizarre to embarrass themselves. Sometimes, therapists may only need to clarify that exposures should be to situations that are likely to occur in normal life; other times, therapists may need to be more explicit that behavior in a proposed exposure would be considered bizarre or off-putting and redirect the family to more appropriate exposures.

Yet another point illustrated by Jasmine's example is that treatment of social anxiety may require explicit guidance and practice with social skills, such as how to start, continue, and end a conversation; how to gracefully enter an ongoing conversation; and etiquette around making social plans. Careful assessment of social skills prior to the emergence of social anxiety disorder may help differentiate if social skill deficits preceded social anxiety or emerged due to avoidance and insufficient practice in the most recent developmental phase(s). Such an assessment may inform how much direct social skill instruction might be necessary. Of course, assessment is typically ongoing, and therapists can learn much about patients' level of social skill by observing them interact with others during exposures. The opportunity to directly observe and assess youths' social competence during interactions is another benefit of group therapy, in addition to the accessibility of peer-to-peer social exposures. If groups are available, we encourage youth to participate, despite initial anxiety, and offer individual therapy only if needed to facilitate group entry.

We next turn our attention to the use of exposure to treat specific phobias.

Specific Phobia

DESCRIPTION

William, an 8-year-old African American boy, lived with his parents, 5-year-old brother, and 10-year-old sister. His mother (aged 39 years) was an executive for a local business, and his father (aged 41 years) was a construction foreman. William was referred for evaluation of a severe dog phobia. A healthy-looking boy, he was very shy, behaviorally inhibited, and initially very reluctant to meet the staff and to participate in the assessment and treatment process. Based on parental report, his fear of dogs had been present for approximately 4 years and interfered significantly with his life and that of his family. His parents reported that whenever they took their son someplace—for example, to school, church, the grocery store, or a park—they had to avoid driving through neighborhoods where dogs might be present; if they did not do so, William would become so upset that he would cry and refuse to get out of the car upon arrival at their destination. Furthermore, on one recent school day, he refused to go to school even before leaving home because the students were supposed to bring their pets and he was afraid that one or more of his classmates would bring their dogs.

William's parents indicated that his fear started when he was approximately 4 years old when a dog chased him and his sister (who was then approximately 6 years old) while they were playing in the front yard of their home. This occurred on a Sunday afternoon and his parents were sitting on the front porch relaxing, talking about an upcoming trip and enjoying the sunny fall day. Although William was chased by the dog, reportedly he was not knocked down or bitten by the dog or hurt other than when he fell down trying to run away from the dog and bruised his face and hurt his left arm. When he fell down, the dog reportedly ran by him and continued to chase his sister as she was also running away; however, she was not knocked down by the dog either. To their knowledge, William never witnessed anyone else being hurt or attacked by this or any other dog. Recently, however, his parents indicated that the new neighbor's dog often barked, ran up to the fence, and growled at children and others when they passed the home. William seemed to recall being chased by a dog when he was a young boy and knocked down by the dog. He could not recall his age at the time or the type of dog or his sister's presence. However, he did report being "scared to death" that the dog would bite him and possibly even kill him. Although some points of recollection differed from those of his parents, it seemed that the same event was being shared.

Approximately 6 months prior to presenting for treatment, while William and his parents were visiting his grandparents (who had a small but "frisky" dog), he hid in a bedroom closet for approximately 3 hours and refused to come out until his parents reassured him that the dog would be put outside and would be kept outside during their visit. During recent months, his fear had reportedly become much worse, precipitating his appointment, after a neighbor purchased a bulldog that looked mean, ugly, and "ferocious" to William. William subsequently refused to go outside to play in his own back yard with his sister and brother, and he asked his parents to ensure the doors to their home were locked at all times so the dog would not get into their home. William's parents indicated they tried to listen to their son's complaints and concerns, but they had become increasingly frustrated with him. They also indicated they tried to reduce his fear and to make him "happy" by avoiding situations in which dogs might be present.

William's parents described his symptoms as having additional effects on the family. His mother endorsed feeling overwhelmed by trying to help William while taking care of her other children, as well as by aspects of her full-time position as a business executive. Although she reported loving her husband and that he was a good father, she wished he would be more involved in helping her deal with William and his fears. William's father, on the other hand, acknowledged his low level of involvement with William. He described William as a major source of frustration for him, that William was not the son he thought he would be, and that he thought William just needed "to grow up and get over it." William's father indicated he spent more time with his younger son who was more outgoing and liked to play various sports than with William or his 10-year older daughter.

William's parents reported they had taken him to a play therapist when he was 6 years old because of his fear of dogs and because he was severely shy and reluctant to try new things or to meet new people. They saw this therapist for 17 sessions and reported that William really liked the therapist and enjoyed going to see her; however, they reported that he did not "really change very much." He continued to have his fear of dogs and to be shy around people—both other children and adults.

ASSESSMENT AND CONCEPTUALIZATION

Upon referral, a comprehensive assessment was conducted. Two therapists independently interviewed William and his parents using the Anxiety Disorders Interview Schedule for DSM-IV Child/Parent version (ADIS-IV-C/P). Based on the parent interview, William was diagnosed with a specific phobia of dogs with a clinician's severity rating (CSR) of 7 out of 8 and assigned a Clinical Global Impression–Severity (CGI-S) score of 5 (markedly ill). In the child ADIS interview, William reported his fear level as an 8 on the ADIS 0–8 rating scale. The child assessing therapist also assigned a CGI-S score of 5. In addition, William's parents endorsed criteria for social anxiety disorder (with a CSR of 6 on the 0–8 scale). Although William was very shy and offered minimal comments, he did not report major fears or anxieties about interacting with his peers or teachers or other adults. Based on these interviews, it was determined that his fear of dogs was most pronounced and troubling and was viewed as the primary reason for referral as well as the primary diagnosis. A behavioral avoidance task was administered in which William was asked to enter a room where a dog was being held on a leash by an assistant and to pet the dog on the head for 10 seconds. However, he refused to enter the room and reported his subjective fear to be a 10 (on a scale from 0 to 10). While standing in front of the closed door, he became extremely agitated, stating "No, no . . . I am not going into the room . . . no way can I go in that room . . . the dog might jump on me and hurt me."

After completing the assessment, a cognitive–behavioral functional analysis was then conducted with William and his parents to understand his symptoms within the anxiety cycle.

During this interview conducted conjointly with William and his parents, William indicated his fears were set off by all dogs, regardless of size or situation. Specifically, his fears were set off not only by physical proximity to dogs but also by seeing them (e.g., through the window) or by situations in which there might be a dog. William was also able to identify a number of danger expectancies that made dogs frightening, including being very sure negative things would happen to him if he were around dogs and that he could not cope with what might happen. For example, he rated "The dog will chase me and bite me and I might die" as very likely to occur and very bad if it were to occur; he rated his ability to cope with such an event as not very likely at all. His rated his second belief, "The dog will bark at me and try to bite me," as also very likely to occur, pretty bad if it did occur, and that he was somewhat able to cope with it.

With the help of the therapist and his parents, William was also able to identify more precisely how he was avoiding dogs. In addition to refusing to go near dogs or places where there might be dogs, he reported checking the doors at home throughout the day and during the early evening to determine if they were locked. Moreover, he admitted shutting the blinds on the windows to avoid seeing their neighbor's dog. When asked if the fear of dogs prevented him from doing things he wanted to do, he indicated he was generally okay as long as his parents did not make him go outside or do things where there might be dogs. However, he was quite aware of his fears and their impact upon him and his family. As such, he acknowledged that he needed help and understood that treatment would involve exposures to approaching and interacting with dogs.

PARENT INVOLVEMENT

William participated in a one-session, 3-hour-long exposure treatment program (described later) that includes significant parent involvement. Both of William's parents participated in the treatment, which is ideal; in many instances, only one parent can be involved due to time and work-related constraints or because the child is from a single-parent family. As illustrated previously, during the assessment phase, both parents contributed, along with William, information about the etiology and maintenance of his phobia, as well as relevant information to arrange appropriate and graduated exposures. In addition, both parents and William received psychoeducation about anxiety and the rationale behind the treatment. During the first hour of the 3-hour treatment, William's parents observed the therapist guide William with graduated exposures to a dog. During this time, his parents learned how to conduct exposures, reinforce appropriate approach behaviors, and decrease avoidance behaviors associated with exposure to the phobic stimulus. In the second and third hours, William's parents joined in the treatment and practiced implementing the observed skills. The therapist provided feedback and gradually transitioned control of the session over to them—a process called "transfer of control." At the end of the session, the therapist assisted the parents in designing exposures for William using a reward system to increase his engagement following treatment and instructed them on ways to deal with their own anxiety when helping William in the exposure situations. After the session, the therapist contacted the parents once a week for 4 weeks to encourage and reinforce ongoing exposures and to troubleshoot difficulties associated with continued exposures outside of session. A sample monitoring form from William's maintenance phase is presented in Box 7.1.

FEAR LADDER

The fear hierarchy was created during the assessment session. William indicated that seeing a dog on the street or in the park without a leash would result in a fear level of 10 out of 10 and that he would likely run away "as fast as [he] can." Seeing a dog being walked on the street—even with a leash—would also result in a fear level of 10, and he would likely "hide behind mom or dad." Approaching and petting a dog off a leash in a safe environment (e.g., at the clinic or in his own home) would also result in a fear level of 10; however, approaching and petting a dog on a leash in a safe environment would still be "very, very scary" but probably only at a fear level of 9. Watching the therapist approach and pet the dog would be a fear level of 8, whereas sitting next to the therapist while the therapist was petting the dog would likely be a 9. Looking at a dog out a window from his home or some other safe place such as the clinic would result in a fear level of 6, and just seeing a dog (unexpectedly) on television would produce a fear level of 4. Moreover, just looking at pictures of dogs in a book would increase his fear level to a 2. Even saying the word "dog" resulted in a fear level of 1. Various steps in between these

Box 7.1

MONITORING FORM

Week 1 2 3 4

Name (Sample Form)

> List the exposure exercise your child will attempt this week on the "Exposure Exercise" line. Enter the day of the week and date in the chart below. For each day listed mark "YES" or "NO" for exercise completed or for reward delivered. Also, list the type of rewards delivered if applicable. On the reverse side of the form please write your comments, e.g., if your child had any anxiety reactions, problems completing the exercises, etc. Please try to complete the exercises at least 3 days a week. This is particularly important during the first 4 weeks after treatment.

Please send me the form at the end of the week.

Exposure Exercise Walk outside with Mom or Dad and go by neighbor dog

DAY	DATE	EXERCISE COMPLETED		REWARD		TYPE OF REWARD*
		YES	NO	YES	NO	
Wednesday	9/29	X		X		Fishing trip with Dad.
Thursday	9/30		X			
Friday	10/1	X		X		Choose movie for family to watch.
Saturday	10/2	X			X	I got too busy.
Sunday	10/3		X			
Monday	10/4	X		X		Praise from parents.
Tuesday	10/5	X			X	It just slipped my mind. I need to make sure I remember to do it.

*Parents should also be rewarded on a weekly basis (e.g., Mom and Dad watched a movie together. Mom and Dad went out to dinner together).

Were parents rewarded this week? Y___ N__ Type of reward:_____

were also determined to construct a 15-item fear hierarchy to be used in therapy. Importantly, at each of these steps, his danger expectancies and his behavioral avoidance responses (as illustrated in the cognitive–behavioral functional analysis presented previously) were also obtained.

SAMPLE EXPOSURE

The following is a description of the first hour of treatment for William's dog phobia, illustrating the nature of the exposure tasks and some of the dialogue between William and the therapist. With William, as with most treatment cases for dog phobias, it is important to have a number of dogs available (ideally three, but at least two) to allow habituation to occur, test out and disconfirm the child's danger expectancies, and help the parents increase their own skills and efficacy. Based on the assessment, the dogs should vary in size (e.g., small, medium, and large), activity level (e.g., calm and active), and ideally color and breed. It is critical to begin the session with each dog in a controlled, safe setting; however, as therapy progresses, it will be important that the dog can be taken to an outside grassy area or walked to a nearby park. The same progression of exposure activities (e.g., looking at, approaching, petting, walking on a leash, playing catch with, feeding, and walking outside on a leash) can be used for each of the dogs introduced to the child.

For William, it was necessary to first look at pictures of a dog and then view the first dog from a window with his parents. A small dog named Izzy was on a leash held by the clinic assistant who was petting the dog. Pictures of other playful dogs were downloaded from the computer along with pictures of dogs in a story book and shown to William. Throughout this first part, information about dogs and their importance to people and society was imparted (dialogue is presented later).

Following this, William and his parents were escorted into the room in which the assistant and the dog were located. The dog was at the far end of the room (10 × 18 feet) and held on a leash by the assistant. The therapist sat with William and his parents on chairs (approximately 15 feet away from the dog) and asked the assistant some questions about the dog, including its name, age, breed, and what it liked to eat and do outside. Then the therapist turned away and asked William to describe the dog (e.g., shape, size, and color). This was done to ensure William was actually looking at the dog, as he tended to look away and crouch behind his mother. William complied albeit somewhat reluctantly and only following much encouragement from his parents (who were prompted to provide encouragement and social reinforcement before the beginning of the session). The therapist then began a series of behavioral experiments whereby William was asked to predict what would happen if the therapist approached the dog. William quickly indicated, "I do not know but I know what he would do to me." The therapist acknowledged William's response and indicated they could still test out what the dog would do to the therapist. In doing so, the therapist carefully modeled how to approach an "unfamiliar" dog (e.g., ask the owner if it is ok to pet the dog on the head and allow the dog to sniff one's hand before petting it) and questioned William about whether his predictions came true as each exposure was undertaken. The therapist crouched down and sat near Izzy and continued to pet her on the head while inviting William to gradually approach the dog. Initially he refused; however, both parents strongly encouraged him to do so. The therapist invited him to stand on one side and asked him to place his right hand on top of the therapist's shoulder while the therapist continued to pet the dog (beginning the participant modeling phase of treatment). For approximately the next 20 minutes, the therapist invited William to place his hand on the therapist's upper arm and then elbow, forehand, wrist, back of hand, and eventually fingers—all the while checking out his beliefs about what the dog would do. Following this, the therapist gradually helped William slide his hand directly onto the dog so that he was petting the dog alone. Throughout this process, the therapist provided profuse reinforcement, education regarding the benefits of owning a dog, the role of dogs in society, and how to approach and handle dogs safely. The following dialogue illustrates some of this process:

THERAPIST: Why do you think people own dogs?

WILLIAM: I'm not sure. I don't want to . . . we do not have a dog.

THERAPIST: Let's ask my assistant and hear what she says.

ASSISTANT: I own a dog because she is my friend and she keeps me company and helps me to stay active. I get to walk her two times every day for about 20 minutes. She also is good at protecting me and my family and barks if someone comes to our door.

THERAPIST: So, you see William, some people own dogs because they make good friends and keep them company. . . . You know William, some dogs even have jobs! Did you know that? What kinds of jobs might they have?

WILLIAM: I do not know. Oh, yeah, I guess guide dogs help people who are blind and also sniffer dogs are at the airport. My grandpa told me about that.

THERAPIST: Good, and yes, dogs help us out in many other ways. Some dogs visit nursing homes to make old people happy or may come into schools so children can read to them, or there are also police dogs too which help police officers find drugs or missing people and even dogs who go to the hospital to help children feel better when they are sick.

WILLIAM: I see. (He turns to his parents with a smile.)

Once William felt comfortable petting the dog (e.g., a fear rating of 5 or less on the 0–10 scale), the therapist moved onto the next step. Typically, children such as William are more fearful when the dog is moving around. The next steps include having the assistant walk the dog around the room and play catch with it. To illustrate further, the therapist and William next walked the dog together around the room on the leash. To do so, the therapist took hold of the lead nearest the dog's head and William was invited to hold the end. When the child feels comfortable, the therapist can let go of the lead and continue to walk beside the child and dog. Eventually, William walked Izzy around the room alone, and then the therapist and William walked the dog around the clinic. William was then prompted to go for a small walk with the dog alone but still within the therapist's (and parents') eyesight (e.g., "I want you to walk with Izzy to the front door and then back to me"). The next task involved letting the dog off the leash. This is often a difficult step for most children (including William) because they perceive the dog is no longer under the assistant's or the therapist's control. For children who are reluctant to proceed with an exposure task or become stuck, "foot in the door" techniques such as those that follow can be used to help the child progress:

> THERAPIST: You did a great job walking our dog. For our next step, I will give you a choice—we could feed Izzy or ask our assistant to let her off her leash? Which one would you like to do first?
>
> WILLIAM: That's not much of a choice! I guess, take her off the leash. She seems like a pretty quiet dog and has not bit me yet.

Prior to beginning this exposure task, William and the therapist sat on the opposite side of the room to the dog and the assistant. Before asking the assistant to let Izzy off the leash, William was asked for his prediction of what the dog would do:

> THERAPIST: In a minute, I will ask my assistant to let Izzy off the leash. What do you think will happen?
>
> WILLIAM: I do not know for sure, but I think she will run towards us and jump on me!
>
> THERAPIST: Okay, I will be here with you. Let's ask our assistant to let Izzy off the leash. Here we go. What happened when she was taken off the leash?
>
> WILLIAM: Nothing, she did not move. She just sat there.
>
> THERAPIST: That's right. Okay, let's just sit here and watch her for a bit longer. . . . She still has not moved. So was your prediction correct?
>
> WILLIAM: No, I guess not, at least not this time.
>
> THERAPIST: What did you learn from this?
>
> WILLIAM: That what I thought would happen did not. I guess I was wrong.

To continue, the therapist and William watched what happened when the assistant encouraged Izzy to move around the room. Eventually, William and the therapist practiced calling the dog toward them several times and throwing a ball for the dog to catch. The final exposure step for William with this dog involved him feeding the dog from his hand. First, as with all steps, the therapist modeled how to feed the dog by placing dog biscuits on one's hand and keeping one's fingers and palm flat. Again, participant modeling was used by having William place his hand under the therapist's hand and then swapping with the therapist's hand under William's and finally William feeding the dog alone:

> THERAPIST: What do you think will happen if you feed Izzy?
>
> WILLIAM: She will bite my hand.
>
> THERAPIST: Okay, you saw me feed her and she did not bite me. Let's try it out together. You put your hand under my hand. . . . Good! You helped me feed her a biscuit. So what happened? Do we still have all our fingers?

WILLIAM: Yes! It felt kind of messy and wet but it was ok. She did not
   bite me.

The task was repeated again with the therapist's hand on top and then following
this three times with William's hand on top until he reported his fear rating to be
a 1 on a scale of 0–10:

   THERAPIST: Okay, you have done so well with me. Let's now see you do it
      alone. Is there anything you worry will happen?
   WILLIAM: I am still worried she will bite me.
   THERAPIST: What is your fear level now? (William held up 8 fingers.) Okay,
      let's try it out to see what happens. (He did so.) You did it! You fed her.
      Great. That is absolutely terrific! So what happened?
   WILLIAM: She didn't bite me, she just licked my hand a lot.
   THERAPIST: What is your fear level now?
   WILLIAM: Only a 2.

The previous steps were all accomplished in the first hour of treatment. This
first hour ended by having William's parents comment on what they had observed
and telling William how proud they were of him.

COURSE OF TREATMENT

William's treatment took place in a brief, massed session, frequently referred to
as one-session treatment. This abbreviated treatment included many standard
cognitive–behavioral techniques (psychoeducation, graduated exposure, reinforcement, cognitive challenges, and participant modeling) with the exposure
massed into a single therapy session lasting approximately 3 hours. This intensive session was then followed by a 4-week maintenance program. William's
exposure session began with the steps described previously. Following a 5-
minute break, the parents took over with another dog, essentially completing
the steps with the therapist in the "background" but helping out by prompting
them at times, modeling at other times, and profusely reinforcing them and
William throughout. The second dog was a larger dog (a collie) but still a relatively calm dog that was very obedient. That hour ended with William, his
parents, and the therapist walking the dog outdoors in a grassy park-like area
adjacent to the clinic. Finally, following another 5-minute break, a third dog
was introduced—this was a bulldog—the very type of dog that lived next door
and that William feared. At first, he was quite reticent to be involved, but with
encouragement and praise he was able to do so. By the end of the session,
William was feeding the bulldog out of his own hand. Following treatment,
the parents instituted the maintenance program at home with weekly phone
calls by the therapist to monitor progress and to help them problem solve
if any difficulties were encountered. For the most part, the weekly exposure
practices went as planned.

William was evaluated at the clinic following the 4-week maintenance stage. On the ADIS-IV-C/P, his clinical severity level was now at a 2—indicating a "mild" subclinical severity level of his phobia but with some lingering wariness of seeing unexpected dogs and dogs not on leashes in the community. To some extent, such wariness is warranted and is part of our program to teach children about dogs, their behaviors, and when and how to approach them. At pretreatment, it will be recalled his CSR was a 7 out of 8 (markedly severe). Also at pretreatment, both the parent and child assessing therapists assigned a CGI–S of 5 out of 7 (markedly ill). At follow-up, he was rated a 3 by the attending therapist—indicating that he was still mildly ill; however, this rating was mainly due to the continued presence of social anxiety disorder with a CSR of 4, still in the clinical range but reduced from the CSR rating of 6 at pretreatment. With regard to the CGI–Global Improvement dimension, he was rated a 2 (much improved). During the readministration of the behavioral avoidance task, William opened the door to the room, approached the dog, and petted it on the head for approximately 5 seconds. He reported his subjective fear to be a 3 out of 10. Finally, both William and his parents indicated high treatment satisfaction at follow-up, indicating they would highly recommend this program to other families.

IMPLICATIONS

The treatment of William's dog phobia illustrates two points that deserve additional discussion. First, because many specific phobias, including a fear of dogs, are specific, tangible, and focused, they provide an accessible example for instruction. For this reason, we use a fear of dogs clinically, and in this book, to illustrate the anxiety cycle and how to do exposures during psychoeducation (introduced in Chapter 5, this volume). Of note, although William's phobia had a likely precipitating event (frightening experience at age 4 years), this is actually unusual for anxiety disorders and obsessive–compulsive disorder. For most patients, including those with specific phobias, families are more likely to report that the child has "always been this way" rather than identifying a specific time when or event after which the symptoms began. Regardless, William's treatment provides excellent illustrations of how to design exposures that gradually titrate the level of difficulty and clearly challenge anxiety-provoking beliefs. For example, titration involved using different distances, levels of support, amounts of participation (i.e., active vs. observing), dog characteristics (e.g., size), and similarity to primary fear (i.e., bulldog). The nature of the feared object, dogs, lent itself to (relatively) easy manipulation so that each aspect could be titrated in the moment to meet William's treatment needs. In contrast, many other fear-provoking stimuli may be much more difficult and/or less intuitive to control at such a granular level. Recall from Chapter 5 that it is not necessary for exposures to proceed in an orderly manner up the fear ladder. However, as William's treatment well illustrates, predictable progression through tasks that very gradually increase difficultly may be necessary to engage fearful youth.

When therapists have difficulty determining how to titrate less controllable exposures, it may be helpful to consider a dog phobia as a template. It may not be possible for a therapist to literally reduce physical support for peer-based social interaction exposures, as the therapist did with William by feeding the dog with his hand below and then above the therapist's hand. However, the therapist and child might jointly start conversations with strangers by first having the therapist initiate contact and then having the child take the lead the next time. Or the therapist might help the family arrange for a friend to provide support when beginning a new activity (as in the social anxiety case presented previously). Similarly, exposure might progress from talking with quiet, well-behaved children to talking with more boisterous children whom the patient views as more likely to tease, just as a child might start with a calm dog before working with an active dog. Moreover, therapists can use examples from dog exposures to help patients understand their own exposure plan. For example, a therapist might state,

> Do you remember when I explained that kids with fears of dogs need to practice feeding dogs, so they can really test whether or not dogs will bite them by having their hand close to the dog's mouth? Well, the same is true for social worries. You need to practice asking questions that might seem obvious, to really test whether people will be rude to you.

As such, the tangible nature of dog phobias and their treatment can provide a useful guide for designing and explaining less intuitive exposure plans.

William's treatment also illustrates a method (i.e., one-session treatment) for increasing the availability of exposure therapy. As discussed previously, access to exposure therapy is limited by multiple factors, including lack of trained therapists and the tendency of therapists to administer other, less effective treatment approaches rather than exposure. As a result, many children do not receive appropriate care and continue to suffer. Time-limited intensive treatment programs, such as the one in which William participated, provide an effective treatment resource to children without options in their home area. Because the interventions are short (1–5 days), families can travel to a specialty clinic, receive care, and then return home. As in the case of William, the success of short-term massed treatment depends on the continued engagement in exposures after the family returns home to maintain and generalize the initial progress. When working with children, training parents to be exposure coaches, along with scheduled check-ins, can facilitate that continued engagement. The success of brief, intensive cognitive–behavioral treatments for treating fears and phobias in children has been supported by a number of studies, with a clear majority of children and adolescents benefitting from them. These treatments have been successfully used to treat specific phobias in children and adolescents from different countries and cultures, including youth with intellectual disabilities and autism spectrum disorders.

William's treatment provides a concise illustration of the fundamental components of exposure therapy as well as a novel approach to increasing access to care. We now turn our attention to the final in vivo case study, which involves the treatment of separation anxiety. This case allows us to explore how to incorporate parents into treatment when their presence is an integral component of the symptom presentation.

Separation Anxiety

DESCRIPTION

Nora was an 8-year-old girl of Asian and Caucasian descent who presented with both parents for anxiety surrounding being alone. The family sought treatment after Nora began refusing to go to school following a brief illness. Although she had recovered from the flu-like symptoms that had kept her home, she continued to complain about stomachaches and feeling sick before school. These complaints crept into worries on weekday nights and culminated in clinging, crying, and refusing to get out of the car before school. With the help of school personnel, the family was generally able to get her to attend school, but during the day she was frequently leaving class to see the nurse. As a result, her parents had picked her up early from school on a few occasions. Nora had also begun resisting attending other activities, such as playdates and dance lessons, unless a parent remained in her sight. This behavior also extended to home life, where Nora wanted to be in the same room as her parents, including when going to sleep. When asked what she was afraid of, Nora was able to list a number of fears about her safety, robbers breaking in and hurting her, and her parents not returning.

Although the current level of distress and dysfunction was new, Nora's parents described a long history of anxiety surrounding separation. She reportedly had more difficulty than her siblings starting day care and school, including increased anxiety at the beginning of the school year and after extended vacations. Her parents stated that Nora had never been comfortable going upstairs or into the basement alone. Her parents had always laid with her in her bed until she fell asleep, and approximately once a week she would awake in the middle of the night and come into their room, co-sleeping until morning. Despite these fears, Nora had always functioned well. Her teachers described her as a good student who was well-liked by her classmates. Outside of school, she historically had been invited to and attended birthday parties and playdates with peers and was involved in regular extracurricular activities, such as dance and soccer. Nora stated that she continued to enjoy school and the other activities in her life, denied environmental stressors, and stated that she would like to engage in her activities if she did not feel so scared.

ASSESSMENT AND CONCEPTUALIZATION

The therapist working with Nora and her parents proposed that her symptoms were best described as separation anxiety disorder. The therapist noted that although Nora's anxiety often occurred in social situations that included an evaluative component, her fears were focused more clearly around themes of separation. Moreover, at times Nora's anxiety would decrease once she was engaged in the activity following separation. Moreover, Nora was particularly fearful in situations in which she would be all alone, such as at home, even without the potential for evaluation. Although Nora and her parents described her experiencing acute panic attacks, these attacks were provoked by separation and Nora did not fear their occurrence, unless they were to occur when her parents were absent. Nora and her parents also reported that she worried frequently, but the content of these worries predominately revolved around themes of separation. As such, although Nora experienced symptoms suggestive of other anxiety diagnoses, at least super-ficially, separation anxiety disorder appeared accurate and sufficient to capture her experience.

After establishing a diagnosis, the therapist worked with Nora and her parents during the first treatment session to conceptualize her symptoms within the cog-nitive–behavioral model. Consistent with the previously mentioned information, physical separation from her parents was identified as the primary stimuli that set off her fears. This physical separation could take the form of playing in a room alone, getting out of the car at school, having parents leave the dance studio, and being dropped off at a friend's house, among others. In addition, two types of thoughts were also identified as setting off her anxiety. The first included anticipa-tion of separation and memories of previous separation, although the latter was to a much lesser degree. As mentioned previously, in the evenings Nora began thinking about separation for school the next day. Occasionally, Nora would also become very upset talking about times when she was required to separate. As such, thinking about separation, in addition to actual physical separation, set off fear and anxiety. Second, the negative events that Nora imagined could occur during separation were additional stimuli that set off anxiety. Specifically, separating from parents at night made her nervous, particularly when she thought that a robber would kidnap her. Moreover, thoughts that her parents might not return to pick her up could provoke anxiety during the school day.

After identifying the items that set off Nora's symptoms, the therapist helped her and her parents identify the beliefs or expectations that made safe situations anxiety provoking. To some extent, Nora feared that bad things would occur when separated from her parents. Because intrusive thoughts, such as "Robbers will hurt me," were identified as stimuli that set off her cycle, the anxiety-provoking expect-ancy was framed as "It is likely that my fears will come true." However, during the discussion, it became apparent that Nora's primary fear was that she would not be able to handle herself or the situation without her parents. Specifically, when discussing her thoughts regarding robbers, she quickly stated that she knew this would never happen. In contrast, she more firmly believed that she could not calm down without her parents. The therapist then shifted to identifying the avoidance behaviors that prevented Nora from learning her anxious beliefs were inaccurate. Chief among them, more so than physical avoidance, were crying, clinging, and other attempts to prevent separation. Even when Nora's parents successfully got her to separate, it routinely occurred after a protracted battle in which she verbally, emotionally, and physically attempted to remain close to her parents. These efforts constituted avoidance in that they not only delayed separation but also proactively decreased the frequency with which her parents expected her to separate. In addition, there were situations in which Nora was able to physically avoid separation, such as sleeping with her parents. She avoided her intrusive thoughts about robbers and upcoming separation by sharing them with her parents, who responded with reassurance, distraction, or efforts to help her replace these thoughts with positive soothing thoughts.

Identifying the stimuli that set off Nora's symptoms, her expectations that made safe situations appear dangerous and her methods of avoidance, led naturally to generating appropriate exposure activities. Most directly, Nora would need to do exposures to being alone without her parents in a variety of situations, both contrived for practice during the session and more naturalistically in the course of daily life. However, in order to handle the intrusive worry thoughts, Nora would need to complete imaginal exposures to feared scenarios. Finally, she would likely need to do exposures to the *process* of separating, in addition to being alone, without engaging in her safety behaviors (i.e., crying and clinging). The goal of these exercises was for Nora to learn that she could handle herself and her environment on her own without her parents (at an age-appropriate level). At the conclusion of the conceptualization, Nora and her parents indicated understanding and agreement with the treatment plan. Nora was understandably wary of exposures but was an energetic and positive girl who felt confident discussing the plans in the abstract. The proposal to repeat scary thoughts, rather than positive thinking, was counterintuitive to the family but made sense to them after having worked through the cognitive–behavioral model of avoidance and how it applied to Nora's experience.

Parent Involvement

Nora's parents were eager to learn new strategies for helping their daughter manage separation. They realized that their current responses to her anxiety were not productive, but they did not know what to do instead. The therapist began by describing how they as parents would learn to be exposure coaches, guiding Nora through setting-up, doing, and learning from planned exposures. In this capacity, they would work with the therapist in session to conduct exposures and would lead Nora through planned exposures at home, such as sitting upstairs alone. Perhaps most important, the therapist also worked with Nora's parents to use their attention differentially to encourage and reward brave behavior. The therapist began by reviewing how Nora's anxious behaviors had been eliciting parental attention. For example, voicing fears of robbers at night brought parents into her room to lay with her until she fell asleep, and complaints of stomachaches before school led, at least initially, to her parents attempting to soothe and comfort her. When she was quiet, Nora's parents assumed she was okay and not in need of additional support. As a result, when Nora wanted help because she was feeling anxious or upset, she expressed these feelings through calling out, crying, and expressing helplessness. If her parents did not immediately respond, whether or not intentionally, she amplified the expression of her anxiety until they provided the support she sought.

To break the anxiety cycle, Nora needed to learn that when she was anxious or upset, her parents would support her efforts to manage these feelings independently rather than handling them for her. Accordingly, the therapist instructed Nora's parents to give her support and attention when she was trying to face her fears and remain calm. In contrast, when she was letting her anxiety win, and not trying to face her fears, her parents should remove their attention. For example, the therapist encouraged Nora's parents to inform her that they would check on her if she was acting calmly by herself. These check-ins could occur very frequently (e.g., every 1 or 2 minutes if necessary) in order for her parents to provide attention and support while she was quiet, before Nora had a chance to call out or leave the situation. The therapist explained that Nora's parents could initially practice this approach during planned in-session exposures to sitting in an office alone by checking on Nora (and collecting anxiety ratings) only if she was quiet. Once they became comfortable with the approach, they should use the strategy in daily activities, most notably at bedtime. Specifically, after putting Nora to bed in her own room, her parents would check on her frequently only if she was quiet. As such, Nora would receive parental attention for facing her fears by staying in bed rather than for avoidance (i.e., insisting that her parents stay with her).

Finally, the therapist worked with Nora's parents to design rewards and consequences to increase her cooperation. Because Nora was generally a highly compliant child, her parents had never felt the need to implement a structured behavior management system. However, based on their recent experience, they anticipated that Nora would be considerably resistant to exposure, particularly when implemented in daily activities. The therapist and parents agreed that at least initially, a plan focused on rewarding her for successful completion of exposures and for progressively remaining calm during daily separation would be sufficient. Nora's parents already removed privileges for minor misbehaviors and thought that they could employ that approach surrounding exposure treatment as well. If differential attention, rewards, and standard discipline proved insufficient, Nora's parents could add a more structured approach to consequences.

FEAR LADDER

The therapist worked with the family during the second treatment session to create a fear ladder. Based on the presenting problem, the goal of therapy was for Nora to be able to separate calmly and to do activities with an age-appropriate level of independence. Based on the conceptualization of Nora's anxiety cycle, the goal of individual exposure exercises was to challenge Nora's beliefs that bad things were likely to occur in her parents' absence and, perhaps more important, that she could manage her feelings and her surroundings without her parents' assistance. The activities required to achieve these goals seemed best categorized into three fear ladders. The first ladder consisted of planned exposures that could be completed in the therapy session and were designed to challenge her anxious beliefs and to prepare her for everyday exposures. These activities included imaginal exposures to worry thoughts and in vivo exposures to separation. The degree of challenge was titrated through the content of the thought, the degree of separation, and combining thoughts and in vivo elements. Nora and her parents generated a short list of common worry thoughts, including "I have to go to school tomorrow," "My parents won't pick me up," "My parents will get hurt," "Robbers will break in," and "Robbers will take me." The in vivo separation exposures included sitting in an office alone with parents checking frequently, sitting in an office alone with infrequent checks, sitting in the dark with a parent, sitting in the dark alone, riding an elevator alone, and going into a store alone.

The second ladder consisted of extending Nora's practice to daily activities that elicited fears of separation and included going to bed on her own, sleeping through the night alone in her room, going to school, playing in a room by herself at home, going upstairs (or downstairs) alone, staying with a babysitter, playing at a friend's house, and being dropped off at dance class.

The third fear ladder consisted of a list of behaviors that Nora engaged at the time of separation, including crying, complaining of a stomachache, getting angry, screaming, clinging, and laying on the ground. Nora's parents agreed that they could temporarily tolerate the initial items on the third list if Nora discontinued the latter, more interfering items.

Sample Exposure

One of the more notable exposures completed by Nora occurred during the fourth treatment session. After completing an imaginal exposure the week before, Nora was now prepared to conduct the first in vivo exposure to sitting in an office by herself. The therapist and the family decided that Nora would repeat the thought "My parents won't come back" while sitting in the room alone because she had prepared for this by completing a number of thought exposures during the week since the last appointment. The exposure began smoothly, with Nora rating her anxiety as a 7 out of 10 and separating from her parents with a minimal number of hugs and requests for reassurance that they would check on her quickly. Her parents responded warmly and tolerated these safety behaviors based on a plan to phase them out in a stepwise process. After leaving the room, Nora's parents returned to check on her within 15 seconds to give her support before she had the opportunity to call out or leave the room. On this first check-in, Nora was calm but appeared nervous.

On the second check-in, after approximately 30 additional seconds, Nora was visibly more anxious and asked her parents to promise that they would check in again soon. Per the initial plan, her parents responded (with prompting from the therapist) by encouraging her to do a worry exposure. Nora began to repeat "My parents won't come back." However, she interspersed her exposure statements with pleading that her parents take her home and physically grabbing onto them. At this point, the therapist intervened and reminded Nora that she had learned during the past week that repeating scary thoughts makes them boring. He also stated that if she wanted her parents to stay with her, she needed to continue her thought exposure. When Nora continued to plead with her parents, the therapist asked her parents to leave the room. Once they had left, Nora was more willing to engage in the exposure, although she remained visibly upset. After she had repeated "My parents won't come back" five times, the therapist praised her, asked if she would like her parents to return, and brought them back into the room when she said yes. However, soon after they returned, Nora again began to plead for them to take her home, and the therapist asked them to leave the room. Again, Nora was compliant with the therapist and repeated her distressing thought. The therapist provided frequent praise for her efforts and encouragement to repeat her thought in a more confident voice. After approximately 5 minutes, Nora's anxiety had decreased, and her parents were asked to return to the room to observe her successfully complete the thought exposure. At this point, the original exposure continued with the therapist and Nora's parents leaving the room.

The remainder of the in vivo exposure was uneventful. Nora's parents checked on her every minute or so to get an anxiety rating and encourage her to continue her thought exposure. When Nora's anxiety was at a 4 out of 10 for the second consecutive rating, the therapist suggested ending the exposure. This decision was based on his impression that Nora had accomplished what she needed to, successfully handling worry thoughts on her own, as well as on time constraints (nearing the end of the session). Following the exposure, Nora's parents praised her profusely for her efforts. They wrapped up by asking whether her fear came true and what happened to her anxiety. Nora responded that her fear did not come true (i.e., her parents did indeed come back) and that her anxiety came down, although she qualified that it only came down a little.

COURSE OF TREATMENT

The previously described exposure occurred early in the course of treatment and was a significant milestone because it gave Nora and her family hands-on practice on how to manage anxiety during exposures, whether planned or as part of daily life. Although Nora had completed thought exposures in preparation for the in vivo exposure, the thoughts in isolation produced relatively minimal anxiety in the absence of separation. In contrast, Nora's worry thoughts during the separation exposure were realistic and provoked significant anxiety. Her success managing her anxiety through direct confrontation of those thoughts significantly increased her confidence. Moreover, Nora's parents benefited not only from the opportunity to witness Nora succeeding with exposure but also from experiencing the effectiveness of using their attention to encourage small steps toward coping. Just like for Nora, her parents' direct experience of tolerating her anxiety without relieving it for her, and Nora being successful, increased their confidence in the exposure process. The week following the first in vivo exposure, Nora and her family conducted comparatively easier exposures at home with Nora playing in a room by herself with her parents close by. This presented a small but manageable step forward from her recent functioning. During the next therapy session, the therapist had the family repeat the same exposure as discussed previously. This time, Nora's anxiety decreased to a 0 out of 10 with minimal reassurance seeking. The family applied this success at home by having Nora do exposures to being upstairs by herself.

At the next session, number 5, Nora's parents expressed interest in beginning to work on her falling asleep by herself. To ensure that each specific stimulus contributing to anxiety around bedtime was addressed, the previous exposure to being alone in a room was repeated with the lights out. The exposure produced little additional anxiety but increased the family's confidence to begin working on falling asleep alone. More important, during the session, the therapist helped the family clarify the plan for home. Specifically, Nora's parents would follow the bedtime routine of reading to her in bed, tucking her in, saying good night, and leaving the room. As long as Nora was quiet, her parents would continue to check on her until she fell asleep. Based on their success as exposure coaches to this point in therapy, Nora's parents felt more prepared to fulfill this role than when initially discussed at the beginning of therapy. Nora and her parents were able to successfully carry out this plan, and after some fits and starts, she was consistently falling asleep in her own bed after 2 weeks. After she was confident she could fall asleep at the beginning of the night, Nora was more compliant with returning to her room if she awoke in the middle of the night.

As the family was working through Nora's bedtime routine, they began addressing separation in other area as well. In-session exposures included doing age-appropriate activities independently in public, such as riding an elevator or purchasing an item in a store. Based on her success with exposures in session and at home, the family began setting goals to separate calmly in daily activities such as school and dance class. Some of these goals included planned exposures, such as scheduling a playdate at a friend's house. Others consisted primarily of parents altering their response to anxiety. For example, Nora's parents gave her points for going to school calmly and cooperatively in the morning. If she complained about stomachaches or anxiety, her parents would offer to assist her with an exposure.

During the course of therapy, which included 10 sessions over 15 weeks, Nora successfully returned to all her activities and her resistance to school ceased. In addition, she became more independent with sleeping alone than she had been before the onset of her acute symptoms. She and her parents became more aware of small examples of avoidance (e.g., the basement) and more likely to tackle these items with exposure.

IMPLICATIONS

The role of Nora's parents in her treatment highlights some of the challenges posed by incorporating parents as exposure coaches. Specifically, there is an inherent paradox in expecting parents to coach their child through separation exposures, when their presence automatically negates the exposure. However, the ability of parents to act as exposure coaches is as important, if not more so, with separation anxiety as it is with the other symptom presentations. Children with separation anxiety tend to be younger and thus require more parental support to conduct exposures outside the session. Moreover, parents are physically involved in practically every instance in which the symptoms occur (i.e., separation from parents) much more consistently than with other symptom constellations, such as those involving specific phobias, peer interactions, contamination, or worries about schoolwork. As such, parents will by necessity continue to guide their children through instances of separation; the question is whether they do so in a manner that promotes independence based on the knowledge and confidence of exposure coaching.

The sample exposure described previously illustrates the potential conflict between exposure coaching and differential attention. When Nora's anxiety increased because of worrying that her parents would not return, her parents helped her conduct a thought exposure. However, her parents' presence during the coaching could have inherently removed her anxiety because they, of course, did not leave and never come back. In addition, as part of the separation exposure, Nora's parents would leave the room again after she successfully engaged in her thought exposure. Under those incentives, Nora has minimal motivation to be successful with the thought exposure because it would lead to more separation. The therapist addressed this problem by taking over the coaching and basing the presence of Nora's parents on successfully displaying calm, brave behavior during the thought exposure. This action shifted the incentives so that continuing to display anxious behavior prohibited parental contact. In response, Nora engaged in the thought exposure and was able to be successful. She was also able to generalize this lesson to the in vivo separation component of the exposure, in that her parents would check on her only when she was behaving calmly.

The potential conflict between parent coaching and differential attention can occur with all anxiety presentations, although it is most apparent with separation anxiety. This challenge typically occurs early in treatment when children require assistance learning how to complete exposures. During initial exposures, parents may provide a significant amount of support, illustrated by sitting with Nora and helping her repeat scary thoughts. This step is a transition from therapist-directed in-session exposure to the child being appropriately independent. However, from the beginning, parents (and the therapist) should use differential attention while coaching exposures. Specifically, if children appear to be resisting the exposure through excessive crying and complaining, parents should remove their attention, including leaving the room. Nora's parents put this into practice during home-based exposures to going to bed alone. When Nora complained about a scary thought during this time, her parents would recommend a thought exposure and then state that they would return to check on her progress if she remained quiet in bed. In this manner, Nora's parents avoided sitting in her room attempting to coach her through a thought exposure that was unlikely to be successful given that success would result in her parents leaving her room. This procedure, however, was based on a foundation of successful thought exposures completed with closer parental contact during coaching.

SUMMARY

The three cases presented in this chapter illustrate the application and issues related to the implementation of in vivo exposures for a variety of symptom presentations. In Chapter 8, we explore the use of imaginal and interoceptive exposures. However, as the cases presented in both chapters demonstrate, many patients' anxiety problems may require application of more than one exposure methodology.

8

Imaginal and Interoceptive Exposure Case Examples

In Chapter 7, we presented three cases demonstrating how to implement in vivo exposures. In addition to illustrating details of application, the cases also explored the broader issues of conducting exposures to situations in which one's fears come true, breaking down exposures into small steps, and incorporating parents. In Chapter 8, we continue our case presentations with a focus on the less commonly used and less intuitive methods of imaginal and interoceptive exposure. We follow the same format as that used in Chapter 7 for presenting cases illustrating exposure application with obsessions and compulsions, general anxiety and worry, as well as panic. As before, we end each case example with discussion of broader concepts related to implementing exposure in clinical practice.

CASE EXAMPLES: IMAGINAL EXPOSURE

Obsessions and Compulsions

DESCRIPTION

Peter was a 15-year-old 10th grader who presented with his mother for treatment of what the family referred to as constant anxiety. They described him as frequently worrying about harming himself or others. These worries were quite distressing to the patient and his parents because they were quite out of character for Peter, who was generally a kind and responsible teenager. His parents expressed concern that he was unable to be rational about these thoughts or accept their logical reassurances that his fears were unfounded. During the past few months, Peter reportedly had been isolating himself from friends and family, preferring to stay in his room alone watching videos or listening to music. More recently, his parents were alarmed when he stated that he wished he were not alive. Peter stated that he worried that he would hurt, specifically stab, himself or family members with a knife or scissors. His mother confirmed that he would often ask if she thought he would stab himself or his siblings and had gotten very

Exposure Therapy for Child and Adolescent Anxiety and OCD. Stephen P. H. Whiteside, Thomas H. Ollendick, and Bridget K. Biggs, Oxford University Press (2020). © Oxford University Press.
DOI: 10.1093/med/9780190862992.001.0001

upset one day because he thought it was dangerous and unnecessary to have so many knives in the house. When asked what other worry thoughts he had, Peter acknowledged there were others but stated he did not know what they were or how to describe them.

The family described Peter's distressing thoughts as having been problematic for the past 3 months but present to a lesser degree for an additional 3 months before that. His mother reported that throughout the years, Peter had experienced anxiety periodically, including episodes of excessive handwashing and worry about school performance. However, these previous bouts had not been impairing, and they had been resolved without intervention beyond parental reassurance and limit setting. The current symptoms had not resolved with a similar approach and instead appeared to be worsening. Peter described his worries as most upsetting when he was with his friends or family and not occupied by a specific activity. This had led him to avoid being in close proximity to his two younger siblings and to not attend a recent family gathering at which there were additional younger cousins. He stated that he generally felt better at school and other times when he could distract himself from his thoughts by focusing on a task, such as academic work or physical activity. In addition to avoidance, his mother reported that he frequently asked for reassurance, such as whether she thought he would hurt someone, whether any of the knives were missing, or whether his siblings were okay. She described these questions as seeming to occur incessantly at times and being quite stressful for her and her husband. When they would attempt not to answer his worrisome questions, Peter would be insistent, at times crying or becoming angry, until they answered. In response to direct questions from the therapist, Peter suggested that he had some neutralizing thoughts and actions that he engaged in to relieve his distress, but he was vague regarding their nature and maintained that avoidance and talking to his parents were his primary means of coping.

Earlier in the current episode of heightened anxiety, the family had consulted with his pediatrician, who had referred him to a therapist. The therapist had diagnosed his symptoms as obsessive–compulsive disorder (OCD), and Peter attended a handful of appointments. The family described the previous therapist as working primarily with Peter alone, although his mother was included at the beginning and end of each appointment to discuss progress. Peter reported that the therapist instructed him in a number of coping strategies that included breathing exercises, focusing on positive images, and bossing-back OCD thoughts. The therapist had also encouraged Peter to stop avoiding knives and discussed doing exposures to sharp objects later in treatment. Peter stated that he liked his therapist, but the family and the therapist were concerned that he was not making progress. Subsequently, they sought care at the specialty clinic.

CONCEPTUALIZATION

Based on the information gathered during the initial evaluation, the current therapist determined that a diagnosis of OCD indeed best described Peter's symptoms. The family readily understood the discussion of OCD as consisting of intrusive thoughts that provoke anxiety or distress (obsessions), efforts to relieve this distress through repeated actions (compulsions), and that because these symptoms interfered with daily life, they qualified as a disorder. The therapist then introduced exposure and response prevention (ERP) as the most appropriate treatment. He explained that Peter would need to do activities and think thoughts that made him uncomfortable, without avoiding or asking for reassurance, until (1) he learned that what he was afraid of was unlikely to happen and (2) he could handle his distress until it decreased naturally. The therapist also explained that Peter's mother (or both parents) would be involved in each of the sessions, learning how to coach him through exposures to help him be successful between sessions and after therapy ended.

When searching online for treatment options, Peter's mother had learned about ERP and was in agreement with the treatment plan. She also appreciated the opportunity to be thoroughly involved in his care and to learn how to respond differently when he sought reassurance. Peter, on the other hand, was skeptical. He reasoned that he was already experiencing these thoughts frequently, sometimes constantly, and he did not understand how exposure therapy would be different. He also expressed reluctance to work closely with his parents on exposures, which appeared to be partly an age-appropriate desire for independence and partly discomfort revealing the content of some of his thoughts. The therapist responded that these concerns were valid, common, and showed that Peter was listening, understanding, and appropriately evaluating the information. The therapist explained that one of the primary differences between experiencing upsetting thoughts in daily life and therapeutic exposures is what happens to make one feel better. Specifically, he explained that in daily life, people typically do not feel better until they escape the thought by distraction or avoidance, so they never learn the thought is not dangerous. In therapy, he continued, they set up controlled experiments in which people focus on the thought long enough to feel better *without* avoiding. This teaches them that the thought itself is not dangerous. The therapist also added that the ultimate goal was for Peter to be able to handle his thoughts on his own, and if he required less parent involvement than other kids, that would be fine. Peter remained ambivalent but indicated he was willing to give it a try.

During the first therapy session following the initial assessment, the therapist introduced the anxiety/OCD cycle to Peter and his mother together and worked with them to apply it to Peter's symptoms. Peter's intrusive thoughts of harming himself or others, as well as other yet undisclosed thoughts, were identified as the primary precipitating stimuli that set off his OCD symptoms. Objects such as knives and situations such as being alone with a younger sibling or his cousins were also identified as stimuli that set off his anxiety by provoking the intrusive thoughts. Next, Peter was able to identify a number of expectations or beliefs that made his unwanted thoughts distressing. First, Peter believed that the presence of these thoughts signaled that something bad was going to happen. Primarily, he believed that having the thought meant he was likely to do the action, perhaps because his thoughts would overwhelm him, making him likely to harm himself or his family. In addition, he believed that having these thoughts meant he must *want* to do the action, and so there must be something wrong with him or he is a bad person. As a result of these expectations and beliefs, Peter not only felt scared and nervous about causing harm but also felt guilty and as if he really was a bad person.

Peter and his mother readily identified his withdrawal as well as his efforts to distract himself with activities and electronics as avoidance. Although perhaps not as problematic, they understood how efforts by Peter to replace his harm thoughts with rational arguments that he would not act on them could also be avoidance. They also agreed that his questioning of his parents about his potential for harm and their offering reassurance that the thoughts were irrational constituted avoidance. Additional rituals to neutralize harm thoughts were minimized by Peter and not pursued further during the discussion. Finally, the therapist helped Peter and his mother identify imaginal exposures to the intrusive thoughts of harming himself and others as the primary mode of exposure. In vivo exposures to handling sharp objects and being in close proximity to his younger siblings were identified as additional, or adjunct, exercises.

The focus on imaginal exposures to the thoughts of harming others followed from the earlier portion of conceptualization that identified these thoughts as the precipitating stimuli. Because these thoughts were cognitions, it would be understandable to classify them as anxiety-provoking beliefs or expectations. Specifically, sharp objects could be viewed as the precipitating stimulus, and the thought "I will stab someone" could be viewed as the expectation that made a safe object seem dangerous. However, such a conceptualization misses the fact that Peter's thoughts were occurring without material reminders and that the thoughts were the primary source of fear. Moreover, such a misunderstanding would suggest that exposure primarily needs to be completed to handling sharp objects, which by itself is less likely to be effective. Another challenge in conceptualizing Peter's symptoms involved separating thoughts of killing himself that elicited anxiety from thoughts that he would be better off dead, which were associated with helplessness and sadness. Whereas the former are targets for exposure, the latter are suggestive of developing depression secondary to OCD. These depressive thoughts required monitoring and efforts to improve mood and instill hope, primarily through successful treatment of OCD.

PARENT INVOLVEMENT

Planning the involvement of parents as exposure coaches was also covered in the first therapy session and presented a few challenges. From the beginning, Peter expressed reluctance to work closely with his parents, whereas his mother found the opportunity for her to be involved a significant improvement over their previous therapy experience. The therapist explained the potential benefits of teaching Peter's parents to be exposure coaches. First, exposure therapy is difficult work, and Peter could likely benefit from parental assistance to regularly initiate and successfully complete at-home exposures. In addition, and equally important in this case, Peter's parents were directly involved in his rituals by providing reassurance and would need to learn a different way to respond to him that promoted exposure rather than avoidance in a manner that was supportive and consistent with his progress in therapy. Similarly, exposures were likely to include his siblings or cousins, and his parents likely would need to facilitate these interactions. Finally, Peter appeared to have intrusive thoughts that he was embarrassed to reveal to anyone, including his parents. Sharing these thoughts with his parents likely would constitute an important exposure for him to learn that he was not a horrible person for having such thoughts.

On the other hand, the therapist acknowledged legitimate reasons to minimize parent involvement. First, at 15-years-old, Peter was appropriately interested in being independent and old enough to meaningfully convey his preferences for the design of his treatment. Not respecting his preferences would likely increase his resistance to therapy. Moreover, given the nature of his symptoms, specifically that sharing some of his thoughts reduced his anxiety, parent involvement in exposures could inadvertently provide reassurance. Specifically, if Peter's parents were to coach him through exposures to his thoughts of harming others, he might attribute safety to their presence rather than the innocuous nature of the thoughts. As such, for treatment to be successful, Peter would likely have to complete exposures not only by himself but also without others knowing that he was completing them. The therapist clarified that the value of parent participation in the exposure depended partly on the expectations that lead to anxiety. For thoughts that Peter feared because they suggested he was dangerous, parental presence could function as avoidance by "preventing" harmful behavior. In contrast, for thoughts that Peter feared because they suggested he was a horrible person, parental presence increased anxiety and provided an opportunity to disconfirm his fears.

To balance the advantages and disadvantages of parental involvement, the therapist recommended beginning with modified parental coaching. Specifically, he recommended that Peter's mother, or father when he attended, practice coaching exposures during the session to learn how to help when needed. However, Peter could conduct exposures on his own between appointments with scheduled check-ins with his mother twice a week to ensure he was staying on track. Neither Peter nor his mother thought adding rewards or consequences would be necessary. The therapist and family agreed to pursue this plan as long as Peter was progressing. If he was not conducting exposures or experiencing improvement in symptoms, they would revisit increasing the degree of parental involvement and possible reinforcement for his efforts.

FEAR LADDER
The therapist built a fear ladder with Peter and his mother during the second therapy session. They began this process by reviewing the goal of exposure, which was to learn that thoughts are not dangerous in that they do not control his behavior or make him a terrible person. To learn the former, Peter would need to handle thoughts on his own, especially with objects and in situations that provided opportunities for harm, and see that he does not act violently. For the latter,

in addition to learning that he was unlikely to act on his thoughts, he would need to share the thoughts with others to learn that others do not shun him. Each exposure would consist of repeating the thought over and over either aloud or silently and recording his anxiety every minute or so. Peter understood that he must resist asking for reassurance or trying to neutralize the thoughts cognitively. The therapist also reviewed the difference between parent support and providing reassurance. If Peter's distress decreased and he did not behave violently, that would suggest that thoughts were not as dangerous as OCD currently had him believing.

The therapist then directed Peter and his mother to make a list of his intrusive thoughts, the situations that were troubling him, and other ways in which his OCD was causing problems. The therapist encouraged both Peter and his mother to contribute to the list because the perspectives of both of them were valuable, and it was fine if they disagreed about the importance of any individual item. Through this process, the therapist and family decided that it would be most helpful to create two fear ladders. The first listed the various thoughts that distressed Peter, and the second listed situations and objects that triggered thoughts or made thoughts more difficult for him to manage. This organization combined stimuli that functioned somewhat differently (i.e., precipitating fear vs. guilt), as well as separated thoughts from their related objects (i.e., harm thoughts from scissors) without specifying particular steps for combining them (i.e., repeating thoughts and then repeating thoughts while holding a knife). However, this strategy seemed to be the most concise manner in which to include all the items that needed to be addressed. The family felt confident that they could titrate the degree of difficulty posed by exposures through combining items as therapy progressed in the absence of a detailed plan.

As Peter began to create his fear ladder, it became apparent that adding thoughts to the list was upsetting and constituted an exposure in and of itself. As had been clear from the beginning, Peter had not revealed some of his intrusive thoughts to anyone because he believed they were too shocking and embarrassing to admit. The therapist explained that this difficulty was common and understandable. Over the course of completing the psychoeducation and creating his treatment plan, Peter had become more comfortable with the concepts of OCD and exposure therapy. As a result, he was now able to engage in a general conversation with the therapist regarding the undisclosed thoughts, which he acknowledged were sexual in nature. Because he was not ready to discuss the specifics of these thoughts, the therapist advised him to enter notes in the fear ladder that represented the different thoughts to him but were not interpretable to others. By the end of the session, Peter had a fear ladder to specific thoughts with a section for harm thoughts (killing a friend, stabbing himself, killing himself, stabbing a parent, choking his youngest sibling, stabbing his other siblings, and killing strangers) and one for sexual thoughts that included four unidentified items. He also completed a second ladder with objects (pens, forks, scissors, butter knives, and kitchen knives of various sizes) and situations (being alone, being with a parent, being with a friend, being with the family, and being with a sibling alone). The items were put in a general order of less to more distressing (as listed here), although Peter understandably had difficulty differentiating the difficulty level of some of his thoughts.

SAMPLE EXPOSURE

Soon after completing his fear ladder and beginning exposure, Peter conducted a series of exposures to a thought that was of moderate difficulty for him (i.e., stabbing one of his parents) that illustrates the general process through which his treatment proceeded. The first exposure was conducted in the office with Peter and his mother. It began with Peter repeating "I want to stab my mother to death." Peter thought that stating "I want . . ." was more upsetting than "I will . . ." because he did not have an object to carry out the thought in the moment. Peter rated his anxiety at the beginning of the exposure as an 8 out of 10. He allowed his mother to query and record his anxiety throughout, although he frequently offered a rating before his mother asked. The interval between ratings ranged from approximately 30 seconds to 2 minutes. He began by repeating the thought out loud, and his anxiety gradually decreased to a 5 out of 10. During the course of therapy, Peter had learned that silently thinking about and picturing a thought was more realistic, and anxiety provoking, than repeating it aloud. When he switched to this modality, his anxiety increased to a 7. For the remainder of the exposure, Peter alternated between out-loud repetition and silent imagination until he felt his anxiety had decreased to 0. At the end of the exposure, Peter was able to state that he believed it was unlikely he was going to stab his mother, even if he concentrated on the thought of doing so. During the next week, Peter practiced this exposure at home. He preferred to start with his father present as a safety behavior, but he was eventually able to complete the exposure with his mother alone.

During the next session, Peter was willing to add a sharp object to his intrusive thought exposure. Again, he and his mother conducted the exposure with direction and assistance from the therapist. Peter held a sharp pencil and said to his mother, "I am going to stab you with this pencil." The plan was for Peter to begin by sitting a few feet from his mother with the therapist in the room, gradually move closer, and then perform the exposure with the therapist out of the room. Peter believed he could manage the thought "I am going to stab you . . ." but that the thought "I am going to kill you . . ." would be too difficult. Because the immediate goal was to introduce the in vivo aspects of the exposure (the presence of sharp objects), the therapist agreed that it was acceptable to begin with a less distressing thought. With the therapist in the room, Peter began to repeat his thought while holding the pencil in front of him with his mother facing him. After his anxiety decreased a few points, he was ready to have his mother turn her back to him. During the next 5 minutes, he gradually moved closer until he was holding the pencil to his mother's neck and repeating his thought, alternating between repetitions aloud and mental imagery. Peter then allowed the therapist to leave the room so that Peter could learn that he did not stab his mother because he did not want to do so, rather than because the therapist was there to stop him. The therapist first returned to the room after approximately 15 seconds to query Peter's anxiety, which had increased significantly with the therapist's departure.

The therapist then left and returned approximately every 2 minutes to monitor Peter's anxiety until it had decreased by half. To end the exposure, Peter noted that he did not stab his mother despite focusing on the thoughts while having the opportunity to do so and also that his anxiety decreased.

COURSE OF TREATMENT

Peter attended 10 sessions during approximately 4 months. His initial ambivalence led to some missed appointments and extended intervals between appointments early in treatment. However, after 2 or 3 sessions in which he successfully completed exposures and then experienced a decrease in distress at home, Peter's engagement increased substantially. He readily engaged in exposures during the session and consistently completed them between sessions. Throughout the process, he continued to prefer to be independent from his parents, completing most of his exposures between sessions on his own. However, he allowed his mother to participate during in-session exposures and to check in with her mid-week to ensure he was progressing as planned.

As described previously, the therapist and family were able to complete psychoeducation in the first therapy session and fear ladder building during the second. The therapist then introduced Peter to the active ingredient of treatment in the third session by having him complete an exposure to the thought of hurting a friend. This was a contrived thought that elicited minimal anxiety and allowed Peter to begin with success. During the same session, he successfully worked on a version of the thought, "I will accidently kill my friend," that he actually experienced and found distressing. These introductory exposures were followed in sessions 4–6 by the exercises described previously for the sample exposure, including repeating the procedures with a knife after the pencil. By session 7, Peter and his mother felt confident they could handle violent thoughts. From this point on, Peter would complete an exposure to a new thought in session (e.g., "I want to choke my brother") and then would repeat the exposure at home in proximity to his siblings and other appropriate objects or situational cues.

The next goal in therapy was to address the remaining thoughts that Peter had not disclosed. As a result of his success addressing his violent intrusive thoughts, Peter was more confident than at the outset of therapy that he could handle the remaining thoughts. He began this process by revealing his thoughts to the therapist individually during session 8. During this discussion, he described having thoughts about touching others inappropriately and having sex with them. These thoughts were generally vague without specific detail. The separate entries on his fear ladder corresponded to inappropriately touching or having sex with different people (i.e., strangers, friends, siblings, and parents). The therapist responded that such thoughts were common OCD symptoms but nonetheless understandably distressing. Peter and his therapist decided that to address his fear that he was a bad person and would be shunned by others, it was important to reveal the nature of his thoughts to his mother, which he did during that same session. Afterward, Peter reported feeling considerably relieved and was confident that he could address these symptoms on his own through thought exposures and eliminating avoidance.

By the end of treatment at the 10th session, Peter's OCD symptoms were in remission. The frequency with which he experienced thoughts was greatly diminished. Moreover, when he had intrusive thoughts, he was able to dismiss them or realize they were "just thoughts" and not dangerous. When necessary, he was able to do impromptu exposures, which were successful. His mother agreed Peter was no longer asking for reassurance nor avoiding sharp objects or his siblings at home. The time he spent alone in his room also appeared to be age appropriate because he was interacting with his family and leaving his room when asked. Although his mother described him as managing OCD on his own, she felt confident that she knew how to help him conduct exposures and that he would continue to accept her support. The therapist then reviewed the likelihood that symptoms would increase from time to time and that they should be prepared to revisit planned exposures when needed. They ended treatment with a reminder that the family was welcome to return whenever needed.

IMPLICATIONS

Peter's case illustrates a number of principles important for the delivery of exposure therapy. First, the nature of his symptoms highlights the importance of an accurate functional assessment and conceptualization. As discussed previously, the design of an effective treatment plan centered on thought exposures was contingent on identifying intrusive thoughts as the stimuli that set off Peter's anxiety. These thoughts were contrasted with suicidal ideation based on an understanding of the precipitating factors and resulting emotions. Similarly, although not discussed previously, OCD harm-related thoughts must be, and were in Peter's case, distinguished from aggressive thoughts associated with actual risk of harming others. Specifically, the latter thoughts are precipitated by believing one has been mistreated and feeling angry and then the thoughts are followed by hostile actions or a desire to follow through on those thoughts. In contrast, OCD intrusive thoughts of doing harm are unprecipitated, or precipitated by innocuous stimuli such as the presence of scissors, and lead to feelings of fear and a desire to protect others from oneself.

A second point of discussion surrounds the delivery of the thought exposures. The content of Peter's thoughts—committing harm and inappropriate sexual behavior—would be distasteful, if not distressing, to most people. Accordingly, parents and therapists may be understandably hesitant to encourage youth to repeat such thoughts, especially when the content of thoughts is not age appropriate. Therapists should keep two principles in mind. First, youth can be encouraged to complete exposures to any intrusive thought they are having, but they should not be encouraged to generate more offensive thoughts. Specifically, if a thought has become entrenched in an OCD cycle of avoidance, then exposure is appropriate no matter how offensive or upsetting the thought is. Avoiding such thoughts places youth at risk for continuing to suffer. On the other hand, especially when working with younger children, therapists and parents are often

able to generate new, more extreme, content than that of the child's thoughts. It
is not necessary, nor advisable, to introduce a child to thoughts or examples that
they have not experienced already. The second principle is to always keep parents
involved. Thought exposures to sensitive topics will generally be more successful
if the therapist first ensures that the parent understands and agrees with the rationale and plan. It is often helpful to have such conversations outside the child's
presence to allow parents to freely discuss concerns at the beginning of therapy
and again when additional sensitive topics arise.

Peter's course of treatment provides a clear example of the traditional use of
thought exposures for the treatment of OCD. The next case example explores
how to apply these concepts to more routine worries in the context of generalized
anxiety disorder (GAD). In addition, we further discuss considerations for combining thought and in vivo exposures.

General Worry and Anxiety

DESCRIPTION

Sam was a 10-year-old fifth grader who presented for evaluation on referral from
his pediatrician who had seen him seven or eight times in the past 6 months for
various somatic complaints. The pediatrician suspected anxiety was influencing
Sam's physiologic distress and symptoms, as well as a reluctance to attend school.
At the initial evaluation with the therapist, Sam's father shared that Sam had been
a colicky baby, had some difficulties separating from his parents when starting
preschool, and tended to be stressed around anticipated transitions such as the beginning of each school year. Sam and his four older siblings had experienced the
loss of their mother in an accident when Sam was 7 years old. Sam had appeared
to have more difficulty with his mother's death compared with his siblings, and
his father described spending substantial energy checking in with how Sam was
doing and providing reassurance for Sam's many "What if . . ." questions. He had
allowed Sam to sleep in his room for the past 2 or 3 years. The family had tried to
transition Sam to sleeping in a room with his brother without much success. Sam
frequently came out of his room to find his father and asked repeatedly to sleep in
his father's room. If his father insisted he stay in his room with his brother, Sam
would be awake for hours before falling asleep. No matter where he slept, Sam was
frequently tired during the day, prone to headaches, and complained occasionally
of difficulties concentrating in class and while doing homework despite teacher
reports of solid academic work and attentive, cooperative behavior at school. His
difficulties seemed to have worsened during the past 9–12 months.

On questionnaire and diagnostic interview, Sam endorsed frequent worrying,
most days. Typically, he would try to push the worries aside, stay busy so he
would not "think too much," or seek reassurance from his father; however, the
worries tended to resurface especially during down times such as at night. Sam
was described as having many "What if . . ." questions and thinking the worst-
case scenario for "everything." His most frequent worries revolved around school

and sports performance (he played in a youth recreational basketball league), the possibility of break-ins or school shootings (although his home and school had professional security systems and no history of break-ins), transitions, and new/ unfamiliar situations and activities. With his schoolwork, he was perfectionistic, and due to worry that he would not perform at the top of his class, he would spend an hour longer on homework than his siblings did at the same grade level in order to check his work or rewrite answers. If he did not perform up to his high expectations in basketball, he would shut down and refuse to speak with his coaches, teammates, or family, even though all expressed expectations he need only give his best effort and focus on fun rather than scoring or winning. Multiple "What if . . ." questions routinely preceded upcoming transitions and in anticipation of doing something new or going somewhere unfamiliar. The family had recently taken a vacation, and Sam needed to know ahead of time every detail of the trip, including where they would be staying, how they would get to and from the airport, and what kind of snacks would be on the plane. At night, he tended to think a lot about how things would go the next day, and he would review in his head whether he had completed all his schoolwork to his standard. He expressed feeling calmer in his father's room at night. He would worry about things more in his room that he shared with his brother, and when falling asleep in that room after his brother had quickly fallen asleep, he would be alert for the slightest sound, worrying that someone might be trying to get into the house to rob them or hurt someone in the family.

When asked about the loss of his mother, Sam expressed that he missed her and was sad when he experienced major milestones without her. He experienced a variety of emotions in response to memories of her but did not endorse symptoms suggestive of complicated grief or post-traumatic symptoms. He worried some about how is father was dealing with being a single father of four children (although he reported no concrete evidence of maladjustment on his father's part) but did not worry about a similar accident befalling his father and was able to leave for school and stay home with siblings while his father was out without any more distress than his usual worries caused. Although he could be irritable at times, especially if he had not slept well or was particularly worried or stressed, neither he nor his father endorsed any episodes of persistently low or irritable mood.

CONCEPTUALIZATION

The therapist discussed with Sam and his father that Sam's symptoms best fit a diagnosis of GAD. Sam's father had been thinking of Sam's distress as primarily stemming from the loss of his mother. However, upon discussion, he agreed that although the loss was difficult and upsetting, Sam's current distress and functional impairment related to frequent and persistent worry about a broad range of topics, most of which did not relate to his mother. Although worry is a common experience, Sam had been worrying nearly daily and to a degree that worries were difficult for him to dismiss and led to difficulties sleeping, low energy, muscle tension in his neck with associated headaches, irritability, and concentration problems. Worry and his efforts to manage anxiety and worry made it difficult for him to engage in and enjoy his daily activities. After explaining this distinction, the diagnostic description of GAD made more sense to Sam's father. To Sam, the description of GAD was quite readily seen as fitting his experience.

The initial evaluation appointment concluded with the recommendation that Sam participate in parent-coached exposure therapy. This therapy was briefly introduced by the therapist as a way of facing fears that would "take the power out of worry." Basically, avoidance of bothersome thoughts can make them "a bigger deal." By spending time focusing on the worry thoughts through structured exposures, Sam would get more bored than bothered by the thoughts. Sam wondered aloud how exposures to his thoughts would differ from his everyday experience of having worry in his head. The therapist explained that exposure would be different in that Sam would be thinking the thoughts without distraction or other relief tactics so that he would have sufficient time to get used to and bored with them. Sam was skeptical but willing to give it a try in hopes of feeling better. His father expressed concern that the therapy approach would further stress Sam out but was willing to try it because the explanation made sense and efforts to calm and reassure Sam had not worked well. For management of somatic complaints, the therapist recommended lifestyle modifications such as improving sleep hygiene (e.g., refraining from screen use 1 hour before bedtime), maintaining regular daily physical activity, and redirecting attention away from physical complaints to daily activities and interests. Although they could spend some time on brief instruction and goal-setting to support Sam's implementation of these self-care recommendations, the primary focus of therapy would be on exposures.

In the first treatment session, the therapist presented education about the avoidance cycle of anxiety and helped Sam and his father apply it to Sam's worry. First, they identified triggers, or *precipitating stimuli*. Primarily, Sam's anxiety was set off by worry thoughts, such as worrying about school performance, not doing well enough at sports, or that someone would break into the house. Sometimes, the thoughts were associated with environmental stimuli, such as having an assignment to do, missing a shot during a basketball game, or sounds at night; other times, the worries seemed to pop up out of the blue. Initially, Sam had difficulty articulating beliefs related to these situations other than that he *had* to do "his best" at school, work, and sports. With more questioning, Sam verbalized that mistakes on his schoolwork would prevent him from doing well academically and qualifying for scholarships to attend college so that he would end up working in the fast-food industry and not be able to support a family. With sports, he feared that he would lose the esteem and respect of his coaches and teammates. At the therapist's prompting, Sam and his father agreed that it was accurate to summarize Sam's anxiety-causing expectations as (1) believing it was likely his worries would come true and (2) that he could not handle thinking about his worries for very long.

Sam and his father initially were not sure how *avoidance* applied to Sam's worries because he was actually highly engaged in his schoolwork and sports. Avoidance became clearer as the therapist explained the function of spending too much time on schoolwork (including checking and redoing assignments) and extra basketball practice as safety behaviors that gave him a false sense of protection against his fears of poor performance. Also, as they talked more about worries at nighttime and with unfamiliar situations and transitions, they identified distraction (e.g., trying to think of other things and using electronics) and reassurance seeking (e.g., asking his father for details on what to expect) as other safety behaviors that served the function of avoidance. Based on the understanding that worry thoughts were the primary stimuli that precipitated anxiety and identification of Sam's methods of avoidance, the family identified broad exposure goals of completing thought exposures to feared outcomes without distraction or reassurance seeking. In addition, he would work toward reducing time spent on schoolwork and practice completing schoolwork imperfectly, as well as set goals to transition to independent sleep. Thought exposures would be important not only on their own but also in accomplishing the latter two goals.

PARENT INVOLVEMENT

Sam was motivated and willing to engage in exposure therapy; however, like many young people seeking treatment for anxiety, his habits of avoidance and safety behaviors were strong, and having his father participate in therapy would be important for getting exposures completed. Furthermore, following the psychoeducation session, Sam and his father were more aware of how some of their interactions were part of Sam's avoidance cycle, particularly around reassurance seeking and reliance on his father's presence for comfort at night. His father also realized that although he was generally firm about expectations for cooperative behavior and followed through with mild consequences for misbehavior or noncompliance, he had relaxed expectations in situations in which Sam could become anxiously distressed or was feeling unwell. He expressed to the therapist a desire for guidance on how to be understanding and supportive without falling into the avoidance and safety behavior cycle. The therapist recommended that Sam's father participate in therapy so that they could jointly develop a fear ladder that defined expectations for gradually facing fears rather than avoiding. In addition, Sam's father could learn how to coach Sam through exposures so that he could practice being firm and supportive around facing fears. They further agreed to work on a behavior plan to solidify expectations around completing exposures and meeting functional expectations (e.g., adhering to homework limits and meeting independent sleeping goals), create a point system and rewards for meeting expectations, and implement mild logical consequences if Sam failed to complete a planned exposure or meet a functional expectation. Sam's father readily understood the concepts behind the behavior plan and expressed confidence that with the additional practice of exposure coaching he would be able to integrate the behavior plan for encouraging exposures and brave behavior into his usual parenting.

FEAR LADDER

During the second therapy session, the therapist worked with Sam and his father to create fear ladders to guide exposure therapy. The therapist encouraged Sam

to start his fear ladder by creating a list of worry thoughts that bothered him. As
Sam created this list, it became apparent that a significant portion of his worries
revolved around performance, so that was identified as one fear ladder. Nighttime
worries constituted another fear ladder. A third fear ladder list was made for "miscellaneous" worries that included various worries about bad things happening and
being unprepared for the unexpected when facing new or unfamiliar situations.

For the first performance-oriented ladder, the therapist guided Sam and his father to list exposures that would help Sam face his identified fears of poor school
performance leading to negative future outcomes and poor sports performance
leading to loss of esteem. This list first included the worry thoughts Sam had initially written down, in general order of difficulty. Because Sam expressed uncertainty about being able to tolerate thought exposures about negative future
ramifications of poor school performance, the therapist guided him to list more
proximal feared outcomes first and the more distal outcomes as higher on the fear
ladder. Because Sam's perfectionistic safety behaviors were interfering with his
ability to learn that normative mistakes are not harmful, the therapist encouraged
Sam to include exposures to making mistakes on schoolwork and during sports.
Sam was clearly anxious about these elements, but he eventually added turning
in a writing assignment with grammatical errors as a highly difficult exposure, as
well as easier exposures of making mistakes on a practice worksheet (not assigned
by the teacher) and then on a worksheet/assignment worth only a few points.
Following the therapist's suggestion, he added reduced homework times to the
list. Easier items included completing single assignments within a time limit and/
or without checking them and turning them into an adult for grading (parent
or therapist was easier, and teacher was more difficult). Based on his father's
estimate that Sam should be able to complete homework within 1 hour, rather
than his usual 2 hours, they included exposures of limiting homework time to
1.5 hours, then to 1.25 hours, and then to 1 hour. For sports, he added items
such as intentionally missing a shot (easier) and dribbling off his foot (more difficult). The therapist explained that integrating thought/imaginal exposures and in
vivo exposures would be important so that Sam could better learn that the worry
thoughts that he so often experienced were not harmful and did not forecast the
future. Furthermore, by purposefully allowing himself to experience feared negative outcomes that are part of the normative human experience, such as mistakes,
he would learn they were tolerable and also not to be feared. Finally, the therapist
explained that combining thought exposures with in vivo exposures would simulate Sam's usual experience of having worry thoughts during situations such as
turning in homework or making mistakes and help him learn that neither the
situation nor the thoughts are harmful.

The fear ladder for nighttime worries proceeded in a similar manner. First, Sam
listed worry thoughts he tended to have at night (e.g., intruders and creepy things
in the shadows) and integrated in vivo exposures of being alone in his dark room
while practicing worry thoughts, looking at shadows, and listening to creepy
noises, first during the day and then at night. As part of his nighttime fear ladder,
Sam and his father negotiated a transition to independent sleep that included first

sleeping on the floor in his father's room and then sleeping in his own room, initially with his father checking in every few minutes and transitioning to less frequent checking. The purpose of these exposures would be for Sam to learn that he could have thoughts of bad things happening at night and even feel scared and could handle those thoughts and feelings independently.

For the final "miscellaneous" fear ladder, Sam listed, in general order of difficulty, imaginal exposures to bad things happening (e.g., school break-ins and school shootings) and ways to practice handling the unfamiliar without reassurance seeking or getting details ahead of time. For the latter, Sam identified that he was worried that he would not be able to handle it if something bad or unexpected happened. Thus, fear ladder items included planning to go for an outing without knowing where, making plans and knowing that his father would change them, and going someplace new and not having information about it ahead of time. For each of these exposures, they agreed ahead of time that Sam's father would answer "I won't answer that" if Sam sought reassurance and that Sam would earn points for refraining from asking questions about the activity or seeking reassurance from his father from the start to the conclusion of the exposure. The exposures in this category were designed to further reinforce that Sam could experience worry thoughts and imagine bad things happening without them coming true, that he could handle the thoughts and distress independently, and to build his confidence that he could handle the unexpected.

SAMPLE EXPOSURE

Sam was eager to reduce stress related to school performance worry and started with several imaginal exposures in the first couple of therapy sessions. He also practiced these thought exposures at home. During the fourth therapy session, the therapist helped him and his father set up an exposure to his worst imagined outcome from a poor grade by instructing him to write out a brief (three to five sentences) story depicting his worst fears coming true. As part of setting up the exposure, the therapist asked Sam what he thought would happen. Sam said that he was afraid that writing out this story would make him so anxious that he would not be able to handle it or that the anxiety would never go away if he kept thinking about his fears coming true. He rated his anxiety prior to writing the story as an 8 out of 10. In creating the story, the therapist instructed Sam to write about a bad grade coming true. She coached Sam to write things in the present tense and change phrases such as "I would be" to "I am." Sam wrote,

> I get the assignment back. It isn't good. I got a D and the teacher wrote on the paper that I should have checked my spelling. Because of bad grades, I do not get into college and cannot get a good job. I turn into a grown up whose dad has to pay for everything and makes me live in his basement. I'm such a loser.

The therapist instructed Sam to repeatedly read the story aloud and asked him after every few times through to rate his anxiety, which started at a 7 prior to reading the story the first time and declined to a 2 after reading the story for approximately 15 minutes. Following this exposure, the therapist asked Sam if his fear had come true and what happened to his anxiety. Sam responded that his fear of getting anxious did come true but that his anxiety eventually came down and he was able to handle it, despite his prediction that anxiety would not go down or would be too high to handle.

After practicing this exposure between sessions with his father during the following week, Sam reported that even the more difficult thought exposures did not bother him much and he was starting to view some of the thoughts as "ridiculous" and not likely to come true. He expressed feeling ready to combine the thought exposures with an in vivo exposure but was clear that he did not wish to be pushed "too hard." He and his father opted to start with completing a mock math assignment with an intentional mistake. Sam asked the therapist to pretend to be the teacher and "grade" the assignment by marking which answers were correct and incorrect. Sam predicted that these actions would trigger worries about not getting into college; thus, he decided that he would combine the in vivo exposure with the thought of "Now, I won't get into college. My dad will have to pay for my things forever. I'll be a complete loser." Although he had practiced similar thoughts many times in the past several weeks and could identify that the outcome was not likely, Sam rated his anxiety as 6 out of 10 at the start of the exposure. His anxiety remained elevated at approximately 4–6 while he completed the assignment and turned it in. The therapist graded it, marking with red the two items answered incorrectly, and handed it back to Sam. Sam looked at the paper with the red marks and said his thought repeatedly out loud. During this time, Sam's anxiety reduced and he started laughing while stating his worry thought. Sam and his father concluded the exposure when Sam's anxiety decreased to a 1 and he appeared quite relaxed. Sam's father followed the procedure they had practiced for wrapping up exposures by asking Sam if his fear had come true and what happened to his anxiety. Sam responded that his fear of making a mistake did come true and that it did trigger the worry thought about not getting into college but that he could handle it and his anxiety decreased very quickly. He described that the anticipation was far worse than the actual outcome. Furthermore, he reported that because he had practiced very similar imaginal exposures prior to this one, he quickly became bored with the thought and even found it funny because after having said the thought so many times, he realized that the college admissions people would probably not care about or even know about this nongraded assignment.

COURSE OF TREATMENT

Generally a people pleaser, Sam tended to be more cooperative in sessions with the therapist than for exposures with his father between sessions. Thus, the therapist's support of the father's use of a behavior plan to reinforce Sam's engagement in exposures (and discourage his avoidance of exposures) was essential to maintaining his progress. Fortunately, Sam's father tended to be authoritative in much of his parenting and benefited from "permission" to apply his usual parenting approach around behavioral expectations to Sam's engagement in exposures in and between sessions.

Following the initial in-session exposures with mock assignments, Sam and his father continued to do similar exposures throughout the week, completing various mock assignments and having different adults "grade" them—including his teacher. Sam was able to report that making mistakes on mock assignments no longer bothered him and that he was becoming bored with thoughts about negative future outcomes for poor school performance. However, his father noted that Sam continued to do a lot of checking of his assignments, leading him to spend too much time on them. Sam acknowledged that he was still afraid of making mistakes on assignments that "counted." The therapist encouraged Sam to move forward with items on his fear ladder that limited completion time or involved errors on actual assignments. Sam thought that if he started with time limits, he would get hung up on whether he had made errors and, with his father's agreement, opted to start with turning in an assignment with a minor error and then more substantial errors and then work on homework time limits. They set up and completed these exposures in a very similar way as the sample exposure. That is, Sam identified the worry thoughts that would likely be triggered by the action and repeated those thoughts as part of the in vivo exposure.

For more difficult in vivo exposures, Sam followed the therapist's suggestion of doing a thought exposure prior to doing the combined in vivo–imaginal exposure. Knowing that reducing homework time would be difficult for Sam, at least initially, his father followed through with the behavior plan. He awarded Sam 1 point for each day that he put his homework away within the time limit. There were also a few times during this process when Sam's father needed to follow through with the planned consequence for Sam exceeding the time limit—that is, Sam needed to create an additional intentional error in the assignment on which he was working. After several weeks, Sam had reduced his homework time to 1 hour most days and reported feeling less stressed about his school performance on typical days. Because he had integrated some sports performance exposures between sessions, he also reported feeling more relaxed though still competitive in sports and better able to have fun. His father observed that Sam was quicker to recover from errors during practice and games and, as a result, was better able to encourage and cheer on his teammates. Sam reported that he noticed he was more stressed and likely to resort to checking and other safety behaviors when stakes were higher (e.g., more important tests and games) but believed that what he was learning through exposures was helping with the worries he experienced during those times.

As his distress around school and sports performance improved, Sam and his father turned toward nighttime worries and independent sleep. At this point, they were 1½ to 2 months into treatment and believed they had mastered imaginal and in vivo exposures. The role of the therapist shifted around this time from providing direct guidance in how to plan and complete exposures to serving as a sounding board as Sam and his father worked through Sam's hierarchy for nighttime fears and miscellaneous fears and worries. Because of the previous practice with imaginal exposures, Sam and his father easily designed imaginal exposures around some simple thoughts about break-ins and creepy things in the dark, followed by imaginal exposures to his worst fears coming true. Sam and his father opted to alternate between doing imaginal exposures only and doing imaginal exposures combined with in vivo exposures of being alone in the dark in his room while either looking at shadows or listening to creepy noises played on a tablet, working their way from easier thoughts to more difficult thoughts. After completing a few imaginal exposures of this type, Sam and his father started following a time line for independent sleep they had set up with the support of the therapist. Again, knowing this process would be challenging for Sam, Sam's father used the behavior plan to reward brave behavior of staying in his room and avoiding reassurance seeking, and they planned that if Sam came out of his room after bedtime, he would forfeit tablet privileges the next day. Knowing that electronics had served as a safety behavior and interfered with good quality sleep, Sam turned the tablet over to his father 1 hour before his bedtime every night.

Toward the end of this process, Sam and his father were feeling confident in their ability to complete exposures, follow the fear ladders for nighttime worries and miscellaneous worries, and use the behavior plan to encourage Sam's continued cooperation. As such, therapy sessions were spaced further apart, every 2 weeks initially and then once a month until they had met their initial treatment goals and could verbalize a plan for how they would use the skills they learned in therapy to maintain gains and approach relapse.

IMPLICATIONS

Sam's case illustrates several important points regarding exposure therapy for generalized anxiety and worry. First, many of the common fears experienced by individuals presenting with GAD do not lend themselves easily or naturally to in vivo exposure. Very often, individuals worry about events that are of very low frequency (e.g., break-ins), events that would be distressing to anyone (e.g., school shootings and the death of family members), or events that are distal outcomes to a proximal event (e.g., not getting into college because of a bad grade in junior high or high school) so that creating an in vivo exposure experience would be impractical, impossible, or harmful. Imaginal exposure is a very useful, although underutilized, tool for these types of worries and fits with conceptualizing GAD from an avoidance and safety behavior perspective. By understanding GAD within the avoidance model of anxiety, the worry thought is the stimulus that provokes anxiety because of a belief that the feared event is likely to come true or that the thought will create unmanageable anxiety that must be avoided or alleviated. Thus conceptualized, imaginal exposure is not just a practical alternative to in vivo exposure; it is the indicated exposure. To learn that worry and thoughts about bad things happening are tolerable, individuals with GAD must engage in thought/imaginal exposures repeatedly until the thoughts no longer elicit high levels of distress.

Conceptualizing GAD with the anxiety cycle brings to light how the process of worry in and of itself can serve as avoidance. That is, as an individual worries, she may jump from worry to worry, moving on to the next worry before the first worry can be fully considered or "faced." In our practice, we have observed anxiety sometimes remaining high during imaginal exposures that include multiple different worry elements or if the individual mentally moves on to other worries before completing the exposure to the first. In these cases, coaching the individual to focus more deeply and consistently on a single element and track their anxiety about that element can lead to a more successful exposure. Future, more challenging, exposures can then integrate multiple worries.

The avoidance conceptualization of generalized worry also brings to light safety behaviors that can be addressed through exposure and response prevention, such as reassurance and proximity seeking, distraction, perfectionistic behaviors, and even self-reassuring. Interestingly, the exposure and response prevention approach runs counter to coping strategies that parents might instinctively encourage and that therapists commonly teach in the treatment of anxiety disorders. Instead of challenging worry thoughts with evidence for and against, utilizing coping thoughts when anxious, or practicing various forms of distraction, the exposure approach is to purposely have the worry thoughts and imagine the worst feared outcome repeatedly *without* safety behaviors. Once the avoidance conceptualization is understood, it is clear that thought/imaginal exposure is necessary to learn that anxiety-provoking thoughts are not dangerous and can be tolerated and that commonly thought of "coping" skills can inadvertently maintain the anxiety cycle when they function as avoidance.

Finally, the case of Sam also illustrates that in vivo exposures remain an important part of treatment, particularly in terms of learning that situations that often set off worry can be tolerated. Sam dealt with some of the most common worries we observe in our practice among youth with GAD—that is, worries about negative outcomes stemming from poor/imperfect performance and fears of not being able to handle or tolerate the unexpected. In both cases, it was helpful for Sam to engage in actives that convincingly evoked his worries with the goal of learning that situations that trigger worry thoughts are tolerable. As such, combining thought exposures with in vivo exposure to situations that triggered worry thoughts (e.g., being alone in the dark, hearing creepy noises, and making mistakes) was very important to his progress.

CASE EXAMPLES: INTEROCEPTIVE EXPOSURE

Panic Related to School Anxiety

DESCRIPTION
Maddie was a 15-year-old sophomore brought in by her parents for evaluation and treatment due to concerns about school attendance. Prompting the initial visit was a notice from the school that the number of missed school days had triggered the truancy process. Maddie identified that extremely uncomfortable anxiety had been preventing her from attending school—initially a few classes

and then increasing to the point that she had not attended for the past 6 weeks. In seeking treatment, her parents expressed a desire for her to feel more comfortable in the school setting and wondered if homebound schooling would be recommended until Maddie started to feel better.

In gathering further information, the therapist learned that Maddie had historically been a strong and conscientious student who enjoyed the academic and social aspects of school. She had been involved in community theater, rock climbing, and playing guitar as hobbies. Within the first few months of ninth grade, Maddie started to express reluctance to go to school and complained of feeling vaguely unwell and uncomfortable. At first, the family attributed it to normative adjustment to high school and a particularly stern biology teacher (symptoms were first noticed in biology class). Maddie expressed feeling anxious or nervous but had difficulty identifying any specific reasons for anxiety other than worrying that she would feel unwell at school. Anxiety symptom complaints and visits to the nurse increased noticeably during her freshman year, triggering a referral to the school counselor. Maddie met a few times with the counselor, whom she said was very nice and a good listener. The counselor recommended distraction and using a grounding technique whenever Maddie felt anxious, and if that did not work, she was welcome to come to the office to see the counselor or take a break before returning to class.

When symptoms did not improve, Maddie's parents took her to a therapist in the community. For a while, Maddie diligently attended weekly therapy sessions and practiced diaphragmatic breathing and other relaxation techniques daily so that she could use them to manage anxious feelings when they arose. The therapist encouraged Maddie to "face her fears" and go to school anyway. They made plans for what she could do when anxious, and she carried around lists of skills she could use. Maddie very much wanted to return to her normal school attendance but struggled increasingly more to stay in school and over time to go altogether. Eventually, she verbalized that "nothing worked" and made many arguments for why it was better for her to be homeschooled. Her parents expressed uncertainty regarding what they should do. On the one hand, the family had always valued education, and they wanted to encourage her to stay in a brick-and-mortar school for both education and socialization purposes. On the other hand, they saw how distraught she was about going to school and did not want to force the issue for fear of putting her over the edge of discomfort she could handle and also for fear of coming across as "mean" or not understanding, which Maddie now often accused them of being.

During diagnostic interview, Maddie endorsed symptoms of panic occurring in rapidly escalating episodes that included increased heart rate, difficulty breathing, feeling hot and flushed, dizziness, and chest tightness. Panic attacks had been occurring since the fall of ninth grade, peaked at a maximum frequency of five or six episodes a day while attending school more regularly, and decreased to approximately three or four episodes a week since she had not been attending school. Maddie identified triggers to these panic attacks as being in school, thinking about school, or "randomly" (i.e., without apparent trigger). She reported that her main worry about going to school was that she would feel anxious to the point that it would spiral out of control and she would not be able to pull herself together. She had started worrying about missing assignments and the effect that would have on her grades as well as the potential for punishment due to truancy, but otherwise she did not worry excessively about school performance and had always been comfortable with the social aspects of school. Maddie noticed that she had begun to dislike crowds since her anxiety started, which led to her avoiding running errands with her mother and turning down invitations from friends. She told the therapist that things were getting worse because a few panic attacks had now occurred outside the school context.

CONCEPTUALIZATION

The therapist explained that Maddie's symptoms met criteria for panic disorder with agoraphobia. This diagnosis did not come as a surprise to Maddie or her parents because this had been the diagnosis provided by her previous therapist. When the current therapist recommended exposure therapy, the family grasped the concept of Maddie needing to face her fears to overcome anxiety. However, they believed that Maddie had tried to do so by attending school, an approach that had been unsuccessful because she continued to have anxiety attacks that prevented her from staying in school. The therapist acknowledged their concerns and briefly explained that to be effective, exposures would need to directly address her panic symptoms, which the previous therapy had not. The family indicated their understanding and agreed to return for a second visit so that they could learn more about anxiety and how modifications to the previous approach had the potential to be more successful.

When the family returned for the second session, the therapist worked with them to apply the avoidance cycle to understand Maddie's symptoms (Figure 8.1). Maddie quickly identified going to school and being in school as triggers for anxiety attacks. The therapist noted that, as is typically the case for panic disorders and based on the history she provided in the initial session, the primary precipitating stimuli were the panic symptoms themselves and that over time she had associated school with those symptoms and, thus, physical symptoms and school-related stimuli would both be considered triggers in her anxiety cycle. Maddie reported that when her panic symptoms began, she would have thoughts such as "Here we go again. The anxiety is coming. I have to get out of here!" When the therapist inquired as to whether Maddie's belief was that something bad would happen because of the symptoms and/or that she could not handle the symptoms, she replied that the latter was very much the case for her. Specifically, it was her experience that anxiety would not go away unless she left the room and that she often needed to go home to obtain relief. Other than thinking anxiety would not subside as long as she stayed in the situation, she had no other fears of what would happen during or as a result of panic attacks.

In identifying means of avoidance, Maddie acknowledged that leaving the classroom, going home, and refusing to go to school or other places outside of the home were all forms of avoidance. The therapist then provided psychoeducation on safety behaviors and how they function as avoidance by preventing her from learning that the situations are safe enough to handle without special precautions.

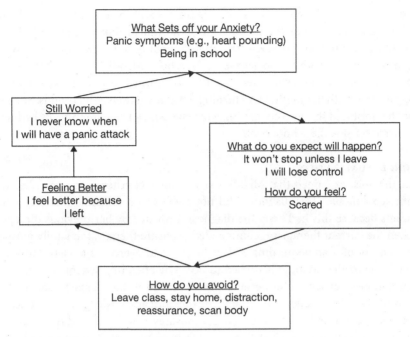

Figure 8.1 Maddie's anxiety cycle (panic).

Maddie and her parents recognized several of the examples the therapist provided as ones Maddie had been engaging in and had even been encouraged to use, such as distraction, reassurance seeking from the school counselor and parents, and mentally scanning her body for signs of symptoms. When the therapist suggested that relaxation exercises could also function as avoidance, the family was inquisitive because they thought this was a coping skill for managing panic symptoms. The therapist explained that relaxation exercises can be effective tools for physiologic self-regulation but that when used to try to prevent or deal with panic symptoms, their use can reinforce the anxious beliefs that panic symptoms are dangerous and need to be avoided. The therapist explained that the overall purpose of exposure would be to help Maddie learn through her experience that panic symptoms were not dangerous and that she could handle experiencing the discomfort of them. Maddie was notably anxious thinking about treatment in this way because she had doubts about being able to manage her panic attacks. In addition, she thought treatment was intended to reduce anxiety, not to make her more anxious. Furthermore, she verbalized that she did not think she could manage a panic attack without using relaxation. The therapist acknowledged her (and her parents') apprehension as normative and made it clear that they would create a plan that would break this task down into smaller steps.

PARENT INVOLVEMENT

Parent involvement was essential in Maddie's case for a number of reasons. First, her motivation to engage in treatment was minimal. She had become quite skeptical of whether treatment could help her, as prior interventions had been minimally effective. She liked the relaxation techniques and believed that she did not need sessions to help her with those skills (and the therapist agreed that would not be a focus of treatment). Further reducing motivation was many months of experiencing avoidance as the primary, if not only, means of symptom relief, albeit temporary. Her parents would need to be involved to encourage and reinforce her participation in exposures both in and out of session. A second reason parent involvement was critical was her parents' involvement in the avoidance cycle. By allowing her to come home or stay home, they had been facilitating avoidance. Understandably, they had felt forced to acquiesce to her insistence on being at home. If they did not, she would "lose it," becoming so emotional and anxious that she would curl into a sobbing pile on the floor and, when she was composed enough to speak, would complain about how they were "heartless" and did not understand what it was like to have anxiety.

Maddie's mother attended the majority of the subsequent treatment sessions with Maddie and explained that her husband's busy work schedule kept him from traveling to appointments. She described him as supportive but anticipated that much of the work would be "on [her]" because she was the one primarily at home with Maddie and her siblings. Anticipating difficulty in getting Maddie to subsequent sessions now that she had a better sense of what exposures would look like for her, the therapist met separately with Maddie's parents at the end of the first therapy session to outline a simple behavior plan for session attendance. The therapist recommended that they be clear that her participation in therapy was her responsibility and that if she attended and participated in all session activities, they would allow a preferred activity following the appointment (e.g., a trip to get frozen yogurt, "window shopping" at the music store, or undisturbed free time for 30 minutes after dinner). If she refused to attend sessions, access to her phone and tablet would be restricted until she attended a session. Consistent with the therapist's prediction, Maddie's mother called during the time of their next scheduled appointment and stated that Maddie refused to get into the car to come to the appointment. The therapist encouraged her to enforce the consequence of removal of tablet privileges. Unfortunately, follow-through was very difficult. When the therapist checked in later that week, Maddie's mother reported that she removed electronics for approximately a day but let Maddie have the tablet back early because she promised to attend the next session.

The day before the next appointment, Maddie's mother called the therapist again, stating that Maddie was refusing to attend. The therapist first confirmed that Maddie's mother continued to be concerned about the course that this was taking and the effect of anxiety on Maddie's school participation and engagement in life generally. Then the therapist reiterated the parents' main job at this point was to get Maddie to a session where she could complete exposures so that she could learn it would not be as bad as her anxiety predicted. The therapist recommended Maddie's parents be clear that if she did not participate in sessions, they would seek a higher level of care for her, such as an intensive outpatient placement, and that they would no longer call in to excuse her school absences unless she had a fever or clearly contagious illness. This latter point took convincing from the therapist, who explained that even if these actions led to truancy, the process would be uncomfortable but could also activate resources to support the parents in getting Maddie to school.

Maddie did come with her mother to the next scheduled appointment. Her mother reported with much relief that Maddie seemed to change her mind about attending when she overheard her mother contacting local intensive outpatient programs. Maddie's desire to avoid this type of program got her to the next several sessions. In addition to weekly therapy sessions focused on exposure, the therapist scheduled a parent-only session in which she worked with Maddie's mother to create a behavior plan that allowed Maddie to earn points for each session attended and each exposure completed (in-session and at home) and identified privileges that would be "on hold" if she refused to attend a session or complete an assigned exposure (i.e., no tablet and phone, no guitar, or no social activities) and would be reinstated after she attended a session or completed the assigned exposure. Furthermore, they clarified that school attendance was expected and made a plan for making staying at home unrewarding in that if Maddie came home or stayed home from school, she would be expected to work on schoolwork during school hours and privileges would be suspended until she completed an extra exposure as a therapeutic consequence in addition to her usual assigned daily exposure.

FEAR LADDER

In the second therapy session, the therapist worked with Maddie and her mother to create a fear ladder of exposure ideas to help Maddie target her main fear that panic attacks would lead to unmanageable distress unless she left or did something to make them stop. Because the primary trigger to her anxiety cycle was the physical symptoms of panic, the therapist introduced the concept of interoceptive exposures as a means of facing fears related to physical symptoms and learning that the symptoms were not dangerous or harmful. The therapist presented a list of common panic symptoms and activities that could be done as exposures to mimic those symptoms. She further explained that by purposely practicing a symptom or two at a time, Maddie could gradually test her fears about panic symptoms becoming unmanageable and not going away. Maddie was still resistant to exposures but was less argumentative about adding fear ladder items involving practicing one or two symptoms at a time. The therapist asked Maddie to use a fear thermometer (or Subjective Units of Distress Scale) to rate the anticipated distress for each of the listed interoceptive exposures that were related to her identified symptoms (e.g., run up and down stairs for increased heart rate, breathe through a cocktail straw for difficulty breathing, and wear a coat and face a hand dryer for feeling hot and flushed). Maddie rated them all as a 100 and then a 10 after the therapist reminded her that 10 was the maximum rating.

After building a fear ladder with the interoceptive exposure items, the therapist urged Maddie and her mother to add in vivo exposures related to school and going places outside the home. Maddie cooperated with adding activities she did as part of previous therapy, such as going to familiar places that were not school, including a store with parents or church-related social functions. Her mother suggested items she thought would be more difficult based on Maddie's level of refusal in avoiding them recently, including sitting in church for services and going to the movies or theater productions. Her mother added that she thought these were more difficult for Maddie in light of statements Maddie had made suggesting concern about getting out quickly from a row of seats if needed.

Of note, several times during this process, Maddie argued with her mother or therapist or simply refused to write anything down. The therapist coached Maddie's mother in utilizing differential attention through ignoring and continuing on with the fear ladder building on her own when Maddie refused to participate balanced with responding positively to Maddie when she suggested or rated fear ladder items. With regard to brainstorming school-related in vivo exposures, Maddie became tearful, curled up in the chair, and refused to respond to her mother's or therapist's inquiries. The therapist verbally recognized that thinking about doing exposures is often an exposure in and of itself. She added that continuing to avoid school was not an option and that having school-related exposures as part of the fear ladder was an important step for addressing anxiety related to school. The therapist encouraged Maddie's participation in the process because Maddie knew best what had been challenging for her in school and would make the most helpful exposure items. When Maddie continued to refuse to participate, the therapist coached Maddie's mother through this refusal by suggesting that if Maddie chose not to participate in this task, her mother would proceed with writing down her own ideas. Maddie argued and tried to interfere with her mother's engagement in this task, so the therapist left Maddie in the office and accompanied her mother to an adjacent room to write down a few ideas.

Together, Maddie's mother and the therapist came up with enough ideas to progress from easier to more difficult school-related exposures—for example, looking at photos of her school, sitting outside the school building, sitting in the office, sitting in an empty classroom, and walking down the hallway. To allow for school-related exposure practice during sessions, they identified exposures that could be done in the clinic setting, such as walking down busy clinic hallways and attending a patient education class. Once back in the room with Maddie, the therapist explained that they would work on exposures from the list, generally progressing from easier to more difficult items and eventually combining interoceptive and in vivo exposures. She explained that by eventually combining physical symptoms with being in school or school-like settings, Maddie would be able to accumulate the practice she would need to learn that she could handle the experience of physical symptoms across a number of settings. Because Maddie was quite firm about her belief that she would not be able to tolerate staying in a situation with panic if she was not allowed to use relaxation techniques to manage her distress, the therapist agreed that in their initial in vivo exposure work, Maddie could use those techniques and the focus would be on staying in the situation long enough to learn that she can handle staying there. The therapist noted that the interoceptive exposures would be very important for Maddie to test her fears about having the symptoms. The therapist predicted that Maddie may feel differently about those symptoms and the need to use relaxation to manage them once she had accumulated experience with interoceptive exposures.

SAMPLE EXPOSURE

The first few exposures were very important for Maddie's progress and started in the third therapy session. Again, Maddie argued with her mother about attending, and Maddie's mother again relied on the therapist's coaching to make clear that the alternative to participating in the session would be an intensive outpatient program and parents no longer calling in her school absences as excused. The therapist suggested starting with the interoceptive exposure lowest on Maddie's fear hierarchy—running up and down stairs to increase her heart rate. Maddie was reluctant and argumentative, but knowing the alternatives, she eventually complied with running up and down stairs as long as her mother did it with her (which her mother agreed to do). The therapist guided them through the setup of the exposure, including identifying the fear that would be tested and how anxious Maddie was that it might occur. Maddie identified that she expected her anxiety would be "out of control" and she would not be able to manage it. She rated her anxiety about starting the exposure as 10 out of 10.

Following the therapist's guidance, Maddie and her mother ran up and down one flight of stairs a couple of times. Maddie reported that her heart had started to beat faster and stronger. The therapist asked her to rate how closely her symptoms matched the symptoms she experienced during panic attacks. Maddie gave a rating of 5 out of 10, noting that the heart rate was somewhat similar to her typical panic symptoms but that she was not experiencing the other symptoms. The therapist also had her rate her anxiety about continuing, which she rated as a 9. When asked what brought her rating down, she said that after getting started things did not seem "as bad," but she was still certain that the symptoms would get worse and spiral out of control. Third, the therapist asked Maddie to rate her physical discomfort, as opposed to anxiety, while running up and down the stairs. Maddie settled on a rating of 8. With that, the therapist recorded both the physical discomfort and the anxiety ratings on a graph, commended Maddie for her bravery in starting the exposure, and instructed Maddie and her mother to start running again. As they ran up and down the stairs, the therapist prompted Maddie to rate her physical discomfort and her anxiety about continuing. Over time, the physical discomfort ratings stayed approximately the same (a 7 or 8), and the anxiety ratings gradually decreased to a 6 after approximately 15 minutes.

Session time was coming to an end, so the therapist reviewed with Maddie what had happened during the exposure. When asked if her fear came true, Maddie stated that it was very uncomfortable but had not gotten as bad as she thought it would and had not gotten to the point of being out of control . . . yet. She attributed the lower than anticipated discomfort to symptoms not being a true panic attack, although slightly similar (i.e., 5 out of 10). She recognized that her anxiety decreased as she got used to her heart beating faster and harder, although she still felt very nervous about the possibility of feeling worse. The therapist highlighted the importance of practicing milder/partial panic-like symptoms to build her confidence about handling symptoms more like her usual panic attacks, commended Maddie for the completion of her first exposure, and scheduled several appointments in close succession during the next several weeks so that they could accumulate a bolus of successful exposures in hopes that she would feel more confident doing these exposures on her own between sessions.

In the following session, the therapist led Maddie through the same exposure of running up and down stairs to bring on the symptom of increased heart rate. This time, Maddie rated her discomfort similarly, but her anxiety rating peaked at a 7 and reduced to a 3 in approximately 10–15 minutes. Maddie appeared relieved as she reported that it was not as bad as the first time. She expressed some doubt regarding how well this exposure would help her with full panic attacks because they were much more uncomfortable. The therapist acknowledged that practicing this one symptom was not the same as dealing with a full panic attack, but it was one step toward doing so. The therapist suggested moving to the next item on Maddie's physical symptom fear ladder, rapid breathing. The therapist led her through similar steps as with the first interoceptive exposure. First, she demonstrated how to hyperventilate, had Maddie and her mother practice doing so for 15 seconds, and asked Maddie to rate how closely the resulting symptoms approximated her panic attacks. Maddie rated symptoms as closer to the real experience, 8 out of 10. Her mother also commented how uncomfortable she felt, to which Maddie expressed delight that her mother could have some sense of what she had been experiencing. They then continued with hyperventilating for 30 seconds followed by a pause to rate discomfort and anxiety. They settled on 30-second intervals because Maddie was reluctant to do it for longer and experienced 8 out of 10 proximity to her usual panic symptoms with this interval. In this exposure, her anxiety rating peaked at 8 and decreased to 4. They planned in the next session to combine the two physical symptom exposures by alternating between running up and down stairs and hyperventilating for longer periods.

COURSE OF TREATMENT

Maddie continued to require contingency management to engage in exposures throughout treatment, and her mother repeatedly requested therapist support enforcing the behavior plan around session attendance, completion of exposures, and school attendance. Maddie's mother often referred to feeling as if she were "on her own" with Maddie, and despite efforts to engage Maddie's father in treatment or at least in supporting Maddie's mother with enforcement of the behavior plan, Maddie's mother continued primarily on her own. With much support and fairly frequent sessions (including participation in a 5-day intensive program), Maddie made progress such that she was attending school daily with minimal visits to the counselor's office (fewer than her usual one to three visits daily).

Maddie alternated between interoceptive exposures (gradually working her way up to the exposures identified as mimicking her worst symptoms) and in vivo exposures (gradually working her way from easier settings, such as going to the store, to more difficult settings, such as being in school). The therapist supported Maddie and her mother in working on a gradual return-to-school plan that followed the general progression of items from her fear ladder associated with being in school. As part of that progression, school classroom participation started with one class period daily and increased by one or two class periods every week.

During that process, Maddie's cooperation with exposures waivered following days during which she had panic attacks at school. The therapist tried to help her frame the experiences as everyday exposure to panic while in school and opportunities to learn that she can get through those experiences. Despite the therapist's prompting her to see that she had managed just fine, Maddie continued to verbalize her experience as "awful" because her fear of having "out of control" anxiety that had come true. The therapist acknowledged that these everyday exposures were more difficult than the planned exposures she had worked on up to that point, specifically interoceptive exposures in the safety of the office or in vivo exposures to avoided situations without inducing panic symptoms. The therapist suggested that it would be helpful to start integrating the two types of exposure, first combining the easier symptoms with easier settings and progressing to more difficult symptoms and settings. With much therapist support of her mother to utilize contingency management for engaging in these exposures, Maddie made some progress and reported feeling better about getting through panic symptoms at school.

One turning point in treatment occurred when Maddie arrived at one of the intensive program group sessions in the middle of a panic attack. She appeared unusually quiet, pale-faced, and focused on her breathing. She did not speak; her mother explained for her that she had started to panic while walking to the office from the car. Her mother expressed hope that the therapist would help. Maddie nodded when the therapist asked if she were experiencing a typical panic attack. The therapist expressed that they could turn it into an opportunity for exposure to full panic symptoms rather than selecting something else from the fear ladder as planned. Following the same procedures—by now, the therapist encouraged Maddie's mother to lead the steps with therapist guidance as needed—Maddie rated similarity of current symptoms to her usual panic symptoms as 10 out of 10 (indicated using her fingers); her ratings for discomfort and anxiety were also 10 out of 10. The panic symptoms continued for the duration of the appointment. Maddie's discomfort remained high (9 or 10), and her anxiety ratings declined initially to 7 out of 10 and then rose to 9 out of 10 when the therapist stated she should stay in the room in response to Maddie pointing toward the door to leave. Maddie did stay in the group room, her anxiety decreased to a 5, and she was speaking by the end of the appointment. Maddie was able to identify that although her fear of feeling uncomfortable did come true, it was unpleasant rather than dangerous and she had been able to function despite it. Her mother added that she had handled it well and differently than usual because she had managed to stay in the room rather than escaping to the bathroom as she normally would. After this point, Maddie continued to express discomfort with interoceptive exposures but appeared more confident with planned exposures.

As the frequency of panic attacks decreased, Maddie became excited about participating in the school play and was motivated to attend school so she could participate. Her mother expressed relief that school attendance was less of a battle. The therapist saw the family increasingly less frequently; appointments were canceled by the family, who sometimes cited conflicts with play practice as the reason for canceling or missing appointments.

After the initial treatment episode, Maddie's trajectory was up and down. She tended to have the most difficulty after school breaks and illnesses. At those times, her mother would contact the therapist and request return calls or appointments due to difficulty getting Maddie to attend school. The therapist would review the importance of sticking with planned exposures even when Maddie had started doing well and of maintaining the contingency management plan. In addition, the therapist continued efforts to reinforce that Maddie and her mother understood the concepts and encourage greater family independence implementing them.

IMPLICATIONS

Maddie's case illustrates the critical value of interoceptive exposure (IE) for panic disorder. Although Maddie had been avoiding school, and one could mistakenly focus on school as the precipitating stimulus, she did not fear school itself but, rather, experiencing unmanageable physical symptoms at school. Thus, IE was crucial to her treatment because she needed to experience physical symptoms in order to learn that these symptoms are not dangerous and that she can handle them. The in vivo exposures she completed in school, and other situations she had associated with panic symptoms, were important for her to learn that she could handle being in those settings. However, she needed to first learn that she could manage panic symptoms directly and then learn, through combining IE with the in vivo situational exposures, that she could handle panic symptoms in those various settings. Similarly, the case illustrates how multiple single exposures (i.e., running up stairs and hyperventilation) can be combined to create more realistic and challenging exposures (i.e., multiple-symptom panic attacks).

Unfortunately, as Maddie's earlier treatment history illustrates, IE is rarely used by clinicians. For Maddie, not receiving the indicated IE had untended consequences of not only delaying improvement but also undermining her confidence in therapy. Conceptually, the well-intentioned encouragement by the school counselor to come to the office when anxious and to utilize relaxation techniques, especially without the use of IE, likely reinforced Maddie's perception of panic symptoms as intolerable. Although her first therapist correctly identified exposure therapy as a fitting evidence-based approach for panic disorder, the focus on encouraging her to "face her fears" by attending school without use of IE left her ill-equipped to tolerate the inevitable panic attacks that occurred while doing so. It is understandable that therapists feel uncomfortable having their patients experience panic symptoms in sessions. In fact, therapists tend to overestimate the likelihood of negative outcomes, such as dropping out of therapy, decompensating, or losing consciousness, despite evidence that the approach is safe in most circumstances, and IE is actually viewed as useful by patients.

An additional concern is that therapists' uncertainty about IE can negatively affect their delivery of this technique. Specifically, therapists with greater concerns about tolerability and risk associated with IE may use less intense forms of IE (e.g., allowing longer rest periods between symptom induction or teaching controlled breathing and/or cognitive reappraisal during exposures) compared to therapists with more confidence delivering IE. Unfortunately, "low-dose" IE with breathing may be less effective than prolonged and intense IE because it provides less of an opportunity to learn that panic symptoms are tolerable. In the current case, relaxation appeared to function as a form of avoidance that prevented Maddie from learning that panic was not dangerous. The power of this safety behavior led the therapist to anticipate that insisting Maddie refrain from relaxation techniques during exposures could create a significant and potentially unsurmountable barrier to her participation in therapy. Thus, use of relaxation was allowed during initial exposures and then removed to make exposures more challenging and effective. The therapist continued to reinforce the concept of safety behaviors and encouraged Maddie to refrain from relaxation during IEs she viewed as less anxiety provoking to build her confidence tolerating uncomfortable symptoms without relaxation. The potential downside to allowing or facilitating use of relaxation or other symptom management skills indefinitely runs parallel to the discussion of safety behaviors elsewhere in this book: Patients may continue to believe that they need those strategies to be "safe" from symptoms and outcomes they view as threatening.

SUMMARY

The cases in this chapter illustrate the use of imaginal and interoceptive exposures. These forms of exposure are powerful therapeutic techniques that are the primary intervention for certain presentations of anxiety and OCD. For other presentations, imaginal and interoceptive exposures can augment the implementation of in vivo exposures. Unfortunately, these two forms of exposures are used infrequently. It has been our experience that many anxious children have symptoms amenable to imaginal and interoceptive exposures, and we encourage clinicians to add these valuable skills to their repertoire. We now turn to the final section of this book, in which we discuss common obstacles to delivering exposure therapy and where to find additional resources.

Troubleshooting

9

Obstacles to Implementation

The chapters in the preceding sections in this book presented the underlying theory of exposure and illustrated the delivery of exposure for a variety of clinical presentations. However, anxiety and obsessive–compulsive disorder (OCD) do not occur in a vacuum, and thus the delivery of exposure is often complicated by obstacles and challenges. As such, we turn in this final section to a discussion of additional issues that sometimes occur when implementing exposure. In this chapter, we discuss common obstacles to exposure therapy, including those emanating from patients, parents, therapists, and the environment. In Chapter 10, we review additional resources that clinicians may find useful to complement the information presented in this book.

CHILD-RELATED OBSTACLES

Exposure therapy is a collaborative process that requires cooperation and active participation by the child or adolescent. Factors that limit the child's ability and/ or willingness to engage in, and learn from, exposures will likely impede the implementation and progress of exposure therapy. Given the frequency of comorbidity, co-occurring behavioral and emotional difficulties are a common source of complication. Here, we discuss some of the more frequent child-related obstacles to exposure therapy.

Defiance

Children who are angry and argumentative are often resistant to engaging in exposure therapy. Sometimes noncompliance is broad, long-standing, and consistent with oppositional defiant disorder. These children frequently respond to requests and limit-setting with anger and arguing, regardless of whether the situation provokes anxiety. For other children, the pattern of general resistance to requests may represent a newer change in behavior that is best viewed as an adjustment disorder or perhaps a parent–child relational problem. Such behavior

Exposure Therapy for Child and Adolescent Anxiety and OCD. Stephen P. H. Whiteside, Thomas H. Ollendick, and Bridget K. Biggs, Oxford University Press (2020). © Oxford University Press.
DOI: 10.1093/med/9780190862992.001.0001

may have originated with refusal in response to anxiety-provoking requests and over time extended to noncompliance with general daily requirements. In either case, parents, and perhaps teachers, have difficulty getting the child to cooperate with simple requests such as getting ready in the morning, doing schoolwork, turning off electronics, playing well with siblings and classmates, and completing household chores.

Typically, defiance must be addressed before treating anxiety symptoms. Children who respond with arguing and refusal to requests to clean their room are unlikely to cooperate with requests to face their fears. Increasing compliance involves working with parents to implement behavior management strategies, such as differential attention, structured reward systems, logical consequences, and time-outs. Clinicians may need to begin with behavior modification techniques even if anxiety symptoms contributed to the development of the disruptive behavior. It can be helpful, however, to distinguish between children who display anger outbursts and resistance solely (or primarily) in the context of anxiety-provoking situations and those who are more routinely and willfully defiant. With the former, using the motivation techniques presented in Chapter 5 to increase engagement in treatment-related activities may be sufficient. Specifically, clinicians can encourage taking small steps, rewarding achievement of short-term goals, and removing attention and privileges for refusal or anxious behavior that interferes with facing fears—all concurrently with exposure. In contrast, when defiance and emotional outbursts are more extreme and extend beyond anxiety-provoking situations, therapists should consider beginning with a more comprehensive behavior management program or at least attending to such issues.

Distraction and Hyperactivity

The co-occurrence of anxiety and symptoms of attention-deficit/hyperactivity disorder (ADHD) can also complicate both assessment and treatment. Anxiety and worry can impair a child's ability to focus, concentrate, make decisions, and complete schoolwork. Young children especially may also respond to anxiety-provoking situations with overly silly, disruptive behavior. Conversely, primary difficulties with focusing, paying attention, or controlling one's impulses and behavior can result in academic problems and disciplinary actions that in turn cause anxiety. Accurately identifying the causal relationship between anxiety and ADHD symptoms is important for developing an appropriate treatment plan. If anxiety is primary, exposure therapy is indicated to reduce these symptoms, which in turn it is hoped should reduce the related attentional and behavioral problems. In contrast, if ADHD is primary, then exposure to stimuli related to poor school performance would be clearly inappropriate. Rather, the child should be given the indicated treatment and support for ADHD, which if successful should alleviate the stress associated with frequently poor performance.

Unfortunately, determining the directional relation between anxiety and ADHD symptoms can be difficult. During the initial assessment, therapists are encouraged to assess the temporal relation between the symptoms. For instance, if fear or worry is the root cause of inattention or off-task behavior, one would expect anxiety symptoms to be observable at other times independent of inattention and for inattention to be primarily observed during times of heightened anxiety. Conversely, if inattention is primary, one would expect anxiety to occur primarily in the presence of negative outcomes from inattention. Moreover, if anxiety is sufficient to cause inattention or other disruptive behavior, there should be other observable symptoms of fear and worry to confirm the diagnoses, with the opposite also being true for ADHD symptoms. A careful functional analysis using the model presented in Chapter 5 can help with accurate diagnoses. Finally, clinicians should also recognize that some children experience difficulties with both anxiety and ADHD symptoms that may or may not affect the presentation of the other set of symptoms.

Like defiance, ADHD symptoms typically should be addressed concurrently or prior to treating anxiety with exposure. As we discussed previously, distress in the context of untreated ADHD may be better understood as a stress reaction, as opposed to an anxiety disorder, and is most appropriately treated by addressing the source of stress as opposed to exposure. Moreover, untreated ADHD symptoms, such as distraction, impulsivity, hyperactivity, forgetfulness, and poor follow-through, can interfere with the delivery of exposure therapy as well as the child's ability to engage in treatment recommendations between sessions (Halldorsdottir & Ollendick, 2016; Halldorsdottir et al., 2015). When clinicians have difficulty discerning the relative contributions of anxiety and ADHD symptoms, it can be helpful to gauge the child's response to the most appropriate initial intervention and use that information to reformulate the treatment plan. For example, if a family has difficulty identifying items for a fear ladder other than situations that would be expected to generate anxiety in most children (e.g., having multiple missing assignments and frequently getting in trouble), it suggests exposure to target unrealistic anxiety-provoking expectations is not the indicated intervention.

Depressed Mood

The presence of depression can significantly interfere with treating anxiety. Exposure therapy is difficult work that requires perseverance and optimism that inviting discomfort in the moment will lead to relief in the future. Depression can negatively affect a child's ability to marshal these internal resources. The sense of helplessness and lack of energy that often accompany significant depression make it difficult for children to feel the agency to engage in exposure. Moreover, hopelessness and feelings of worthlessness can impair depressed children's ability to believe that their effort will be successful. In more severe cases, concerns regarding a child's safety due to suicidal ideation take precedence over other therapeutic activities, such as exposure. As such, severe depressive symptoms typically need to be addressed before exposure therapy can be effective. However, given the frequency with which anxiety and depression are comorbid, the presence of the latter is by no means a blanket contraindication for exposure therapy.

In many cases, anxiety precedes and is the root cause of depression. In addition to the direct burden of often feeling scared and worried, the avoidance that is central to anxiety disorders often reduces a child's participation in home, school, social, and extracurricular activities. The absence of these experiences, especially as adolescents become aware of the amount of enjoyable activities they are missing relative to their peers, can lead to sadness and more severe depressive symptoms. In these cases, treating anxiety through exposure is essential for relieving depression in the long term. However, in situations in which secondary depression has become severe enough to impede exposure therapy, those symptoms should be addressed first, regardless of the causal connection.

Treatment for depression is beyond the scope of this book, but it has strong similarities to that for anxiety. Cognitive–behavioral therapy (CBT) enjoys the strongest evidence base for both, with increasing support for the primary importance of behavioral components for both conditions (Arora, Baker, Marchette, & Stark, 2019; Weersing, Jeffreys, Do, Schwartz, & Bolano, 2017). Whereas therapy for anxiety hinges on the completion of exposures, depression treatment primarily involves behavioral activation (i.e., scheduling and engaging in pleasant activities that improve mood). Additional coping and cognitive strategies are also included to increase a child's ability to manage her mood. At their core, exposure and behavioral activation both involve improving symptoms through participating in activities that have been avoided because of negative affect. Perhaps the most important distinction for our current purposes is the role of fear and worry. When planning behavior activation to reduce depression in preparation for exposure, the chosen pleasant activities will likely need to be limited initially to those that cause minimal anxiety. For example, a child with depression and social anxiety might be encouraged to increase enjoyable activities with her family at home and social interactions with a few close friends. Once the child's mood has improved sufficiently to restore hope and personal agency, exposures to more challenging social interactions (that also function as behavioral activation) can be further pursued.

Autism Spectrum Symptoms

Given the increasing frequency with which children are diagnosed with autism spectrum disorder (ASD), clinicians are likely to see these children for anxiety treatment. Comorbid ASD symptoms present complications surrounding diagnosis and treatment. As discussed previously, anxiety disorders, for which exposure is appropriate, involve exaggerated fear or worry in response to a generally safe stimulus. In contrast, stress, for which exposure is not appropriate, involves expectable levels of anxiety in response to current or recent upsetting life circumstances. Differentiating anxiety disorders from life stress can be challenging in children with ASD symptoms because daily life for these children can be very stressful. For example, a child with ASD symptoms may be very anxious around peers because he does not understand the unspoken or nonverbal aspects of interpersonal interactions nor have the skills to navigate the give and take of a conversation. Because his anxiety accurately reflects the likelihood that peer situations will end poorly, treatment should be designed to improve his social skills rather than face his fear of social mishaps. Additional diagnostic questions can surround the emotions associated with a given behavior. For example, a child with ASD symptoms may be withdrawn and play by himself because of a lack of interest in others rather than social anxiety. Or, the child may engage in repetitive or rigid behaviors, such as hand flapping or nonfunctional routines, because these are self-stimulating or enjoyable activities, as opposed to OCD rituals to prevent feared outcomes.

Children with ASD or related symptoms may certainly experience anxiety that is independent of skill deficits or is excessive after accounting for the skills deficits that are present. In these cases, exposure-based treatment is appropriate and indicated. However, ASD traits can complicate treatment, and clinicians should prepare to work with these patients effectively. First, skill deficits should be addressed. For instance, a child with social anxiety and ASD symptoms may need more assistance generating questions prior to a conversation exposure than would a similar-aged peer without ASD. Moreover, youth with ASD symptoms may require additional structure to guide their learning from exposures. Difficulty reading social cues, heightened sensory sensitivity, and cognitive inflexibility can interfere with a child's ability to recognize that a feared outcome did not occur, tolerate anxiety during exposure, or change her expectations in response to exposures. As a result, progress may be slower and require additional time devoted to preparing for and learning from exposure. However, exposure-based CBT programs have been found to be successful for children with ASD (Ung, Selles, Small, & Storch, 2015).

Developmental Level

A child's developmental level, whether or not it is consistent with his chronological age, can present a variety of challenges within treatment. As with ASD-related symptoms, developmental delays can lead to anxiety that is better characterized as environmental stress rather than as an anxiety disorder. For instance, a child who experiences frequent failure at school, both academically and socially, due to intellectual abilities below those of her same-age peers may understandably experience anxiety, but which would be inappropriate for exposure therapy. Moreover, although exposure is a behavioral exercise, as discussed in Chapter 2, symptom change is thought to be learning based as opposed to a more passive habituation process as was once believed. Youth are actively involved in the cognitive tasks of identifying fear-provoking expectations, evaluating whether exposure experiences support or refute those expectations, and generalizing those experiences to other settings. Because such tasks will likely be more difficult for young children and youth with developmental delays, clinicians may need to modify their delivery of exposure accordingly. For instance, the pace of therapy may be slower, or the role of parents guiding exposures outside of session may be especially important. In addition, less intuitive forms of exposure, such as worry or interoceptive exposures, may need increased explanation. Finally, more emphasis may need to be placed on tangible rewards and behavior management strategies. Fortunately, such modifications are possible, and exposure-based therapy is often successful with very young children and youth with developmental disabilities (Freeman et al., 2008; Obler & Terwilliger, 1970; Rudy, Zavrou, Storch, & Lewin, 2017).

PARENT-RELATED OBSTACLES

Parents are intricately involved in the development and maintenance of their child's anxiety symptoms. The established pattern of interaction between parent and child will affect progress whether or not the clinician directly includes parents in the delivery of treatment. Consequently, as we have suggested throughout this volume, we encourage therapists to work with children and parents together to teach them how to engage in exposure exercises as a team and integrate those principles into daily life. We assume that all parents have their child's best interests at heart and are open to learning a new approach to managing anxiety. However, parenting a child with anxiety can be difficult, and parent-coached exposure therapy can be challenging for youth and their parents. We now turn our attention to some parent-related issues that can arise during treatment.

Overaccommodation

Parents naturally respond to their child's anxiety and distress with nurturance and caretaking. This is an appropriate response that provides children the support they need to manage new and challenging situations and prevents anxiety from bringing daily life to a standstill. However, as discussed previously, when a child's anxiety becomes problematic because it is excessive and misdirected, efforts by parents to soothe and accommodate inadvertently maintain, rather than reduce, that anxiety over time. Helping parents recognize excessive accommodation and replace it with exposure coaching is a standard component of therapy. Including parents in in-session exposure provides an opportunity for them to directly address their own anxiety about their child's ability to be successful—essentially a parental exposure. At times, this process can be especially difficult for parents and impede progress.

Anxious children often have anxious parents, and a parent's own problematic anxiety can interfere with addressing accommodation patterns. When a parent has fears or worries similar in nature to those of the child's, she may have more difficulty recognizing when the child's fears, and her response to the child's fears, are unreasonable and in need of change. Alternatively, a parent's general worry, or difficulties tolerating distress, may make it exceedingly difficult for him to allow his child to be anxious without intervening. Parental anxiety may present early in treatment in the form of hesitancy or resistance to engage in exposure therapy. Other times, parents may agree with the treatment plan but have difficulty executing the appropriate response in the moment. In response, clinicians should normalize the parent's concern and make efforts to avoid blaming the parent for the child's symptoms or lack of progress. Communicating that parental uncertainty is expected, appropriate, and directly addressed through their participation in treatment can be helpful. Occasionally, it may be necessary to encourage parents to seek treatment for their own anxiety. Participating in their child's treatment and observing the positive effects can also inspire parents to seek exposure therapy for themselves.

Overenthusiasm

Parents often feel enthusiastic about the potential for their child's anxiety to improve through exposure therapy. Moreover, taking an active role in their child's treatment can be empowering, and virtually all parents want to help their child get better as quickly as possible. Although these responses are for the most part positive and to be encouraged, clinicians should be prepared to reign in overenthusiastic parent exposure coaches. For instance, parents, especially if they are not anxious themselves, may underestimate how challenging seemingly manageable exposures are for their child. As a result, they may propose beginning treatment with items from the fear ladder that are too difficult and unlikely for the child to complete. Or they may push their child to move up the fear ladder more quickly than the child is prepared for. As a result, children may resist engaging in exposures or may cooperate, out of an abundance of compliance, but not be afforded sufficient time and support to process their emotional response and learn from the exposures. Similarly, parents at times respond to early success during an exposure exercise with thoughtful ideas for how to immediately increase the degree of challenge. In response, children can feel "punished" for being successful, or they can simply feel irritated.

Parental overenthusiasm is often well intentioned and a sign that parents are involved and actively trying to implement the therapist's direction. As such, clinicians should respond with education and efforts to temper, rather than extinguish, the parent's behavior. Specifically, clinicians can encourage parents to adhere more closely to the fear ladder, which presents exposure exercises in a general order of increasing difficulty. Parents can also be encouraged to base their expectations on the child's recent level of performance and suggest exposures that represent only small increases. Parents should also be encouraged to specify, as clearly as possible, and adhere to what constitutes successful completion of a given exposure. If the task proves to be easier than expected, parents can certainly suggest methods for increasing the difficulty, but those suggestions are optional and not required. The child should be allowed to decline changes suggested midstream while still being successful. In general, from the beginning, clinicians should validate parents' understandable desire for their child to progress and improve as quickly as possible, while also encouraging parents to be patient.

Sources of Stress

Despite the emphasis we have placed on refraining from attributing a child's anxiety symptoms or lack of progress to parental factors, there are times when parents' behavior is a significant contributor to the genesis or maintenance of their child's distress. In these circumstances, the child's symptoms often should be viewed as resulting from environmental stress and as not being an appropriate target for exposure therapy. In the most extreme cases of abuse or mistreatment, the clinician should ensure the child's safety and implement the appropriate mandated-reporting mechanisms. In less severe situations, when parents have difficulty providing a stable and predictable setting for their child, perhaps due to their own mental health or other issues, therapists may work with the family to voluntarily connect with county or home-based services. Tension between parents, whether living together or separated, can be a significant source of stress for children through being exposed to conflict, being placed in the middle of parental disagreements, having to navigate inconsistent behavioral expectations, or filtering negative information about one parent provided by the other. In such instances, the clinician can encourage the parents to seek couples counseling, mediation, or legal assistance as appropriate for their situation. Finally, parents may contribute to stress through unreasonable expectations. When parents demand unattainably high levels of achievement in school or other activities, children may respond with anxiety and/or resentment. In all of these circumstances, adverse elements in the child's family circumstances should likely be viewed as either the source of the child's anxiety that needs to be addressed directly or perhaps a complicating factor that needs to be improved before exposure therapy for unreasonable fears and worries can be implemented.

Parent-related stress can also complicate the delivery of exposure therapy with youth. Parent-coached exposure therapy involves parents managing their own fears and frustrations, maintaining patience, and providing warm support for small steps by the child that can seem miniscule to the parent. A parent's ability to engage in these tasks can be impeded by a variety of factors, including a history of frustration and conflict with the child, other parenting responsibilities, unrelated family or financial strains, lack of emotional support, and marital conflict. As a result, parents at times may respond to their child with frustration, by arguing with the child, or with a lack of warmth. Such actions not only make it more difficult for a child to participate in exposure therapy but also cause additional distress. In such circumstances, clinicians should attempt to understand and address stressors that the parent is experiencing and encourage the use of parenting techniques to increase positive parent–child interactions, such as special time, praise, and reward systems. In other cases, the non-coaching parent may be perceived as a source of stress. For example, a child who is accompanied to therapy by her mother might have "talking to Dad" on her fear ladder. In cases such as this, the therapist should work with the family to determine the degree to which these fears reflect an accurate reaction to the father's behavior (e.g., yelling) versus an anxious overreaction (e.g., Dad's deeper and louder voice). The therapist can then help the family implement the appropriate balance between exposure and changing family interaction patterns.

THERAPIST-RELATED OBSTACLES

Exposure therapy begins with the therapist. Implementing exposure therapy requires the therapist to correctly assess the child's symptoms, know that exposure is the appropriate treatment and how to implement it, and choose to use exposure and deliver it well. Here, we explore obstacles to exposure therapy that reside with the clinician.

Misdiagnosis

For therapy to be effective, the treatment modality needs to match the patient's presenting problem and goals for treatment. If the treatment and diagnosis do not match, the intervention is likely to be unsuccessful and unsatisfying for both the family and the clinician. A negative treatment experience can leave a child symptomatic and discourage a family from continuing to pursue help. Moreover, if a therapist perceives that his delivery of a treatment modality ended unsuccessfully, he will be less likely to use that modality again, even if it is the most appropriate intervention for a future patient. One common misdiagnosis concerns the difference between environmental stress and an anxiety disorder, a topic we have discussed throughout this book. Few therapists would likely recommend exposure therapy for a child currently experiencing stressful life events, such as bullying or mistreatment. However, confusing anxiety disorders with environmental stress has the potential to erode the therapist's focus on exposure. First, if therapists perceive that exposure is recommended for their patients experiencing environmental stress, they may dismiss this advice as incompatible with their practice, including for patients with anxiety disorders. Alternatively, therapists may generalize the appropriate use of coping strategies with environmental stress cases to youth with anxiety disorders, diluting their use of exposure. As such, it is important for clinicians to bear in mind the difference between anxiety disorders and environmental stress.

Clinicians may also diagnose anxiety to fill the void from lack of another diagnosis. For example, a child with difficulties focusing at school may be diagnosed with anxiety because he does not meet full criteria for ADHD–inattentive type and gets upset about unfinished schoolwork. In this case, the symptoms may be better conceptualized as subclinical inattention with secondary stress related to the consequences of incomplete work. Alternatively, persistent requests for desired items, such as being allowed to go to a friend's house, and refusal to accept "no" might be diagnosed as OCD (because of repetitive behavior) or general worry (because of concern about what is going to happen in the future). Of course, these behaviors are likely better conceptualized as disruptive behavior or noncompliance, whether or not the child meets criteria for oppositional defiant disorder. In cases such as these, misdiagnosis may reflect a misunderstanding of the child's symptoms or the nature of anxiety by the clinician, a desire to provide a clear diagnosis for ambiguous or subclinical symptoms, or an attempt to give a more socially acceptable diagnosis (i.e., the child is acting out of fear rather than disobedience). Regardless, a diagnosis of anxiety must be based on the positive identification of symptoms consistent with the disorder as well as a cogent functional analysis rather than the absence of symptoms confirming other differential diagnoses.

Lack of an accurate functional analysis can also contribute to misdiagnosis. As indicated in Chapter 5, anxiety disorders are characterized by benign stimuli and unrealistic expectations that provoke anxiety, which are relieved through avoidance, ritual, or safety behavior. Observed behaviors in the absence of the accompanying emotions likely represent another disorder. For example, avoidance of social interaction that is preceded by lack of interest and followed by satisfaction with solitary play is likely more related to ASD-type symptoms than to anxiety. The same would be true for repetitive behaviors that cause enjoyment to reduce boredom or that express excitement. Similarly, thoughts of suicide that occur when a child is very sad and lead to a sense of resignation that death is the only solution are depressive in nature and should be responded to by ensuring the child's safety. Alternatively, a child's thoughts of killing his mother that are precipitated by seeing a knife despite a neutral mood, and prompt the child to frantically confess these thoughts to his mother so she will reassure him that he would not do it, are probably OCD in nature. Misdiagnoses such as the ones illustrated here are more likely to occur when clinicians rely solely on categorical diagnoses rather than attempting to understand the function of the behavior and its dimensionality.

Crowding Out

As introduced previously in this book, exposure is most commonly presented in a multicomponent CBT package. In addition, other treatments have some empirical support (e.g., acceptance and commitment therapy), and new exciting treatment approaches often come to therapists' attention before they can be empirically established. As a result, therapists can feel a strong pull to augment exposure with additional techniques from CBT, other approaches, or nonspecific therapeutic principles. In fact, therapists are more likely to use CBT coping strategies (e.g., relaxation and cognitive techniques), mindfulness, and thought stopping than exposure (Whiteside, Deacon, Benito, & Stewart, 2016). Even when clinicians have the intention of applying exposure to a child's symptoms after other preparatory activities, they may run out of time given the short nature of real-world therapy (Whiteside et al., 2016). As such, clinicians should have a clear focus on beginning exposure as early as possible with families and minimizing the use of other techniques.

We encourage therapists to feel comfortable beginning in-session exposure by the second or third treatment session (Whiteside et al., 2015). As discussed previously, it is typically not necessary to spend time implementing relaxation, cognitive strategies, or mindfulness techniques before exposure. In addition, a warm therapeutic relationship can be established while providing psychoeducation, and thus separate rapport-building exercises, such as games, are generally unnecessary. Clinicians should also carefully evaluate whether there is added benefit to pursuing an eclectic approach. Augmenting exposure with other techniques, whether mindfulness, eye movements, or biofeedback, should be based on a clear conceptualization for why exposure alone has not been, or is unlikely to be, effective. It is our experience that if a diagnosis of anxiety or OCD is based on a well-formulated functional analysis, additional therapeutic techniques are rarely needed. When clinicians decide to forgo exposure, it may reflect their own anxiety and negative beliefs rather than characteristics of the patient (Meyer, Farrell, Kemp, Blakey, & Deacon, 2014; Whiteside, Deacon, et al., 2016).

Timidity

Exposure is thought to be most effective when the child's expectations of danger are as thoroughly and clearly challenged and disconfirmed as possible. To accomplish this, therapists may need to help families plan exposures in which the child completes activities without direct adult support that are more challenging than everyday experience. Such activities can stretch the comfort level of therapists, especially those new to exposure. Feeling uncomfortable with exposure can lead therapists to deliver it more cautiously, such as by planning and selecting less challenging activities or by attempting to minimize the patient's anxiety during the exposure (Farrell, Deacon, Kemp, Dixon, & Sy, 2013). As a result, the child will not be provided the experience to learn that she can handle the most challenging situations independently and is at risk for continuing to experience excessive fear and worry.

When deciding whether an exposure is appropriate, we encourage therapists to consider if it represents a situation that similar-aged youth could be expected to handle. For example, although children do not specifically grasp a door handle and then rub the germs on their faces, the sequence of events of opening a door and then touching one's face or eating a finger food happens frequently. Similarly, although adolescents do not intentionally order food that is clearly not on a restaurant's menu, most people ask questions or make statements that they realize after the fact were unnecessary. To increase their confidence, clinicians are encouraged to consult with other exposure therapists. Finally, clinicians should keep in mind that exposure therapy does not lead to more dropouts than other forms of psychotherapy and that patients are often open to exposure even though they know it will be challenging (Meyer et al., 2014). We have had multiple children state that although they did not enjoy exposure therapy, they believe it was just what they needed.

ENVIRONMENT-RELATED OBSTACLES

Some obstacles to exposure therapy do not emanate from the participants (child, parents, or therapists) but, rather, from the environment or circumstances in which therapy is operating. Some of these barriers may be outside the clinician's control, but they are still important to consider.

Leaving the Office

More realistic exposures will provide a more powerful and generalizable learning experience compared to those that are more of a practice simulation. Planning realistic exposure involves traveling to the location of feared stimuli or bringing those stimuli to the office. Some exposure targets are readily available in the office and can be implemented with little or no planning, such as hyperventilation. For exposures that require specific items to be transported to the office (e.g., contaminated clothes, pictures, or spiders), therapists and families will need to plan ahead. This can be accomplished by clarifying what the family needs to bring with them the next session, although it can be helpful to have a backup plan if the family forgets those objects. For items that are too large to transport, perhaps a contaminated couch, the family can transfer contamination to another item, such as towel, and bring that item in for a preparatory exposure. This can be more challenging when families are traveling a distance for a short-term treatment or massed exposure and cannot return home between sessions to collect items for exposures. In such case, the therapist likely will have to do some initial triage, perhaps even before the in-person assessment, to prepare the family for their visit. Therapists may also consider having some standard items available for exposures, such as cocktail straws for interoceptive exposures, needles for injection phobias, websites with videos of vomiting for emetophobia, or a connection with an owner of a companion dog (i.e., one approved to be in the clinic) for dog phobias.

For exposures that cannot be completed in the office, being located in a busier, more populated area can be very beneficial, although often not within a clinician's control. Locating an office in a hospital or clinic can provide access to support staff for social exposures, full waiting rooms for exposures to have panic symptoms in a crowd, heavily trafficked public surfaces for contamination exposures (door handles and waiting room magazines), or a second office for separation exposures. Location in a commercial district can provide stores and restaurants for social or agoraphobia exposures, taller buildings or parking structures for exposures to a fear of heights, and buses for exposure to a fear of accessing public transportation independently. When the situations and stimuli that provoke anxiety are not accessible from the office, the therapist can either assign those exposures as homework or meet the family on location. The former is significantly more feasible for many therapists and in many cases, especially with good parent exposure coaches, sufficient. However, if the family is having difficulty completing a necessary out-of-office exposure, perhaps because it is difficult to design lower level exposures that can be completed in the office, therapists are encouraged to either physically meet the family at the location or provide support from a distance, such as by phone. In fact, some therapists regularly offer home visits to conduct exposures. Fortunately, in our experience, through a combination of the strategies discussed previously, exposure therapy typically can be effectively administered in *and around* the therapist's office.

Ethics

Some therapists have concerns about the ethical implications of exposure therapy and its delivery. For example, leaving the office to conduct exposure can make it more difficult to protect the patient's confidentiality. Other therapists have concerns that exposure therapy can be dangerous, raising the risk that the patient will deteriorate. Others have concerns about recommending a treatment that they believe patients will refuse. However, as indicated previously, there is no evidence that exposure therapy is associated with more dropouts or negative side effects compared to other forms of therapy (Meyer et al., 2014; Öst & Ollendick, 2017). Moreover, exposure therapy is highly collaborative and consistent with the principles of informed consent. Therapists thoroughly outline the rationale and mechanism of action underlying therapy during psychoeducation, clearly communicate and agree on what will be expected of the child and family while building a fear hierarchy, and continually reassess the child's and the family's consent when identifying feared beliefs prior to each exposure. This level of informed consent is much higher than that with a treatment in which parents are not included within the session or that is predicated upon unconscious processing of dynamic themes during play or other activities. Finally, as discussed in Section 2, exposure therapy has the most empirical support of any intervention and thus offers patients the best chance to experience symptom relief and improvement in functioning. As such, providing exposure therapy for childhood anxiety disorders is most consistent with the primary ethical principle of benefitting those with whom a therapist works.

SUMMARY

As with any endeavor, writing and reading about how to do exposures are much easier than implementing them in real life. In this chapter, we identified some of the more common barriers that can impede the implementation of exposure therapy. In Chapter 10, we discuss additional resources that therapists may find helpful when using exposure therapy, including to address some of the obstacles discussed in this chapter.

REFERENCES

Arora, P. G., Baker, C. N., Marchette, L. K., & Stark, K. D. (2019). Components analyses of a school-based cognitive behavioral treatment for youth depression. *Journal of Clinical Child and Adolescent Psychology, 48*(Suppl. 1), S180–S193. doi:10.1080/15374416.2017.1280800

Farrell, N. R., Deacon, B. J., Kemp, J. J., Dixon, L. J., & Sy, J. T. (2013). Do negative beliefs about exposure therapy cause its suboptimal delivery? An experimental investigation. *Journal of Anxiety Disorders, 27*(8), 763–771.

Freeman, J. B., Garcia, A. M., Coyne, L., Ale, C., Przeworski, A., Himle, M., . . . Leonard, H. L. (2008). Early childhood OCD: Preliminary findings from a family-based cognitive–behavioral approach. *Journal of the American Academy of Child & Adolescent Psychiatry, 47*(5), 593–602.

Halldorsdottir, T., & Ollendick, T. H. (2016). Long-term outcomes of brief, intensive CBT for specific phobias: The negative impact of ADHD symptoms. *Journal of Consulting and Clinical Psychology, 84*(5), 465–471. doi:10.1037/ccp0000088

Halldorsdottir, T., Ollendick, T. H., Ginsburg, G., Sherrill, J., Kendall, P. C., Walkup, J., . . . Piacentini, J. (2015). Treatment outcomes in anxious youth with and without comorbid ADHD in the CAMS. *Journal of Clinical Child and Adolescent Psychology, 44*(6), 985–991. doi:10.1080/15374416.2014.952008

Meyer, J. M., Farrell, N. R., Kemp, J. J., Blakey, S. M., & Deacon, B. J. (2014). Why do clinicians exclude anxious clients from exposure therapy? *Behaviour Research and Therapy, 54*, 49–53. doi:10.1016/j.brat.2014.01.004

Obler, M., & Terwilliger, R. F. (1970). Pilot study on the effectiveness of systematic desensitization with neurologically impaired children with phobic disorders. *Journal of Consulting and Clinical Psychology, 34*(3), 314–318.

Öst, L. G., & Ollendick, T. H. (2017). Brief, intensive and concentrated cognitive behavioral treatments for anxiety disorders in children: A systematic review and meta-analysis. *Behaviour Research and Therapy, 97*, 134–145. doi:10.1016/j.brat.2017.07.008

Rudy, B. M., Zavrou, S., Storch, E. A., & Lewin, A. B. (2017). Parent-led exposure therapy: A pilot study of a brief behavioral treatment for anxiety in young children. *Journal of Child and Family Studies, 26*, 2475–2484.

Ung, D., Selles, R., Small, B. J., & Storch, E. A. (2015). A systematic review and meta-analysis of cognitive–behavioral therapy for anxiety in youth with high-functioning autism spectrum disorders. *Child Psychiatry and Human Development, 46*(4), 533–547. doi:10.1007/s10578-014-0494-y

Weersing, V. R., Jeffreys, M., Do, M. T., Schwartz, K. T., & Bolano, C. (2017). Evidence base update of psychosocial treatments for child and adolescent depression. *Journal of Clinical Child and Adolescent Psychology, 46*(1), 11–43. doi:10.1080/15374416.2016.1220310

Whiteside, S. P., Ale, C. M., Young, B., Olsen, M. W., Biggs, B. K., Gregg, M. S., ... Homan, K. (2016). The length of child anxiety treatment in a regional health system. *Child Psychiatry and Human Development, 47*(6), 985–992. doi:10.1007/s10578-016-0628-5

Whiteside, S. P. H., Ale, C. M., Young, B., Dammann, J., Tiede, M. S., & Biggs, B. K. (2015). The feasibility of improving CBT for childhood anxiety disorders through a dismantling study. *Behaviour Research and Therapy, 73*, 83–89. doi:10.1016/j.brat.2015.07.011

Whiteside, S. P. H., Deacon, B. J., Benito, K., & Stewart, E. (2016). Factors associated with practitioners' use of exposure therapy for childhood anxiety disorders. *Journal of Anxiety Disorders, 40*, 29–36. doi:http://dx.doi.org/10.1016/j.janxdis.2016.04.001

10

Additional Resources

In this chapter, we discuss additional resources to aid therapists in the delivery of exposure therapy for childhood anxiety or obsessive–compulsive disorder (OCD). We begin with materials and sources specific to the delivery of exposure. Next, we review resources for addressing other aspects of child emotional and behavioral problems that may co-occur with anxiety and that require other techniques. Finally, we list some avenues for locating other practitioners with an interest or expertise in exposure for child anxiety. It is important to note that although all the sources cited in this chapter were current and operational at the time of writing, with the passage of time they will become dated and, especially in the case of web pages, may no longer be accessible.

ADDITIONAL EXPOSURE RESOURCES

In this book, we have attempted to present a thorough, yet concise, introduction to exposure therapy for childhood anxiety and OCD. For those interested in learning more about exposure and its implementation, we review other resources regarding research and clinical practice, both in print and electronic. However, we begin by presenting a session-by-session outline to guide the delivery of exposure therapy with youth.

Session-by-Session Outline

The following session outline is based on our clinical experience delivering parent-coached exposure, as well as related research studies (Ollendick et al., 2015; Whiteside et al., 2014, 2015; Whiteside, Dammann, Tiede, Biggs, & Hillson Jensen, 2018). The approach to exposure therapy that we have presented in this book is intentionally flexible and intended to be customizable to the patient, family, and provider. As such, we do not have a structured protocol in which clinicians must complete specific therapeutic tasks in specific sessions. That level of structure and prescription assumes a degree of uniformity and predictability

Exposure Therapy for Child and Adolescent Anxiety and OCD. Stephen P. H. Whiteside, Thomas H. Ollendick, and Bridget K. Biggs, Oxford University Press (2020). © Oxford University Press.
DOI: 10.1093/med/9780190862992.001.0001

that is not desirable and rarely possible in clinical practice. In reality, symptom severity, comorbidity, family factors, clinician comfort and expertise, frequency and consistency of appointments, and other factors influence the content and delivery of treatment. With these caveats in mind, we present the following time line as a guide to demonstrate how parent-coached exposure can be implemented in the majority of cases. The order in which therapeutic tasks are implemented is based on a logical progression from learning to planning and execution, but neither the order nor the individual impact of each step has been empirically tested. Because patient and provider factors affect treatment delivery, clinicians should not feel the need to adhere rigidly to the following session outline. However, if clinicians find themselves frequently deviating from the guide in significant ways, we encourage them to examine their practice and reflect upon their approach. Deviations that reflect the clinicians' learning curve or unique patient needs are appropriate and acceptable. However, deviations resulting from clinician discomfort with the approach or belief that other techniques must routinely be added to exposure should be examined for their consistency with the available research literature and likelihood of benefiting patients. Upon reflection, most decisions to delay or avoid in-session exposure likely stem from clinician habits rather than patient needs.

Session 1

The first treatment session typically focuses on psychoeducation. This session occurs after the diagnostic assessment establishing the presence of anxiety or OCD. The goal of the first session is to orient the family to treatment, including the activities in which they will be participating, the typical number of sessions (8–10 in our experience, although sometimes fewer when we use brief intensive treatments), and the expected outcomes. Within this session, experienced therapists can typically present the anxiety/OCD cycle, help the family apply those concepts to their presenting complaints, identify the type of exposures the child will need to engage in, teach the steps for conducting exposures, and introduce strategies for maintaining motivation. As such, the family can leave the session with a clear understanding of exposure therapy and the expectations they might have for how it will work for them. Moreover, the therapist can ask them to discuss their reactions, questions, and concerns prior to the next session and to bring those items to the attention of the clinician at the beginning of the next session.

Session 2

The second session can typically focus on treatment planning. The therapist should begin by revisiting the psychoeducation from session 1 and inquiring whether the family has any questions or concerns. Then, the therapist uses the information gathered while applying the anxiety/OCD cycle to the child's symptoms in the previous session to build fear ladders. The primary goal of session 2 is for the family to leave with a specific treatment plan in the form of at least one but often two or three complete fear ladders. Prior to the next appointment, the family should review the fear ladders and add to them as needed. If time permits, the content of sessions 1 and 2 outlined here can be combined into a single session. For example, psychoeducation and fear ladder building can be completed in a single 75- to 90-minute group setting with multiple families (Ollendick et al., 2015; Whiteside et al., 2018). Indeed, some patients and therapists are able to begin exposure in session 2 (Whiteside et al., 2015).

SESSION 3
Clinicians should typically be able to begin exposure in session 3 (Whiteside et al., 2015). The purpose of this initial exposure is to provide the child and parents with hands-on experience in how to set up, do, and learn from an exposure. The target of the exposure should be manageable and elicit minimal fear. The therapist should guide the child through the exercise and allow the parents at least to observe, if not assist. If this introductory exposure is completed quickly, a second exposure that elicits more anxiety can also be conducted in this session. In our experience, it is not unusual for children to challenge themselves from the beginning with a moderately anxiety-provoking exposure, and this should not be discouraged. At the end of session 3, the therapist should help the family identify exposure activities in the home and instruct them to complete daily exposures prior to the next meeting.

SESSION 4
During the fourth session, if not before, the therapist should strive to have the child complete a challenging exposure. At this point in therapy, youth can typically engage in exposures that present a moderate degree of difficulty. It is hoped that the family completed the introductory exposures during the previous session and some amount of home practice during the intervening period. The degree of exposure difficulty will vary significantly among children and their families, but therapists can expect and should encourage children to complete exposures that meaningfully target the fears that precipitated treatment. In addition, the therapist can expect the parent and child to set up the exposure independently, although she should review the plan and provide direction before the family actually begins the exposure.

SESSIONS 5 AND 6
The goal for sessions 5 and 6 is for the family to transition from learning how to do exposures to actively engaging in exposures that challenge the core fears that brought the family to therapy. The therapist should be actively involved with helping the family stay on track, but the family should be able to design and complete in-session exposures with minimal assistance. In addition, the family should be completing regular exposures between sessions, working on challenging exposures that provoke anxiety and relate to the primary therapy goals, and have checked off several fear ladder items as mastered. Again, there will be significant variability among patients in the pace and initial success, but most are able to make meaningful, independent progress by this point.

Now that the family has begun conducting exposures, the role of the therapist and the therapy sessions is to support and promote these exercises in three primary ways. First, meeting with the therapist provides supportive accountability (Mohr, Cuijpers, & Lehman, 2011). Knowing that they will be meeting to review the exposures they have completed between sessions can help families keep up with their home practice. As such, it is very important for therapists to begin each session with a review of the exposures completed between sessions and to prioritize addressing obstacles that interfere with home exposures. Second, the sessions provide an opportunity for skill refinement. Exposure therapy requires practice to ensure that exercises are clearly targeting the child's fears and are providing a corrective learning experience. Therapists should encourage the child and parent to work together to design and implement exposure with increasing independence, while also providing instructive feedback regarding the principles outlined in Chapters 5 and 6. Third, therapy appointments provide an opportunity for children to complete more challenging exposures. The clinician's expertise and confidence, combined with the safe structured office setting, can help families engage in exposures that were too difficult to do at home on their own because of the complexity, novelty, or anxiety level. In summary, after teaching the family the why and how of exposure therapy, the therapist's role shifts to supporting the completion, refinement, and progression of exposure.

SESSIONS 7 THROUGH TERMINATION

During the remaining sessions, the therapist supports the family working up the fear ladder, tackling the most anxiety-provoking items, and mastering items as they progress. Patients should be experiencing decreases in symptoms, and parents should be observing improvements in functioning. Therapists can expect that, on average, families will attend 8–10 sessions (Gryczkowski et al., 2013; Vande Voort, Svecova, Brown Jacobsen, & Whiteside, 2010; Whiteside et al., 2016). We suggest discussing the outline of treatment presented here with patients, including the major tasks (education, planning, and exposure) and the typical time commitment—8 to 10 sessions in addition to daily home practice over 4 or 5 months. Although these time frames are estimates, they can help families make an informed decision regarding engaging in treatment. In reality, many patients discontinue care by the 6th session and 85% are done by the 14th session, although considerably more work needs to be done to understand how much treatment is adequate in clinical settings. Despite this uncertainty, the estimates provided here serve as a useful guide to the commitment needed to improve and minimize the chance of relapse.

Individual patients will fall outside these guidelines; some, for example, may receive sufficient benefit from two or three sessions. Indeed, we have successfully shown that some anxiety disorders, particularly the phobic disorders, respond to a concentrated dose of exposure therapy delivered in one 3-hour session, with a 3- or 4-week maintenance phase (Ollendick et al., 2009, 2015). Other families might require regular appointments for 6 months or more. However, in these circumstances, therapists should strive to have a clear conceptualization of the factors contributing to the divergence and ensure that the treatment course is optimally addressing the patient's needs and delivered as intended. Moreover, if clinicians find that their practice routinely deviates from the 8–10 sessions as presented here, they are encouraged to reflect upon their approach and seek consultation. Because there are appropriate reasons why a patient's care or a therapist's practice may differ from the typical time line present here, reflection and consultation may not lead to change. However, because it is often initially unclear whether our practice reflects patient need or our own habitual comfort zone, practice review can often be a valuable endeavor.

Further Reading on Exposure

HOW TO DO EXPOSURE

There are a number of additional resources that therapists may find helpful to further explore some of the topics introduced in this book. Therapists searching for more detailed information regarding the execution of exposures may find the *Handbook of Exposure Therapies* (Richard & Lauterbach, 2006) and, specifically, *Exposure Therapy for Anxiety: Principles and Practice* (Abramowitz, Deacon, & Whiteside, 2011) instructive. Because *Principles and Practice* is not directed to a child population, therapists who treat anxiety and related disorders in patients across the life span may find it to be complementary to the current book. In addition, Section II of *Principles and Practices* includes chapters devoted to the conceptualization, planning, and implementation of exposure for different symptom presentations. As such, the information presented in Chapter 6 of this book is elaborated upon, including more detailed directions for exposure completion.

Clinicians may find two studies regarding interoceptive exposure helpful for increasing their confidence in delivering this modality. The first details how to deliver high- versus low-intensity interoceptive exposure and demonstrates the increased efficacy of using higher intensity exposure (Deacon, Kemp, et al., 2013). The second examines the degree to which therapists tend to overestimate the likelihood of negative outcomes such as dropping out of therapy, decompensating, or losing consciousness, despite evidence suggesting the approach is safe and acceptable in most circumstances and viewed as useful by patients (Deacon, Lickel, Farrell, Kemp, & Hipol, 2013).

MECHANISM OF ACTION

Therapists interested in learning more about the different theories of how exposure therapy works and leads to symptom improvement are encouraged to read a special section on the exposure process in the *Journal of Obsessive–Compulsive and Related Disorders* (Conelea & Freeman, 2015). As the journal name implies, the articles are specific to OCD and are based primarily on the adult literature. Nonetheless, as we explored in Section 2 and have demonstrated in other publications (Ale, McCarthy, Rothschild, & Whiteside, 2015), examination of research completed in adults and in OCD, respectively, can provide valuable insight into issues that are yet to be fully examined in the child anxiety literature. The articles in the special section allow therapists to compare and contrast the habituation, cognitive, acceptance, and inhibitory learning theories of the process by which exposure leads to symptom reduction and the practice implications of each theory. Further understanding of theoretical underpinnings of different aspects of exposure therapy can help clinicians refine their use of various techniques and increase confidence in their implementation.

EMPIRICAL SUPPORT

Clinicians can also increase their confidence in exposure therapy through a direct review of the supporting literature summarized in Section 2. A qualitative review by Oar, Johnco, and Ollendick (2017) and a meta-analysis by Wang et al. (2017) provide two of the most thorough and up-to-date reviews of the literature on child anxiety treatment. The Cochrane Library, which gathers evidence to inform health care decision-making, published an overview of reviews that provides another convenient synthesis of the research literature (Manassis, Russell, & Newton, 2010). Another review was conducted more recently and provides a synthesis of breadth of data supporting the efficacy of exposure-based therapy for anxiety and related disorders (Crowe & McKay, 2017). In addition, Higa-McMillan, Francis, Rith-Najarian, and Chorpita (2016) comprehensively review the support for cognitive–behavioral therapy (CBT) and exposure specifically. Regarding the relative importance of exposure, two meta-analyses provide an empirical examination of this question (Ale et al., 2015; Whiteside et al., in press). Finally, two small studies and one larger study support the specific parent-coached exposure therapy described in this book. An article in *Behaviour Research and Therapy* supports the effectiveness of parent-coached exposure when used in a once-weekly individual manner with anxious youth (Whiteside et al., 2015). A study in *Psychiatry Research* supports the application of parent-coached exposure in youth with OCD in a time-intensive manner (Whiteside et al., 2014). The randomized control trial by Ollendick and colleagues (2015) describes and evaluates the use of this approach with 97 youth with various specific phobias. All of the previously mentioned references provide a convenient and direct source for therapists to demonstrate the empirical support for implementing exposure therapy.

Further Training in Exposure

Professional organizations provide a number of opportunities for clinicians to receive additional training in exposure therapy. For example, the Association for Behavioral and Cognitive Therapy (ABCT) and the Anxiety and Depression Association of America (ADAA) offer a number of live and recorded webinars on topics related to exposure, such as exposure therapy for OCD symptoms. In addition, the International OCD Foundation (IOCDF) provides in-depth training through its Behavior Therapy Training Institute. This training ranges from introductory to advanced courses and also includes online consultation groups. All of these organizations hold annual conferences or conventions, and others, such as the Miami International Child & Adolescent Mental Health Conference, often include trainings in exposure-based treatments.

Self-Help Books

Clinicians often find it helpful to have additional reading to offer patients. Such resources may be intended as stand-alone treatments in lieu of face-to-face, office-based therapy or as an adjunct to therapy. However, a note of caution must be stated. The market is full of self-help programs with little or no connection to the empirical literature. As such, clinicians should be cautious in their selections and thoroughly review the content of any resources they might recommend. The highest bar for appropriateness of a self-help book would be consistency with the evidence base and direct evidence of the benefit of using the program (i.e., testing through a randomized controlled trial). Unfortunately, direct empirical testing is very rare, and although some books are consistent with exposure therapy, many are not. Providing patients with reading material that presents other strategies than those emphasized in the therapy runs the risk of diluting the evidence-based exposure offered in session by competing for the family's time and attention. To help clinicians find self-help books consistent with the empirical literature, Farrell, Ollendick, and Muris (2019) provide a review of evidence-based self-help books. Moreover, organizations such as ABCT and ADAA make recommendations that are accessible through their websites. However, clinicians are encouraged to use such resources to winnow the field of potential books rather than as a replacement for a careful review for fit with their own practice.

Technology

Technology has the potential to facilitate the delivery of exposure through multiple modalities. Applications for mobile devices (i.e., apps) are likely the technology most easily accessible to therapists and patients. Unfortunately, due to the proliferation of mobile applications that are inconsistent with the literature, it is very unlikely that therapists or patients will encounter an appropriate program through a simple search of available applications (Kertz, MacLaren Kelly, Stevens, Schrock, & Danitz, 2017). However, there are some mobile applications that, although lacking direct empirical support, are consistent with the evidence base. For example, Mayo Clinic Anxiety Coach is an iOS application (i.e., iPhones and iPads) designed to facilitate the delivery of exposure for anxiety and OCD in youth and adults. The application allows individuals to build a fear ladder with the assistance of a library of exposure exercises, track their anxiety in real time during the completion of exposures, and track their progress through symptom ratings and mastery of fear ladder items. Therapists may find the application useful for generating ideas to populate fear ladders, replacing paper records, and collecting more detailed information about their patients' engagement in exposures (e.g., duration and anxiety levels). Mobile application development occurs very quickly, and unfortunately, grant-funded applications consistent with the evidence base often do not remain active for long (Bakker, Kazantzis, Rickwood, & Rickard, 2016). However, interested clinicians can consult databases available through professional organizations that independently review the quality of mobile applications, such as the partnership between ADAA and PsyberGuide.

Computer-based therapy is another avenue to use technology in the delivery exposure. Some programs are designed to be used entirely as self-help, whereas others are designed as an adjunct to therapy. The latter may include computer programs that guide the therapist–patient interaction during the session or that supplement face-to-face sessions with content delivered electronically to patients in their homes. To date, computer-based programs appear to successfully improve symptoms of child anxiety (Ye et al., 2014), especially if they include exposure (Donovan & March, 2014). Computer-based therapy is likely more useful for extending therapy to those without access to clinicians rather than for helping clinicians deliver exposure. As with all supplemental resources, however, we encourage clinicians to thoroughly review the content of technology-based programs to ensure consistency with their evidence-based exposure practice.

ADDITIONAL TREATMENT RESOURCES

Because mental health problems frequently co-occur, therapists often need to provide exposure therapy in conjunction with other evidence-based techniques. As discussed in Chapter 9, clinicians may need to treat depression or disruptive behavior before exposure therapy can be successfully introduced. Here, we review additional resources that clinicians may find useful to complement exposure therapy.

Disruptive Behavior

As mentioned in Chapter 9, arguing, anger outbursts, and noncompliance can interfere with the delivery of exposure therapy. When severe, these behaviors may warrant a diagnosis of oppositional defiant disorder. The actions of other children may be less severe or occur primarily in response to anxiety-provoking situations or expectations to begin exposures. Presentations consistent with the latter may respond to a simple reward system (e.g., small prize after every five exposures) combined with loss of privilege (e.g., electronics) and removal of attention for avoidance of exposure. For anger and defiance that is more severe or pervasive (i.e., general noncompliance), families may benefit from integrating a structured behavioral management program. A commonly used program, *Defiant Children: A Clinicians' Manual for Assessment and Parent Training* (Barkley, 2013), is in its third edition and was evaluated by Ollendick and colleagues (2016) in a randomized clinical control trial. The program clearly presents the basic strategies for helping parents improve the behavior of school-age children. When working with families with older children, clinicians may consider the *Defiant Teens* version, which combines the standard behavior management techniques with family communication and problem-solving strategies (Barkley & Robin, 2014). Both manuals include handouts and a companion parent manual. When working with younger children, clinicians might also consider parent–child interaction therapy (McNeil & Hembree-Kilgin, 2010), an evidenced-based treatment program.

Behavior management strategies to improve compliance and decrease anger outbursts have been studied and used clinically for decades. Over time, a large number of programs and manuals have been developed and are available. The manuals mentioned previously are commonly used, but clinicians are encouraged to explore others or may already have access to a particular program. We encourage clinicians to review the empirical support for any program they use. Reviews of the literature have most consistently identified encouraging good behavior through praise and structured reward systems and responding to misbehavior with ignoring and time-outs as the most important components of behavior management (Chorpita, Daleiden, & Weisz, 2005; Garland, Hawley, Brookman-Frazee, & Hurlburt, 2008; Kaminski, Valle, Filene, & Boyle, 2008; Murrihy, Kidman, & Ollendick, 2010).

Depression

Due to the high comorbidity between anxiety and depression, clinicians working with the former will want to have familiarity with the latter. As with anxiety, CBT is the most empirically supported treatment for depression, but it is also a heterogeneous, multicomponent intervention (Weersing, Jeffreys, Do, Schwartz, & Bolano, 2017). As such, clinicians should try to acquaint themselves with the literature regarding which techniques appear to be most closely associated with treatment response and adopt a treatment approach consistent with that evidence. As with anxiety, behavioral components, such as behavioral activation and problem-solving, may be the most powerful components of CBT (Arora, Baker, Marchette, & Stark, 2017). Treatment manuals for both CBT and interpersonal therapy are consistent with the evidence base and may be a good starting point for clinicians who want to complement their anxiety specialty (Lewinsohn, Rohde, Hops, & Clarke, 1991; Mufson, Dorta, Moreau, & Weissman, 2004). Moreover, the Unified Protocol and MATCH program provide frameworks to integrate anxiety and mood treatment (Chorpita & Weisz, 2009; Ehrenreich, Goldstein, Wright, & Barlow, 2009). Therapists may find these resources helpful when needing to address comorbid depressive symptoms, but we encourage them to use the principles outlined here to ensure the robust delivery of exposure for anxiety and OCD.

Trauma

Exposure is a central component in the treatment of post-traumatic stress disorder (PTSD). However, PTSD differs from the anxiety disorders and OCD due to the presence of a distinct identifiable traumatic experience. Although anxiety and OCD can be associated with a clear precipitating event, they often are not; even when they are, the events are not usually traumatic. The occurrence of a traumatic event can have a number of ramifications and associated problems that a clinician must address beyond a child's fear of memories and associated reminders. For instance, trauma can alter a child's relationships, living arrangements, or support structure. Trauma in children can also be associated with multiple behavioral and emotional symptoms, including anxiety, depression, and defiance. As such, clinicians working with trauma in children are encouraged to pursue additional training. Trauma-focused CBT is a commonly used approach with empirical support that also has a process for training clinicians. Farrell and colleagues (2019) review several other programs for youth with PTSD.

Obsessions and Compulsions

Obsessive–compulsive disorder differs from anxiety disorders by the presence of compulsions and the frequency of distressing emotions other than fear or worry, such as disgust or the sense that things are just not right. These differences may be more of degree, rather than qualitative, because anxiety disorders can be associated with repetitive avoidance behavior such as asking for reassurance. Furthermore, phobias can be based more in disgust than fear. Regardless, clinicians treating OCD in children may find it useful to consult additional recent OCD-specific resources, such as *Treating OCD in Children and Adolescents: A Cognitive–Behavioral Approach* (Franklin, Freeman, & March, 2018).

CONNECTING WITH OTHER PROFESSIONALS

Often in learning, there is no substitution for ongoing support from a teacher, mentor, or colleague. Written material can provide the information needed to get started learning about exposure and acquiring pointers on how to address new situations. However, translating what one learns on the written page to actions with a patient can be daunting. Visual demonstration of techniques, such as hyperventilation induction or social mishap exposures, can increase a clinician's confidence in how to properly implement them with patients. Moreover, even seasoned experts—including us—encounter challenging cases that they need to review with colleagues, even if only for an outside perspective about proceeding appropriately. As such, we encourage clinicians to make personal connections with others delivering exposure therapy.

Trainings through professional organizations provide one such opportunity to connect with other clinicians. For example, ABCT's Child and Adolescent Anxiety Special Interest Group aims to provide a forum for collaboration and networking. A similar group through ADAA provides monthly peer video consultations. As mentioned previously, the Behavior Therapy Training Institute offered through IOCDF includes online consultation groups. Participation in such groups provides opportunities to discuss cases and practices in a supportive environment that can help clinicians feel more confident that they are implementing exposure therapy appropriately.

SUMMARY

This chapter brings our book to a close. We began by striving to build a persuasive foundation for exposure therapy by introducing the history and theory behind it as well as the research supporting its use. Next, we sought to provide a specific framework for delivering parent-coached exposure and sufficient examples to illustrate how to apply exposure with youth presenting with a variety of anxiety and OCD symptoms. Finally, we attempted to anticipate the common obstacles experienced when implementing exposure therapy and to provide guidance for seeking additional training. We thank you for dedicating your time and expertise to helping children and adolescents suffering with anxiety and OCD. We are hopeful that we have provided information to make your work not only more efficient and more effective but also more fun and fulfilling.

REFERENCES

Abramowitz, J. S., Deacon, B. J., & Whiteside, S. P. H. (2011). *Exposure therapy for anxiety: Principles and practice.* New York, NY: Guilford.

Ale, C. M., McCarthy, D. M., Rothschild, L., & Whiteside, S. (2015). Components of cognitive behavioral therapy related to outcome in childhood anxiety disorders. *Clinical Child and Family Psychology Review, 18,* 240–251. doi:10.1007/s10567-015-0184-8

Arora, P. G., Baker, C. N., Marchette, L. K., & Stark, K. D. (2017). Components analyses of a school-based cognitive behavioral treatment for youth depression. *Journal of Clinical Child and Adolescent Psychology, 48*(Suppl. 1), S180–S193. doi:10.1080/15374416.2017.1280800

Bakker, D., Kazantzis, N., Rickwood, D., & Rickard, N. (2016). Mental health smartphone apps: Review and evidence-based recommendations for future developments. *JMIR Mental Health, 3*(1), e7. doi:10.2196/mental.4984

Barkley, R. A. (2013). *Defiant children, third edition: A clinician's manual for assessment and parent training.* New York, NY: Guilford.

Barkley, R. A., & Robin, A. L. (2014). *Defiant teens, second edition: A clinician's manual for assessment and family intervention.* New York, NY: Guilford.

Chorpita, B. F., Daleiden, E. L., & Weisz, J. R. (2005). Identifying and selecting the common elements of evidence based interventions: A distillation and matching model. *Mental Health Services Research*, 7(1), 5–20.

Chorpita, B. F., & Weisz, J. R. (2009). *MATCH-ADTC: Modular approach to therapy for children and adolescents with anxiety, depression, trauma, or conduct problems.* Indialantic, FL: PracticeWise.

Conelea, C., & Freeman, J. (2015). What do therapists and clients do during exposures for OCD? Introduction to the special issue on theory-based exposure process. *Journal of Obsessive–Compulsive and Related Disorders*, 6, 144–146.

Crowe, K., & McKay, D. (2017). Efficacy of cognitive–behavioral therapy for childhood anxiety and depression. *Journal of Anxiety Disorders*, 49, 76–87. doi:10.1016/j.janxdis.2017.04.001

Deacon, B., Kemp, J. J., Dixon, L. J., Sy, J. T., Farrell, N. R., & Zhang, A. R. (2013). Maximizing the efficacy of interoceptive exposure by optimizing inhibitory learning: A randomized controlled trial. *Behaviour Research & Therapy*, 51(9), 588–596.

Deacon, B., Lickel, J. J., Farrell, N. R., Kemp, J. J., & Hipol, L. J. (2013). Therapist perceptions and delivery of interoceptive exposure for panic disorder. *Journal of Anxiety Disorders*, 27, 259–264.

Donovan, C. L., & March, S. (2014). Computer-based treatment programs for youth anxiety: A systematic review. *Psychopathology Review*, 1, 130–156. doi:10.5127/pr.033613

Ehrenreich, J. T., Goldstein, C. M., Wright, L. R., & Barlow, D. H. (2009). Development of a Unified Protocol for the treatment of emotional disorders in youth. *Child & Family Behavior Therapy*, 31(1), 20–37. doi:10.1080/07317100802701228

Farrell, L. J., Ollendick, T. H., & Muris, P. (Eds.). (2019). *Innovations in CBT for childhood anxiety, OCD and PTSD: Improving access and outcomes.* Cambridge, UK: Cambridge University Press.

Franklin, M. E., Freeman, J. B., & March, J. S. (2018). *Treating OCD in children and adolescents: A cognitive–behavioral approach.* New York, NY: Guilford.

Garland, A. F., Hawley, K. M., Brookman-Frazee, L., & Hurlburt, M. S. (2008). Identifying common elements of evidence-based psychosocial treatments for children's disruptive behavior problems. *Journal of the American Academy of Child & Adolescent Psychiatry*, 47(5), 505–514. doi:10.1097/CHI.0b013e31816765c2

Gryczkowski, M. R., Tiede, M. S., Dammann, J. E., Brown Jacobsen, A., Hale, L. R., & Whiteside, S. P. H. (2013). The timing of exposure in clinic-based treatment for childhood anxiety disorders. *Behavior Modification*, 37, 113–127.

Higa-McMillan, C. K., Francis, S. E., Rith-Najarian, L., & Chorpita, B. F. (2016). Evidence base update: 50 years of research on treatment for child and adolescent anxiety. *Journal of Clinical Child and Adolescent Psychology*, 45(2), 91–113. doi:http://dx.doi.org/10.1080/15374416.2015.1046177

Kaminski, J. W., Valle, L. A., Filene, J. H., & Boyle, C. L. (2008). A meta-analytic review of components associated with parent training program effectiveness. *Journal of Abnormal Child Psychology*, 36(4), 567–589. doi:10.1007/s10802-007-9201-9

Kertz, S. J., MacLaren Kelly, J., Stevens, K. T., Schrock, M., & Danitz, S. B. (2017). A review of free iPhone applications designed to target anxiety and worry. *Journal of Technology in Behavioral Science*, 2(2), 61–70.

Lewinsohn, P., Rohde, P., Hops, H., & Clarke, G. (1991). *Leader's manual for parent groups: Adolescent coping with depression course.* Eugene, OR: Castalia.

Manassis, K., Russell, K., & Newton, A. S. (2010). The Cochrane Library and the treatment of childhood and adolescent anxiety disorders: An overview of reviews. *Evidenced-Base Child Health, 5*, 541–554.

McNeil, C. B., & Hembree-Kilgin, T. L. (2010). *Parent–child interaction therapy* (2nd ed.). New York, NY: Springer.

Mohr, D. C., Cuijpers, P., & Lehman, K. (2011). Supportive accountability: A model for providing human support to enhance adherence to eHealth interventions. *Journal of Medical Internet Research, 13*(1), e30. doi:10.2196/jmir.1602

Mufson, L., Dorta, K., Moreau, D., & Weissman, M. (2004). *Interpersonal psychotherapy for depressed adolescents* (2nd ed.). New York, NY: Guildford.

Murrihy, R. C., Kidman, A. D., & Ollendick, T. H. (Eds.). (2010). *Handbook of clinical assessment and treatment of conduct problems in youth*. New York, NY: Springer.

Oar, E. L., Johnco, C., & Ollendick, T. H. (2017). Cognitive behavioral therapy for anxiety and depression in children and adolescents. *Psychiatric Clinics of North America, 40*(4), 661–674. doi:10.1016/j.psc.2017.08.002

Ollendick, T. H., Greene, R. W., Austin, K. E., Fraire, M. G., Halldorsdottir, T., Allen, K. B., . . . Wolff, J. C. (2016). Parent management training (PMT) and Collaborative & Proactive Solutions (CPS): A randomized control trial for oppositional youth. *Journal of Clinical Child and Adolescent Psychology, 45*(5), 591–604. doi:10.1080/15374416.2015.1004681

Ollendick, T. H., Halldorsdottir, T., Fraire, M. G., Austin, K. E., Noguchi, R. J., Lewis, K. M., . . . Whitmore, M. J. (2015). Specific phobias in youth: A randomized controlled trial comparing one-session treatment to a parent-augmented one-session treatment. *Behavior Therapy, 46*(2), 141–155. doi:10.1016/j.beth.2014.09.004

Ollendick, T. H., Öst, L.-G., Reuterskiold, L., Costa, N., Cederlund, R., Sirbu, C., . . . Jarrett, M. A. (2009). One-session treatment of specific phobias in youth: A randomized clinical trial in the United States and Sweden. *Journal of Consulting and Clinical Psychology, 77*(3), 504–516.

Richard, D. C. S., & Lauterbach, D. L. (Eds.). (2006). *Handbook of exposure therapies*. San Diego, CA: Academic Press.

Vande Voort, J. L., Svecova, J., Brown Jacobsen, A., & Whiteside, S. P. (2010). A retrospective examination of the similarity between clinical practice and manualized treatment of childhood anxiety disorders. *Cognitive and Behavioral Practice, 17*, 322–328.

Wang, Z., Whiteside, S. P. H., Sim, L., Farah, W., Morrow, A. S., Alsawas, M., . . . Murad, M. H. (2017). Comparative effectiveness and safety of cognitive behavioral therapy and pharmacotherapy for childhood anxiety disorders: A systematic review and meta-analysis. *JAMA Pediatrics, 171*(11), 1049–1056. doi:10.1001/jamapediatrics.2017.3036

Weersing, V. R., Jeffreys, M., Do, M. T., Schwartz, K. T., & Bolano, C. (2017). Evidence base update of psychosocial treatments for child and adolescent depression. *Journal of Clinical Child and Adolescent Psychology, 46*(1), 11–43. doi:10.1080/15374416.2016.1220310

Whiteside, S. P., Ale, C. M., Young, B., Olsen, M. W., Biggs, B. K., Gregg, M. S., . . . Homan, K. (2016). The length of child anxiety treatment in a regional health system. *Child Psychiatry and Human Development, 47*(6), 985–992. doi:10.1007/s10578-016-0628-5

Whiteside, S. P., McKay, D., De Nadai, A. S., Tiede, M. S., Ale, C. M., & Storch, E. A. (2014). A baseline controlled examination of a 5-day intensive treatment for pediatric obsessive–compulsive disorder. *Psychiatry Research, 220*(1–2), 441–446. doi:10.1016/j.psychres.2014.07.006

Whiteside, S. P. H., Ale, C. M., Young, B., Dammann, J., Tiede, M. S., & Biggs, B. K. (2015). The feasibility of improving CBT for childhood anxiety disorders through a dismantling study. *Behaviour Research and Therapy, 73*, 83–89. doi:10.1016/j.brat.2015.07.011

Whiteside, S. P. H., Dammann, J. E., Tiede, M. S., Biggs, B. K., & Hillson Jensen, A. (2018). Increasing availability of exposure therapy through intensive group treatment for childhood anxiety and OCD. *Behavior Modification, 42*(5), 707–728. doi:10.1177/0145445517730831

Whiteside, S. P. H., Sim, L. A., Morrow, A. S., Farah, W. H., Hilliker, D. R., Murad, M. H., & Wang, Z. (in press). A meta-analysis to guide the enhancement of CBT for childhood anxiety: Exposure over Anxiety Management. *Clinical Child and Family Psychology Review.*

Ye, X., Bapuji, S. B., Winters, S. E., Struthers, A., Raynard, M., Metge, C., . . . Sutherland, K. (2014). Effectiveness of internet-based interventions for children, youth, and young adults with anxiety and/or depression: A systematic review and meta-analysis. *BMC Health Services Research, 14*, 1–9. doi:10.1186/1472-6963-14-313

Figures are indicated by *f* following the page number

For the benefit of digital users, indexed terms that span two pages (e.g., 52–53) may, on occasion, appear on only one of those pages.